A SHORT HISTORY OF

CHINA

AND SOUTHEAST ASIA

Short History of Asia Series

Series Editor: Milton Osborne
Milton Osborne has had an association with the Asian region for over forty years as an academic, public servant and independent writer. He is the author of eight books on Asian topics, including *Southeast Asia: An Introductory History*, first published in 1979 and now in its eighth edition, and, most recently, *The Mekong: Turbulent Past, Uncertain Future*, published in 2000.

A SHORT HISTORY OF CHINA AND SOUTHEAST ASIA: TRIBUTE, TRADE AND INFLUENCE

By Martin Stuart-Fox

First published in 2003

Calligraphy by Anita Chang
Maps by Robert Cribb

Allen & Unwin
83 Alexander Street
Crows Nest NSW 2065
Australia
Phone: (61 2) 8425 0100
Fax: (61 2) 9906 2218
Email: info@allenandunwin.com
Web: www.allenandunwin.com

National Library of Australia
Cataloguing-in-Publication entry:

Stuart-Fox, Martin, 1939– .
A short history of China and Southeast Asia : tribute, trade and influence.

Bibliography.
Includes index.
ISBN 1 86448 954 5.

1. China – Foreign economic relations – Asia, Southeastern.
2. Asia, Southeastern – Foreign economic relations – China.
3. China – Foreign relations – Asia, Southeastern. 4.
Asia, Southeastern – Foreign relations – China. 5. China –
History – 1900– . I. Title.

382.951059

Set in 11/14 pt Goudy by Midland Typesetters, Maryborough, Victoria
Printed by South Wind Production (Singapore) Private Limited

10 9 8 7 6 5 4 3 2

Contents

Preface and acknowledgments

It has taken almost two centuries, but China is once again becoming a great power—at a time when the United States stands alone as the actual global hegemon. Some see the rising power of China as a threat, to regional if not global stability. Others see it as a challenge: how can Chinese ambitions be accommodated? But threat or challenge, Southeast Asia will be a principal arena for the exercise of growing Chinese political influence and military power.

Relations between China and Southeast Asia will thus clearly be crucial in the early years of the twenty-first century. These relations go back over two millennia, during which they were mostly conducted in accordance with a tributary system imposed by China and accepted by Southeast Asian kingdoms. Over this long period, the peoples of China and Southeast Asia came to understand and accommodate each other, despite their very different cultural assumptions and expectations. This is a rich and varied story, which a book of this length can only tell briefly and schematically.

I have approached this task with some trepidation, for relations between China and Southeast Asia have been much studied over the years, from a variety of perspectives. Moreover, I come to this study not as a China scholar, but as someone whose research and teaching have focused on continental Southeast Asia. But then, this is not a book only about China's relations with Southeast Asia, but about the relationship from both sides. It could just as well be titled 'Southeast Asia and China'.

As an historian, my approach is historical, not just because I want to tell a story, but because history continues profoundly to influence relations between China and Southeast Asia. History is central to the way both Chinese and Southeast Asians understand the world.

Western scholars may take history less seriously (and international relations analysts are particularly prone to do so), but no-one disregards history in China or Southeast Asia.

The other important dimension of understanding that we must bring to the study and interpretation of China–Southeast Asian relations is of their respective worldviews. 'Worldview' refers to the structure of cognition that shapes both habitual behaviour and considered action in response to confronting situations, for national leaders as for individuals in their everyday lives. Worldviews are built up over time through upbringing (the learning of language, values, etc.), formal education, socialisation and life experience. We all perceive the world through the prism of our individual yet more or less shared worldviews.

What I have tried to do in this book is to show how certain elements of the different ways both Chinese and Southeast Asians viewed the world not only characterised their relationships until the middle of the nineteenth century, but have persisted into the present. This is not to argue that worldview is unchanging. Far from it. All Chinese know that China no longer stands alone as the superior Middle Kingdom, even though this is the name they still call their country. And the peoples and governments of Southeast Asia will hardly accept a return to an outmoded tributary system.

What I maintain is that a new pattern of power relations is emerging, one that harks back in significant ways to earlier times. The era of Western domination in Asia is drawing to a close. The United States has withdrawn from mainland Southeast Asia and will not return, leaving China the opportunity to regain its historic position of regional dominance. Much will depend on how Beijing chooses to exercise what will amount to its de facto hegemony; but in arriving at ways of accommodating a much more powerful China, the countries of Southeast Asia will not only naturally respond in terms of their own views of the world, but also reach back into the long history of their relations with the Middle Kingdom. In fact, I would argue that this is already evident: in the 'ASEAN way' of conducting diplomacy, for instance, and in the steadfast refusal of Southeast Asian nations to enter into any formal balance-of-power coalition to 'contain' China.

As an amateur in the field, I am happy to acknowledge my debt to all those scholars whose research has revealed the varied dimensions of China–Southeast Asia relations. A number of these are mentioned in footnotes and suggestions for further reading, though I have referred there to very little of the journal literature to which I am also indebted. One scholar in particular requires special mention, and that is Wang Gungwu. To Professor Wang, all who write on China–Southeast Asia relations are indebted.

I am most grateful also to the many international relations scholars, political analysts, historians, and diplomats in Beijing, Hanoi, Bangkok, Viang Chan, Manila, Singapore, Kuala Lumpur and Jakarta who kindly gave me of their time. The opportunity to visit these capitals was provided by a University of Queensland Foundation Grant. The International Institute of Asian Studies in Leiden kindly provided me with a Visiting Fellowship to conduct part of the historical research. My thanks, finally, to Robert Cribb, who drew the maps, to Milton Osborne, general editor of this series, and to John Iremonger and all the production team at Allen & Unwin.

Abbreviations

AFPFL	Anti-Fascist People's Freedom League
APEC	Asia–Pacific Economic Co-operation
ARF	ASEAN Regional Forum
ASEAN	Association of Southeast Asian Nations
BCE	before the common era
BCP	Burmese Communist Party
CCP	Chinese Communist Party
CE	common era
Comintern	Communist International
DRV	Democratic Republic of Vietnam
FDI	Foreign direct investment
GMD	Guomindang (Nationalist Party)
ICP	Indochina Communist Party
MCP	Malayan Communist Party
NATO	North Atlantic Treaty Organization
PAVN	People's Army of Vietnam
PKI	Partai Komunis Indonesia (Indonesian Communist Party)
PRC	People's Republic of China
PRK	People's Republic of Kampuchea
ROC	Republic of China
SEATO	South-East Asia Treaty Organization
SRV	Socialist Republic Of Vietnam
UMNO	United Malays Nationalist Organisation
UN	United Nations
USA	United States of America
USSR	Union of Soviet Socialist Republics
Vietminh	Viet Nam Doc Lap Dong Minh (Vietnam League for Independence)
VNQDD	Vietnamese Nationalist Party
VOC	Dutch East India Company
ZOPFAN	Zone of Peace, Freedom and Neutrality

1 INTRODUCTION

This book sketches in broad outline the history of 2000 years of contact between the peoples and governments of China and the peoples and governments of Southeast Asia. This is an ambitious undertaking that presents some obvious problems. China itself has not always been unified and Southeast Asia is a wonderfully varied region that historically has comprised many more independent kingdoms and principalities than the ten modern states making up the Association of Southeast Asian Nations (ASEAN). Moreover frontiers have shifted over these two thousand years, and once powerful independent kingdoms in what is now southern China have disappeared.

Historians do not just recount past events, however: they also interpret them, often by pointing out patterns that impart meaning. The early twenty-first century provides a convenient vantage point from which to do this for China–Southeast Asia relations. European powers have withdrawn from Southeast Asia, and after a period of weakness and humiliation lasting more than a century, the People's Republic of China (PRC) has restored much of China's former influence and status. The United States is the only power outside Asia that still plays a significant role in shaping regional relations. The reduction of direct foreign interference leaves China and the countries of Southeast Asia freer than at any time in their modern histories to construct their own mutually acceptable relationships.

Until the nineteenth century, relations between China and Southeast Asia were conducted in accordance with what has come to be known as the 'tribute system'. This was a world order that was both sinocentric and orchestrated by China. The weakness of the late Qing dynasty at the end of the nineteenth century was not unusual in the context of Chinese history, as it conformed to the pattern of dynastic rise and decline. The replacement of the Qing dynasty by the Republic of China could even be viewed as the start of a new 'dynastic' cycle. But the move from empire to republic was in response not just to loss by the Qing imperial line of their mandate to rule granted by Heaven, but also to entirely new international pressures that forced China to accept a radically different world order of contending empires and nation-states. Even though these pressures for change had been building for over a century, the transition was a painful one. The collapse of the Qing ushered in a period of turmoil and war that only ended with the victory of the Chinese Communist Party (CCP) in 1949, at a time when the peoples of Southeast Asia were themselves gaining independence.

Both the PRC and the newly independent countries of Southeast Asia were born into a world divided by the Cold War. Their mutual relations were buffeted by the winds of global competition, to which China in particular reacted with sudden policy shifts. Not until the leadership of Mao Zedong gave way to that of Deng Xiaoping did some predictability come to characterise Chinese foreign policy. In the meantime, the countries of Southeast Asia coped with China in their different ways. Some, like the Philippines and Thailand, relied on American protection. Some, like Burma and Cambodia, sought to win Chinese approval through a policy of strict neutrality. Some, like

Vietnam and Laos after 1975, turned to the Soviet Union. And some, like Indonesia after 1965, eschewed all contact with the PRC.

At the same time as the countries of Southeast Asia were responding so differently to the exigencies of the Cold War, they increasingly realised the need for concerted regional policies. In 1967 Indonesia, Malaysia, the Philippines, Singapore and Thailand formed the Association of Southeast Asia Nations (ASEAN). Thirty years later, ASEAN grouped all ten Southeast Asian states. A new and important multilateral dimension had been introduced into relations between Southeast Asia and China.

Two events—American defeat in Vietnam and the disintegration of the Soviet Union—had profound impacts on relations between China and Southeast Asia. While the former threw into question American willingness to guarantee the security of mainland Southeast Asian states, the latter deprived Vietnam of Soviet support. Both drove countries that had depended on outside powers (Thailand on the United States; Vietnam on the Soviet Union) to seek accommodation with China.

The impact of both events on China itself was less immediate, though in the longer term, just as significant. The aftermath of the Vietnam War exacerbated China's fear of the Soviet Union, and while the collapse of the Soviet empire removed that fear, it also severely undermined the ideological pretensions of Chinese communism. The CCP regime survived, but only by introducing free market economic reforms and by drawing increasingly on nationalism to legitimise its monopoly of power. China's continuing quest for status as a great power owes nothing now to Marxism–Leninism, but a great deal to China's cultural pride and its reading of its own history.

This brings me to the second purpose of this book, which is to try to interpret the recent history of China–Southeast Asia relations. What I shall argue is that as the influence of extra-regional powers has diminished, and as China's own political, economic and military power has grown, so traditional modes of interaction have come increasingly to reassert themselves in shaping relations between China and the countries of Southeast Asia. The multilateral dimension of ASEAN–China relations stands in the way of this development going too far, but if it should continue, resulting tensions within ASEAN will test regional solidarity to the limit. How these tensions are dealt with will depend on how aggressively China pursues its strategic goals, how the other two principal interested major powers (the US and Japan) react, and how the ASEAN states singly and collectively move to assure their own interests and security.

The present evolving relationship between China and the countries of Southeast Asia cannot be understood simply in terms familiar to hard-headed realists among international relations analysts.[1] It is not enough to compare political institutions, economic strengths and weaknesses and military force levels: while these considerations are obviously important they do not of themselves determine how states will relate to other states in crisis situations. Other, often emotive, factors come into play, such as national pride or traditional enmity. A good example of how such 'irrational' factors influence decisions on interstate relations is provided by the events of 1978–79 that saw militarily weak Cambodia provoke war with Vietnam, which in turn risked war with China by invading Cambodia. In both cases, cultural presuppositions and the histories of relations between Cambodia and Vietnam and Vietnam and China significantly influenced decisions by political leaders that risked, and eventually led to war.[2]

Cultural and historical influences on international relations decision-making often go unanalysed because their causal impact is difficult to theorise and define. Yet they remain crucial for an understanding of relations between states, for history and cultural presuppositions influence not just strategic and military considerations (when and why force was considered a legitimate or necessary option or response),[3] but also how peaceful intercourse with other states should be conducted (including diplomacy, trade, and the treatment of foreign nationals).

The principal way in which cultural factors influence the way states and nations relate to one another derives from how their foreign policy elites understand the world. This worldview, which a foreign policy elite shares for the most part with the broader political elite, includes both how the world is constituted (believed to be in a descriptive sense) and how it should be constituted (in an ideal and prescriptive sense.) They thus constitute systems of belief that are centrally informed by religion. Worldview shapes and is shaped by culture, while its temporal dimension defines how time and history are understood. Both culture and history contribute significantly to our sense of identity. How we think about ourselves as belonging to a community or national group, and how we think about others, using what metaphors and analogies, drawing upon what prejudices and stereotypes, are important cultural influences on international relations. Culture also influences decision-making processes through the education and socialisation of political elites, the politics of personal power and ambition, and the functioning of national institutions (parties, parliaments, ministries of foreign affairs, etc.).

Analysis of such influences on the behaviour of states and nations towards each other reveals many of the presuppositions underlying foreign policy decisions and action. These presuppositions include values, norms, and expectations with respect to the proper conduct of international affairs. Together they constitute what I shall call the *international relations culture* of a traditional polity or modern nation-state. Historically international relations cultures have been much more diverse (take the case of the European powers and China in the nineteenth century) than they presently are in our globalised modern world. Even so, differences in international relations cultures still frequently act as irritants in relations between states. We need to understand, therefore, how worldviews differ and how differences can be reconciled. This can only be done by examining the cognitive assumptions embedded in worldviews, systems of values, and strategic goals. Where these coincide, the conduct of relations between two states will often not require shared commitments to be spelled out; they will be taken for granted—which may cause some amazement to those who do not share them. An example would be the willingness of certain Southeast Asian states (Thailand, Burma) to make use of 'family' metaphors in referring to their relations with China, a form of words that would not come naturally even to fellow members of ASEAN (Indonesia, the Philippines).

In order to understand the current state of relations between China and Southeast Asia and where they are leading, we also need to understand why historically relations took the form they did. Until the nineteenth century, China, by virtue of its size, its economic and military power and the uncompromising nature of its worldview, imposed what amounted to a hegemonic international order on all aspects of its relations with other polities. The question is: why did Southeast Asian kingdoms go along with this? Did they do so for purely pragmatic reasons in order to promote profitable trade? Were there other reasons that had to do with security, both internal and external? Or were Chinese demands not resented because they could be accommodated within Southeast Asian views of the world, and so were not considered outrageous in the way they seemed to be to nineteenth century European envoys?

Towards the end of the nineteenth century, China was forced to come to terms with an entirely different international order, based on a completely different view of the world and of how relations between states should be conducted. This was a world of competing empires, in which the Chinese empire attempted to claim some status, until humiliated by the West and Japan. Yet the Chinese empire remained essentially intact. Even after the fall of the Qing dynasty, though it lost its hegemonic influence in Southeast Asia, China continued to rule over non-Chinese peoples beyond its core cultural area (Mongols, Tibetans, Uighurs). This was a difficult transitional period, even after China became a republic, for the world system of nation-states was itself evolving. Only after the Second World War, when the countries of Southeast Asia regained their independence, did the United Nations—as a forum of nominally equal sovereign states—come to embody the contemporary world order. It was in this context, in which the Peoples' Republic of China after 1949 was initially a pariah state excluded from the UN, that relations between the new China and the newly independent states of Southeast Asia had to be negotiated. The first stages of this process were complicated by the continued presence of former colonial powers, by the intervention in the region of the United States, by China's revolutionary ambitions, and by the internal politics of Southeast Asian nations. The later stages are still in the process of being worked out. What their form will be into the twenty-first century is unclear, though it is possible to discern certain trends.

What this book will attempt to do, in summary, is to trace the changing relations between China and Southeast Asia from the points of view of both sides. How both sides, as regions—China as unified empire (for most of the time) and Southeast Asia comprising a collection of kingdoms and states—related to each other evolved over time and according to circumstances. The international relations cultures of both China and Southeast Asian polities—comprising cognitive, cultural, political, diplomatic, economic, and military factors—also changed over time. Bilateral interaction between China and Southeast Asian polities came to constitute a set of relationships that I have called a *bilateral relations regime*.[4] In the modern world, a bilateral relations regime between two states might be given formal expression in a bilateral treaty, but more often regimes rest simply on some sharing of principles, norms and expectations, which presuppose a sensitivity by each party to the other's interests. In large part the principles underlying early bilateral relations regimes between China and Southeast Asian kingdoms were dictated by China, but they came to be accepted by Southeast Asian ruling elites as defining expected behaviour on both sides in matters of diplomacy, security and trade. These bilateral relations regimes evolved not just out of a coincidence of interests;

they also necessarily rested on a degree of compatibility of worldviews and shared historical experience, factors which still impact upon contemporary relations between China and the states of Southeast Asia. To these worldviews and this shared historical experience we shall now turn.

2
THE CHINESE VIEW OF THE WORLD

中國

The birthplace of Chinese civilisation was on the North China Plain, watered by the Yellow River and its tributaries. It was inland and inward-looking, far from any other centre of civilisation. It was also a superior civilisation whose fine pottery, bronze metallurgy and invention of writing clearly differentiated the early Chinese from surrounding peoples. From as early as the Shang dynasty (sixteenth to eleventh century BCE), China's isolation and its sense of superiority shaped not only Chinese attitudes towards other peoples, but also their conception of themselves. From this period date key characteristics of the Chinese view of the world. Among these were a belief that the Chinese stood at the centre of the universe, that theirs was the 'Middle Kingdom', surrounded in all four directions by less culturally advanced, 'barbarian' peoples.

Belief in a powerful protective deity, Shang Di, probably the original ancestor of the ruling house, encouraged a sense of community. Shang Di was never thought of as creator of the world. Rather, Shang Di presided over organically connected divine and human realms, whose mysterious processes could be discerned through the use of oracles. Divination and the keeping of records together encouraged a well-developed sense of precedent, and a belief that one could learn from the past. Society was hierarchically structured, with political power exercised by an authoritarian ruling elite, whose lavish lifestyle and impressive tombs rested on the extraction of surplus production from toiling peasants.

In overthrowing the last of the Shang kings, the Zhou dynasty (eleventh to third century BCE) elaborated and reinforced this developing Chinese worldview. The Zhou came from the western fringes of the Shang culture area, a people who had been influenced by and adopted much of Shang civilisation. They brought with them their own ancestral deity, whom they called *tian*, meaning Heaven, and identified with Shang Di. The Zhou kings called themselves Son of Heaven (*tian-zi*), thereby claiming both moral power and a divine mandate to rule (*tian-ming*). In Zhou cosmology, the Son of Heaven, representing humankind, stood as the crucial link between Heaven, the human world and the Earth itself. It was the duty of the Zhou kings to sustain that linkage on behalf of all humankind through ritual worship at the temples of Heaven and Earth.

The Shang was a great literate and artistic culture, as demonstrated not least by its incomparable bronze metallurgy. For centuries the dynasty had ruled the core Chinese cultural area. By what right, then, could the Zhou claim the Shang mandate to rule? The Zhou legitimised their seizure of power by means that were both ethical and historical. The Zhou painted the last of the Shang kings as not just weak and ineffective, but as morally corrupt, a man who had lost all moral right to rule, and so who could no longer fulfil his assigned role in the Heaven-ordained natural and political order. This established two important principles: first, that Heaven was a moral force, which meant that the Son of Heaven presided over what was a moral world order; and second, that history provided crucial evidence for the working out of those processes over which Heaven presided.

The acute Chinese consciousness of history had two further ramifications. One was that history had a pattern: each dynasty moved inexorably from the heroic exploits of its founder to the miserable exit of the last emperor in the dynastic line. The second was that the model to be emulated by each new dynasty lay in the past. History provided no record of progress for the Chinese. What it provided was moral example, established in the 'golden age' of the early Zhou kings. Historians sat in judgment over the past, and on those judgments rested future policy—in foreign relations, as in government.

The kingdom over which the early Zhou kings ruled was by no means a centralised state. Rather, it was feudal in structure, made up of dozens of principalities whose aristocratic rulers acknowledged Zhou suzerainty. In 771 BCE, the power of the Zhou kings was forever destroyed when their capital was overrun by an alliance of barbarians and rebel vassals. Powerful feudal lords rescued the dynasty and established a new capital further to the east, but the Eastern Zhou kings were thereafter mere figureheads. The Chinese cultural area fragmented politically into a number of autonomous principalities which, by the fifth century BCE, were in a state of almost constant conflict with each other. This was the time of the 'warring states'. It was also a time of innovation in technology, in culture, and in philosophy.

The Confucian worldview

The greatest of China's philosophers, judged by the influence he has had on Chinese civilisation, was Kung Fu-zi, known to the West as Confucius, who lived from 551 to 479 BCE. The importance of Confucius lies in the direction he gave to Chinese thought, to its rationalism, to its humanism, and to its social and political focus. Confucius had one overriding concern: to restore social order and moral propriety in an age of growing political anarchy and social chaos. For a model he naturally looked to the past, to the foundation of the Zhou dynasty by King Wu, and his faithful and principled brother, the Duke of Zhou. Confucius believed that social and moral order rested on universal recognition and acceptance of social and political hierarchy. It was essential that everyone should know their place in the world, accept their duties and responsibilities, and recognise their superiors and inferiors. Moral example should be provided by those at the apex of the hierarchy, and emulated by their inferiors. Confucius believed that social anarchy and political immorality happened because the rulers of states refused to recognise that the powerless Zhou kings still possessed the mandate of Heaven.

How was this state of affairs to be redressed? As an itinerant philosopher, with only his tongue to protect him, Confucius was not in a position to dictate to princes. What Confucius taught as the basis of good government was 'the rectification of names', summed up in a famous saying: 'Let the lord be a lord; the subject a subject; the father a father; the son a son' (Analects 12.11). Elsewhere he spelled out what he believed rested on the proper use of language:

> If the names are not correct, language is without an object. When language is without an object, no affair can be effected. When no affair can be effected, rites and music wither. When rites and music wither, punishments and penalties miss their target. When punishments and penalties miss their target, the people do not know where they stand. (Analects 13.3)[1]

Both these sayings taught the same thing: people must be what they say they are, and if they occupy some office they must act accordingly. Unless language reflected reality, whatever principles and rules were enunciated would fail to have the desired effect. So punishments and penalties imposed for contravening those rules would not bring about social order, and people would become bewildered, and not know what was expected of them. This opened the way to anarchy and chaos. It should be added that in the Chinese worldview there was no supreme deity, no universal lawgiver, and no belief in punishment after death. It was thus up to human beings to construct a human order.

An ordered society, Confucius believed and taught, required three things: the inculcation of moral qualities; a defined social hierarchy; and the proper example of those who stood at the apex of society. The moral qualities Confucius prized included first and foremost *ren*, sometimes translated as 'human-heartedness' or 'humaneness', meaning something like philanthropic benevolence towards others and concern for their well-being. It became recognised as the essential quality of Chinese humanism. Other qualities included filial piety (*xiao*) and the duties that went with it; loyalty (*zhong*) to a principled superior; courage (*yong*) to act and speak out; righteousness (*yi*) expressed particularly in commitment to a just order; reciprocity (*shu*); and that combination of intellect and integrity (*xian*) that is the essential quality a minister must possess in order to advise his lord as he should. One who embodied and expressed these qualities was a *jun-zi*, a 'gentleman' in the ideal Confucian sense of one whose thought and action reflected his true moral worth. It was the goal of Confucius and the school of thought he founded to educate and produce such men, who would provide the moral core of the Chinese social and political order.[2]

Confucius was no democrat. There is never the slightest notion of social equality in his thinking. For him, the proper and harmonious ordering of society required the recognition and active reinforcement of social hierarchy. The *jun-zi* formed a cultured elite; but not for a moment should they think of usurping the hereditary right of rulers to rule. Their duty was to give advice to rulers, not to become philosopher-kings of the Platonic kind. Such high-principled men were formed through moral education, which all should undertake. Candidates were not confined to sons of the aristocracy and Confucius accepted disciples from all social levels, but the upward social mobility this provided was designed to reinforce social hierarchy, not undermine it.

The means by which social order was given overt expression and reinforced was through *li*, meaning literally 'ritual', but denoting a much wider range of religious and secular ceremony down to what we would call social etiquette. The term derived from the formal ritual performed during the rites of divination, and was subsequently extended to performance of all collective religious ceremonies. By further extension, *li* came to refer to the polite behaviour expected of individuals in everyday social intercourse. For Confucius there was a prescribed way to behave towards both superiors and inferiors. Each such behaviour, graciously performed, reinforced the social order.

The Chinese way of war

Confucius conspicuously failed to achieve what he had hoped to in his lifetime. The warring states continued to war. From this period dates an entirely different, but similarly practical, body of writings, not on government, but on the conduct of war. Six of the texts traditionally making up the seven military classics of ancient China date from the time of the warring states. These texts advise rulers on the strategy and tactics of warfare, with one end in mind—complete victory over the enemy.[3] To this end, all available means are justified, including espionage, sabotage and deception, in order to inflict defeat at the least cost to one's own forces. Morality is sacrificed to expediency. Indeed the writers of these treatises on war stand closer to Machiavelli than they do to Confucius.

Much has been made of these military classics as embodying a Chinese way of war which all later Chinese commanders, down to Mao Zedong, drew upon and applied. They have been extensively commented upon by both Chinese and Western scholars, who have pointed out how little reference they make to Confucian morality.[4]

Three brief comments can be made in relation to these military texts. The first is that they reflect the period in which they were written, just as did Machiavelli's advice to rulers in sixteenth-century Italy. We should not expect them to be imbued with Confucian values, for they were written centuries before these had become accepted as the basis for government. The second point is that pursuit of victory, forcefully and decisively, does not actually conflict with the Confucian ideal of social order once the texts are applied not to civil conflict between warring Chinese states, but between the Middle Kingdom and threatening barbarian enemies. Preservation of social harmony as endorsed by Heaven always extended beyond China's frontiers, a moral mission that justified the means used to achieve it. The third point, of importance for Southeast Asia, is that the Chinese way of war was much more consistently applied along China's northern and northwestern borders, against powerful nomadic empires, than it was against neighbouring kingdoms in the south and southwest, where the security threat was usually much less.

The Confucian ideal was taken up and elaborated more systematically by Master Kung's followers. The most important of these, Meng-zi (Mencius) and Xun-zi, both lived in the later Eastern Zhou period in the fourth and third centuries BCE, and both grappled with the problem of the proper use of force in a civilised society. In so doing they elaborated an important distinction between *bing* meaning war in an aggressive sense, which Confucianists condemned, and *zheng* referring to the use of violence in a punitive sense. The latter presupposed a moral and social order that had regrettably been violated, whether by rebels or barbarians, and thus needed to be restored. Punitive expeditions were justified, as much in sorrow as in anger, as necessary for the restoration of the social harmony that reflected Heaven's way. Their purpose should never, therefore, be to gain at the expense of others, neither for conquest nor booty, but rather to re-establish universal acceptance of the moral authority of the Son of Heaven. Time and again throughout Chinese history, China's use of military force has been described as 'punishment', most recently when China 'punished' Vietnam in 1979.

While Confucius's moral teachings may have fallen on deaf ears during his lifetime, his belief in social order and hierarchy, and his glorification of the early Zhou dynasty, when the Chinese cultural area was unified under Heaven, struck a resonant chord in the hearts and minds of later rulers and their ministers alike. When China was eventually united in a single empire by Qin Zi Huangdi in 221 BCE, however, it was not by an emperor acting upon the advice of a Confucian-educated elite. Rather, it was through the ruthless application of an entirely different philosophy of governance, known as Legalism.

The Legalists were convinced that social order could only be maintained through a totalitarian system of draconian laws administered by an impersonal bureaucracy. Human beings, they taught, responded only to punishments and rewards. It was not necessary for people to be educated to the need for social order; it was enough that they obey the decrees of their emperor. Nor did the Legalists believe that all wisdom lay in the past; situations should be examined on their own terms, and sensible solutions found.

If Legalism was preferred during the Qin dynasty (221–207 BCE), the succeeding Han dynasty (206 BCE–220 CE) incorporated elements of Legalism into a dominant Confucian framework. Actually, Legalists and Confucianists had much in common. Both sought social order, and both affirmed a strict social hierarchy, with the emperor at its apex. Both also believed that proper conduct (court ritual and social etiquette) were essential to reinforce this hierarchical social order. Where they differed was over whether people could be educated to the need for such conduct, and so act appropriately out of conviction; or whether they had to be forced to do so through fear of draconian punishment. The end they held in common; it was essentially the means over which they differed. Chinese government applied both.

Empire and world order: Qin and Han

The Qin dynasty re-established two things crucial to the Chinese worldview: the political unity of the Chinese culture area; and the exalted role of the emperor as the Son of Heaven. The significance of political unity lay in the concentration of power (*de*) it made possible. But the concept of *de* also carried the ancient sense of 'virtue', and so included a moral dimension. Internally *de* brought about good government; and it was this example, later thinkers agreed, that led barbarian rulers freely to acknowledge Chinese suzerainty.[5] The notion of *de* was reinforced by the concept of *dao*. This term has complex meanings, but as the core concept of the Taoists it denotes the 'way' of the natural world, and so refers to the unitary natural order of things. Once differentiated, *dao* gives rise to the contending forces of *yin* and *yang*, the universal principles of, respectively, female and male, dark and light, cold and heat, and so on. Equilibrium between these forces produces harmony (*ho*) within both the individual and society.

The synthesis of all the various elements contributing to the Chinese worldview was achieved during the Han dynasty. The core belief is that Heaven, humankind and Earth ideally constitute a single, harmonious, natural order. This order is both balanced, through the interaction of *yin* and *yang*, and moral, in that its ideal harmony rests on an ethical basis. The central figure in this scheme of things—the point, as it were, where Heaven and Earth converge—was the emperor.[6] As the Son of Heaven, he was the point of contact between the macrocosm and the microcosm. By the sacrifices he performed at the temples of Heaven and Earth, he ensured cosmic balance and harmony; by his personal behaviour he ensured, or failed to ensure, Heaven's blessing. Any moral failure on the part of the emperor, any failure of *de*, would provoke Heaven's displeasure, made known by signs and portents, in the form of such remarkable and unseasonable events as the appearance of shooting stars, floods, and earthquakes, or by increasing human misery and social chaos.

The Emperor ruled 'all under Heaven' (*tian-xia*), the entire human world as cosmically constituted. In a cosmic sense, the Son of Heaven was a universal ruler; not just his capital, but he himself was the centre of the world. The realm over which he ruled was the Middle Kingdom, a term that acknowledged that other kingdoms lay beyond it in the four directions. The Chinese worldview was sinocentric, but this did not mean that it ignored the existence of other peoples. Beyond the core area of Chinese civilisation lived barbarian peoples (*yi-ti*), inferior in every way to the Chinese, yet still existing under Heaven and so part of the great 'family' presided over by the Son of Heaven. Though Chinese superiority was primarily cultural, this easily slipped into attitudes that were essentially racial. Non-Chinese were likened to animals and stood well below Chinese in the socio-cultural hierarchy. Redemption was possible only for those who were culturally assimilated. Until this happened, non-Chinese were to be treated with paternal benevolence, as objects of the emperor's protection.

The place of non-Chinese in this view of the world was arrived at over the course of time. The Chinese had always been surrounded by those they termed 'barbarians', for their lack of civilisation (*wen*). In unifying the empire, Qin pushed back the barbarians in the north and northwest, and protected the Chinese core cultural area by construction of the Great Wall. It was in the southeast, however, that the greatest gains were made. There new military/administrative commanderies were created, colonised by a motley collection of criminals, fugitives from military service or forced labour, bonded servants, and small traders and retailers who stood at the bottom of the social scale. Continuing internal migration during the Han dynasty eventually brought all the non-Chinese coastal peoples, known collectively as the Yue, inhabiting the region from Fujian to Guangdong and south to the Red River delta (in what is now northern Vietnam) under Chinese political control and cultural influence.

The progress and significance of this southern expansion for relations with Southeast Asia will be examined in the next chapter. Here, what is important is how Qin and Han conquests reinforced Chinese thinking about how non-Chinese peoples should be incorporated into the Chinese world order. The most powerful of these non-Chinese peoples, the Xiongnu, precursors to the Huns, inhabited the steppe lands to the northwest. As their mobility and fighting prowess made Chinese conquest impossible, appeasement was the only possible recourse. Rich annual payments of silk, alcohol and foodstuffs and dispatch of Chinese 'princesses' were used to buy off Xiongnu rulers. A treaty signed in 198 BCE not only established the Great Wall as the frontier between Han China and the Xiongnu confederacy, but also formally noted the equivalent status of the two 'brother' kingdoms. This was for the benefit of the Xiongnu. For the Chinese, brothers were never of equal status: one was always the elder, the other the younger. Even so, such a situation rankled for the Chinese, for it threatened their own understanding of the world, and the respective places of Chinese and barbarians in it. Moreover, as the treaty stipulated that the Han would provide a substantial annual 'gift' of silk and other commodities in return for a Xiongnu commitment not to raid Chinese settlements within the wall, it was a moot point who was paying tribute to whom.[7]

Despite the treaty of 198 BCE, therefore, the Chinese never for a moment accepted the Xiongnu as their equals. The Chinese view of the world that had evolved by the later Han period (the first two centuries CE) conceived it in the form of five concentric zones or regions (*wu-fu*), whose relations to each other were strictly hierarchical. At the centre stood the royal domain, the area under the direct rule of the emperor himself. Beyond lay the zone controlled by the great feudatory lords of the kingdom, who were loyal to the emperor. Then came those areas, known as the pacified zone, that were culturally Chinese, but had had to be conquered in order to be brought into the empire. These three zones comprised the Middle Kingdom, beyond which lay two further barbarian zones—an inner one or controlled zone for those barbarian tribes who accepted Chinese suzerainty, and an outer or wild zone for those who did not. The five zones combined thus constituted 'all under Heaven'.[8]

The hierarchical relationship between these zones was defined by the frequency with which tribute was presented to the emperor. In the central zone, this was on a daily basis in the form of produce and services rendered to the court. The lords were required to present their tribute once a month, while tribute from the pacified zone was expected every three months. Controlled barbarians presented tribute annually, while those beyond, in the wild zone, were expected to appear only once at court, a symbolic appearance that signalled their inclusion within the Chinese world order.

While this was clearly an idealised schema, during the Han dynasty it did roughly reflect the division, within the Chinese cultural area, into a well-guarded capital territory, commanderies under central administration, and feudal kingdoms that had declared allegiance to the Han emperor. Over time, most of these kingdoms reverted to the direct control of the central administration, particularly after the conquests of Han Wudi, who finally brought the Yue coastal region into the empire. Even after these conquests, the Yue counted as inner or controlled barbarians, or 'dependent countries', from whom annual tribute was expected. The Xiongnu, by contrast, were classified as outer or wild barbarians beyond Chinese control, and so not expected to pay regular tribute.

The tributary system was not fully institutionalised under the Han, but it did evolve in response to particular circumstances. Because it applied, as noted above, to Chinese as well as barbarians, the system was in a sense inclusive rather than divisive. It included barbarians within the Chinese world order, but created a clear distinction between inner and outer barbarians, between those effectively colonised through imperial expansion, and those allowed independent status. Non-Chinese peoples within the empire were placed under

Chinese administration and progressively sinicised. Those beyond the empire's frontiers were under no such pressure, though the Chinese could pretend that eventually these too would come to accept the superiority of Chinese civilisation.

Han conquests brought new barbarian peoples within the empire. These included the southern Yue, whom we now know as the Vietnamese. It did not include the peoples of Yunnan, where the later kingdoms of Nanzhao then Dali retained their independence until conquered by the Mongols in 1253 CE. While most of the peoples incorporated into the Han empire became sinicised over the centuries, some stubbornly maintained their own cultures, including the Vietnamese, the Miao (Hmong) and other mountain tribes and minorities. Some, including the Tai, migrated south, away from Chinese domination, to establish their own independent principalities. No kingdom on China's frontiers to the south, however, ever posed an equivalent military threat to the steppe peoples of the north.

In summary, therefore, by the time of the later Han dynasty, when expansion of the Chinese cultural area had brought Chinese peoples increasingly into contact with those of Southeast Asia, a specifically Chinese view of the world was already firmly established, though the institutions by which foreign polities were ritually incorporated into this worldview (the tribute system) were not yet fully in place. The key elements of this worldview included the unity of Heaven, Earth and humankind; the notion of Heaven as a moral force imposing a moral order; social harmony as Heaven's way; and the emperor as Son of Heaven at the apex of, and presiding over, a hierarchical social world in which all were assigned their status, including non-Chinese. The Middle Kingdom comprised the Chinese cultural area whose superior civilisation was available to less cultured peoples. Eventually, the Chinese were convinced, barbarian peoples would be drawn by the virtue of the emperor to recognise the superiority of Chinese civilisation and voluntarily to embrace it. In the meantime, they were expected symbolically to recognise that superiority, and along with it the cosmic status of the emperor, by deferentially offering their tribute at court and gratefully receiving gifts in exchange. They were also expected to keep the peace along China's frontiers, for the notion of social harmony necessarily extended beyond the Middle Kingdom to embrace 'all under Heaven'. In other words, China brought to its earliest relations with Southeast Asia an already evolved foreign relations culture.

3
EARLY RELATIONS

中國

Indirect trading contact between China and the Nanyang, or Southern Ocean, the name by which the Chinese referred to Southeast Asia, goes back as far as the Shang dynasty when cowrie shells were used as currency. During the Zhou dynasty a variety of luxury products, including ivory, rhinoceros horn, tortoise-shell, pearls and birds' feathers, found their way to the Chinese capital. Little is known about early trade routes, or the traders who plied them, but it would seem likely that while most of these products reached China overland, some arrived too on small coastal vessels crewed by 'Malay' or Yue seamen. How far merchandise travelled by sea and in what early entrepôts it was exchanged during the later Zhou period, we can only guess.

What we do know from Zhou period texts is that the Chinese were acutely aware of the difference between themselves and non-Chinese 'barbarians', and of their own cultural superiority, no matter what desirable products the barbarians might possess. It is clear, however, that intercourse with non-Chinese peoples, while it might reflect Chinese assumptions of superiority, had yet to become formalised into what was later known as the 'tributary system'. That in its fully elaborated form was the outcome of centuries of development from the Han to the Ming dynasties.

Trade was an important source of wealth for the Yue peoples of coastal China south of the Yangze River. That wealth, and access to luxury products from Southeast Asia, seems to have motivated the first Qin emperor to send his victorious armies against the Yue kingdoms. Chinese domination was brief, however, and in the chaos that followed the overthrow of the Qin dynasty, many of the Yue peoples regained their independence. It was left to the emperor, Han Wudi, in the early first century BCE, finally to extend Chinese power to the southern coastal province of Guangdong, and to the Red River delta of northern Vietnam.

In the meantime Chinese migration into the Yue coastal regions had increased, as families fled unrest or persecution, or sought new opportunities. These migrants brought with them Chinese culture and the Chinese system of writing. Though extensive borrowing occurred, northern Chinese (Mandarin) never succeeded in replacing the Yue languages, which continue to this day in the form of Chinese 'dialects' (including Wu, Min, and Cantonese). The Yue languages of coastal China became monosyllabic and tonal, like Mandarin Chinese. In this form they could easily be written using Chinese characters. The capacity of the non-alphabetic Chinese writing system to provide the crucial adhesive that held China together as a unitary, centrally administered kingdom can hardly be overestimated. It provided access for the coastal peoples to Chinese classical literature and the worldview it took for granted, and led them to identify themselves eventually as Chinese. This process of sinicisation was long and drawn out, seeping down over the centuries from the literate elite to shape the thinking of the mass of the population. Only the Vietnamese in the end were able to resist this process and retain their separate identity as the Lac people, or southern Yue (the character for which is pronounced Viet in Vietnamese).

By the beginning of the first century BCE, conditions existed for an expansion of Chinese contacts with Southeast Asia. Yet this was slow to happen. Yue vessels do not seem to have ventured far beyond their coastal waters. The few bold Chinese merchants, adventurers, and eventually envoys, who sailed to Southeast Asia did so on ships probably crewed by more accomplished Austronesian-speaking sailors whom we can broadly designate as 'Malay'. There are several reasons why the Chinese failed to exploit trading possibilities with Southeast Asia at this time. For one thing, after Han Wudi's reign no official encouragement was given to overseas trade, though if we are to believe the historian Ban Gu writing almost two centuries later, tributary (essentially trade) missions were received from as far away as south India. Also, the products of Southeast Asia were relatively little known. The luxury items most prized by the Chinese came from India and further west, overland along the fabled Silk Road. Sea trade was dangerous, and as foreign vessels continued to make port in northern Vietnam and southern China, bringing pearls, coral, tortoise shell, precious stones and bird's feathers to exchange for silks and gold, there was little need for Chinese merchants to sail their own ships into the Southern Ocean.

The few Chinese traders who voyaged by sea at this time would first have come into contact with the Cham, a people speaking an Austronesian language who had settled along the coast of central Vietnam. Merchants who ventured further into the Gulf of Thailand would then have encountered proto-Khmer and Mon speakers of Austroasiatic languages who had established riverine or coastal settlements. Further to the south Malay peoples were already present along the coasts of peninsula Malaya, and had populated much of maritime Southeast Asia. All were poised to construct their own small and localised kingdoms, and eager to borrow any ideas that would help. The failure of the Chinese to take to the sea left the way open for Indian influence to dominate state formation in Southeast Asia.

Early Southeast Asia

Little is known about Indian trade and contact with Southeast Asia during this early, but crucial period. What we do know is that important trade routes ran from the mouth of the Ganges down the coast of Burma, and from south India across the Bay of Bengal. These converged on the Kra Isthmus where low-weight, high-value luxury goods from as far away as the eastern Mediterranean were transported overland to be reshipped in the Gulf of Thailand. From there small ships hugged the coast all the way to Canton. Another trade route must at least by the early centuries CE have led south through the Strait of Melaka to southern Sumatra and northern Java, though at this stage there seems to have been no corresponding link between Indonesia and China.

It was along these maritime trade routes that Indian civilisation reached Southeast Asia. From Burma to central Vietnam and from Sumatra to Borneo, the peoples of Southeast Asia borrowed elements of Indian religion and ritual, statecraft and social organisation, language, literature and art. Most Indian traders were probably either Tamils from south India or perhaps Sinhalese from Sri Lanka, whose pearls were in high demand. For them, trade east to Suvarnabhumi, the fabled 'land of gold', promised great profit. But these merchants did not come alone. By the first century CE, they were accompanied by Brahmin priests and Buddhist monks literate and learned in all aspects of Indian culture and religion. Southeast Asian seamen meanwhile reached India, and returned with their own accounts of Indian civilisation.

The process by which local chieftains throughout Southeast Asia adopted and adapted elements of Indian civilisation that would legitimise their rule and enhance their power is usually referred to as Indianisation. It proceeded, especially over the first two centuries CE, initially in coastal trading ports, but in time penetrated inland to influence larger land-based kingdoms in Burma, Java, Cambodia and Thailand. We cannot follow in detail the rise of various early Southeast Asian kingdoms, but we will give some attention to the first of these, known to the Chinese as 'Funan'. By what name it was known by its own people, we do not know.

Funan was the first kingdom in Southeast Asia to which Chinese envoys were sent. Apart from a few references in inscriptions, the fragmentary reports of these envoys are the only records that remain of Funan, apart from archaeological evidence. The Chinese mission arrived probably around 228 CE, on behalf of the state of Wu, the southernmost of the three kingdoms into which China was divided after the collapse of the Han dynasty in 220 CE. Contact with the Southern Ocean during the later Han had been intermittent at best, as the principal trade route to Persia and India was still overland through Central Asia. For the Wu rulers, however, cut off as they were from northern China, only the maritime route was available.

It was probably to promote the potential benefits of increased trade that Chinese envoys were dispatched to Funan, perhaps in response to an earlier Funanese trade mission. From the accounts they recorded, along with a few later inscriptions, we can gain some idea of the economics and politics, the power and extent, of Funan. What emerges is a polity owing its economic prosperity to a combination of its agricultural base (a peasant population producing a surplus of rice) and its geographic location about mid-way between southern China and the Kra Isthmus.

Funan owed both its origins and most of its cultural borrowing to Indian traders and the occasional Brahmin priest who had put into its principal port of Oc-eo over the two centuries before the Chinese envoys arrived. It was founded, the Chinese reported, as a result of a marriage between an Indian Brahmin and a female ruler, a probably mythical union symbolising the syncretism of Indian and local culture. But we should beware of placing too much credence in Chinese descriptions of Funan—or of other early Southeast Asia kingdoms.[1]

This is because the Chinese envoys described what they saw and learned through Chinese eyes. Theirs was a centrally organised kingdom, in which a powerful court appointed officials to administer districts and provinces in the name of the emperor. But Southeast Asian kingdoms were not so organised and administered, for they owed their philosophy of government and political structure not to China, but to India.

Powerful empires did arise in India—the Mauryan empire under Ashoka in the third century BCE and the Gupta empire under Chandragupta II in the second century CE are obvious examples. But these empires were constructed through the incorporation of neighbouring kingdoms as functioning units. Often the ruling family would remain in place, provided they acknowledged the suzerainty of their new overlord. The empire was held together through formal oaths of loyalty backed by regular payment of tribute, the provision of troops when called upon, a well-developed network of spies and informers, and the capacity of the centre to punish any ruler tempted to renounce his allegiance. When the centre was weak, particularly during succession disputes, outlying territories tended to break away and declare their independence. Often a new ruler, preoccupied with establishing his own right to rule, could do nothing but let them go. Frontiers were thus much less stable than in a centrally administered empire like China.

The Indian model was eminently suitable for Southeast Asia. By the early centuries CE, centres of power had developed in several areas where agricultural resources were more extensive and population could expand. There 'men of prowess' arose who enforced their rule over neighbouring territories.[2] A powerful regional ruler might appoint his sons to rule outlying areas. When he became frail or died, however, these same sons would often contest the succession, backed by competing powerful families and court factions. Kings used every means to concentrate power by demanding tribute from regional leaders and requiring them to serve at court.

Early Southeast Asian rulers and elites borrowed from India, above all, the means to legitimise and consolidate their power. These included a system of writing and the language (classical Sanskrit) and literature that went with it, principles of statecraft, and a set of religious beliefs that rested on the identity of local deities with gods of the Indian pantheon. Kings ruled as representatives of a high god, their right to rule reinforced by the central role they played in religious rituals designed to ensure the prosperity of the kingdom through control over cosmic forces. This Indian system of power relations did nothing, however, to overcome the inherent political instability of early Southeast Asian kingdoms. Instead it reinforced the segmentary structure of Southeast Asian polities in the form of what have become known as *mandalas*, in order to differentiate them from modern territorial states.

To call a Southeast Asian kingdom a *mandala* is to draw attention, metaphorically, to relations of power that connected the periphery to the centre. The *mandalas* of Southeast Asia were constellations of power, whose extent varied in relation to the attraction of the centre. They were not states whose administrative control reached to defined frontiers. Power diminished with distance from the centre, frontiers fluctuated, and relations with neighbouring *mandalas* tended to be antagonistic, as each attempted to expand at the other's expense. As a key Sanskrit text, the *Arthaśāstra* explains, neighbouring kingdoms should be distrusted as potential enemies, while the enemies of enemies should be treated as friends.[3] A more different world from that familiar to Chinese merchants and travellers would be hard to imagine.

We should think of Funan, therefore, not as a centralised kingdom extending from southern Vietnam all the way around to the Kra Isthmus, but rather as a *mandala*, the power of whose capital in southeastern Cambodia waxed and waned, and whose armed merchant ships succeeded in enforcing its temporary suzerainty over small coastal trading ports around the Gulf of Thailand. What gave Funan the edge over other such centres of power was clearly its position astride the India–China trade route. Its power, however, is unlikely to have spread far inland. Further north, on the middle Mekong and on the lower Chao Phraya River, other power centres were establishing themselves that in time would challenge and replace Funan.

Six Funanese tributary missions to China are recorded as arriving during the third century. Then comes a gap of seventy years, a single embassy in 357 CE, then eighty years before a group of three embassies arrived between 434 and 438 CE. After a further gap of some fifty years, ten embassies arrived between 484 and 539, and three more between 559 and the last embassy in 588, after which Funan gave way to Zhenla, which itself was replaced by the Khmer kingdom of Angkor in 802.

What are we to make of this patchy record? Why were embassies sent so infrequently, and why by some kings and not others? And what did they mean to both parties? Of course, it may be that embassies did arrive more frequently and were not recorded, or that the records of their arrival have been lost. But China was a bureaucratic state, and records were important. Moreover, embassies from other countries were just as intermittent. It seems likely, therefore, that the list of Funanese embassies is relatively complete.

So what conclusions can we draw? The first is that these were not tribute missions in the sense that applied between the segmentary parts of Southeast Asian *mandalas*. Funan was not required to send large amounts of produce to China, nor were Funanese kings required to take loyalty oaths to the Son of Heaven. Embassies were sent not in response to Chinese directives, but for the benefit of Funanese rulers. For the Chinese, on the other hand, all official missions, even those solely concerned with trade, were designated as 'tributary' in order to conform to the Chinese sinocentric view of the world. Embassies from barbarian kingdoms served to reinforce the way in which the Chinese understood the world and their own place in it. Their purpose, in Chinese eyes, was as much ideological as economic. The emperor graciously accepted the 'tribute' offered, but gave more expensive presents in return. Of course, foreign embassies also brought goods for trade, and the Chinese well appreciated their commercial value.

A second conclusion is that the frequency of official embassies by no means indicated the extent and volume of trade between China and Funan. Private trade fluctuated, depending on political conditions in both China and Southeast Asia, but it certainly did not dry up for decades on end. 'Smuggling' continued even when official sanctions against trade were enforced, for local officials could always be bribed.

So why did Southeast Asian rulers send official embassies to China? Some went in response to the invitation of Chinese emperors who sought exotic products or the gratification of barbarian submission. Some Southeast Asian rulers dispatched embassies in order to reinforce or legitimise their own power. Presentation of fine clothing, titles and regalia raised the status of rulers of small kingdoms like Funan, giving them the edge over their rivals in the cutthroat politics of Southeast Asian *mandalas*. Most embassies, however, were sent to promote trade, particularly in Chinese luxury products, such as silk and later fine porcelain, desired as status symbols by Southeast Asian elites.

There is still something odd about proud and independent Southeast Asian rulers accepting even nominal vassal status in the form of Chinese investiture, even if this was to their temporary political advantage. In order to understand why so many were prepared to do so, we need to look more carefully at the worldview of Southeast Asia, for this rested on entirely different cosmological as well as political, institutional and economic foundations from the Chinese understanding of the world outlined in the previous chapter.

Most early Southeast Asian rulers borrowed from Hinduism the idea that the king was the representative on earth of the great god Shiva (or more rarely Vishnu). Prosperity depended on the extent to which an earthly kingdom reflected the heavenly realm of the gods. The more nearly this was achieved, the closer the identity between king and god, and the greater the power of the king. Kings thus set out to recreate in microcosm the macrocosmic geography of the divine realm, with the palace at the centre representing the abode of the gods on Mount Meru, the world axis. The impressive rituals at which they officiated only added to their aura of cosmic power.

Belief in karma and reincarnation provided further legitimisation. Karma as an inexorable natural law of moral cause and effect provided an explanation for both individual fortune and social status. The king ruled as king because through previous lifetimes he had accumulated the necessary karma to do so. In this way karma powerfully reinforced social hierarchy, for everyone was born into the social situation they deserved.

Kings sought to maximise their sources of social power: military, economic, political, and ideological. Ultimately the goal of a powerful king was to become a universal ruler, or *chakravartin*. As no ruler could know how far his karma might permit him to go in realising this ideal, the potential was always there. A more powerful ruler would have superior karma, but this was recognised only as a temporary phenomenon, for who knew what a ruler's karma had in store, or that of his successor? This was a worldview that accounted for and reinforced hierarchies of power; and did so without discredit, for all such hierarchies were always open to change.

The temporary nature of political power is even more evident in Buddhism than in Hinduism, for in Buddhism impermanence (*anicca*) is one of the three 'signs of being', along with the inevitability of suffering (*dukkha*) and the non-existence of a permanent self or soul (*anatta*). As all earthly phenomena are impermanent, so are all configurations of power. One can therefore accept the greater power of another kingdom, in the knowledge that this will change in time. The mighty will be laid low, and new powers will arise. The fluidity of this conception of the world as process contrasted markedly with the order and stability of the Chinese worldview.

These very differences in worldview allowed Southeast Asian rulers to accommodate the pretensions even of the emperor of China.

An important factor here was the different way in which tribute was understood. Superior karma and thus status was recognised in the *mandala* through a net transfer of power to the centre, both economic—through tribute paid in the form of goods and food supplies—and military—through provision of a contingent of troops when called upon. Tribute in Southeast Asian *mandalas* was thus the principal means by which political elites extracted and concentrated surplus resources. In an economic sense, tribute constituted a 'mode of production'. Instead of taxing people, land, or agricultural produce at a fixed rate, tribute from a subordinate ruler required delivery of specified amounts of valuable local products, which might be gathered (such as aromatic woods and resins, rare wildlife, or spices), mined (gold, silver and other metals), grown (mainly rice), or manufactured (including weapons and luxury handicrafts). Some of these would be retained for use by the king and his court; others would be traded, often as a royal monopoly. All that was offered in return was status as a lord of the realm and protection against the depredations of neighbouring kingdoms.

Tribute in a Southeast Asian context was thus very different from the tribute demanded by Chinese emperors from vassal kingdoms. For the Chinese tribute denoted not the transfer of economic resources, but symbolic submission. The presents the emperor gave in return were consistently of higher value than the tribute offered, in order to demonstrate imperial magnanimity and benevolence. China pretended that it needed nothing material from barbarians. Tribute for China was thus not a means of accumulating wealth (even through accompanying trade), but symbolic recognition and reinforcement of China's superior status in its own sinocentric world order.

For Southeast Asian kings, tribute 'paid' to China did not carry the same connotation as tribute demanded from their own vassals, just because more valuable gifts were given in exchange. What was tribute for the Chinese was for Southeast Asian rulers the polite exchange of gifts as a formality that went with mutually beneficial trade. The accompanying ceremonial established status hierarchy, but not vassalage in the Southeast Asian sense. It was acceptable for envoys to show proper respect to the Chinese emperor, just as Chinese envoys paid their respects to Southeast Asian kings; but with the exception of Vietnam, no ruler of a major Southeast Asian kingdom ever voyaged to Beijing to pay homage in person.

The differing understandings of what the tributary relationship entailed are evident in an incident in October 1592 when King Narasuan of Ayutthaya offered Siamese naval assistance to the Ming court in its struggle to contain the depredations of Japanese pirates. The offer was refused, for from the Chinese point of view it would have been demeaning, and an admission of Chinese weakness, to have accepted. In the *mandala* world of Southeast Asia, however, it was usual for an ally to contribute military assistance in time of war. Narasuan may have hoped for some quid pro quo in his own conflict with the Burmese, but his offer, and the Ming refusal, point to essential differences in worldview.

Differing interpretations of the meaning of the ritual of diplomatic intercourse enabled entirely different Chinese and Southeast Asian cultures of international relations to find compromise in mutually acceptable bilateral relations regimes. These necessarily built on certain congruities. Both Chinese and Southeast Asian worldviews acknowledged hierarchy as the natural order, both in their own societies and in relations between polities. Both sought to maximise power through manipulation of ideologies of legitimation and world order. But what for the Chinese was the permanent order of the relation between Heaven, Earth and humankind represented by the emperor was, for Southeast Asian rulers, the temporary configuration of the ever-changing play of karma. And what for the Chinese was tribute offered in submission to the Son of Heaven was, for Southeast Asian rulers, polite recognition of superior status as a prerequisite for mutually beneficial trade.

Rulers of early Southeast Asian kingdoms were ready to recognise the superior power and status of China, even though most had never witnessed this for themselves. Chinese emissaries extolled the emperor's glory; merchants brought back stories of the extent and wealth of China; and Southeast Asian envoys reported on the impressive pomp and ritual that accompanied their presentation at the Chinese court. China did not have to send its armies into Southeast Asia for regional rulers to accept China's formal demand that visiting officials prostrate themselves before the Son of Heaven. The exchange of presents was for Southeast Asian rulers a matter of courtesy; but if the Chinese insisted on the formalities of a 'tributary' relationship, then this could be accommodated in the context of Southeast Asian Hindu/Buddhist worldviews.

Little of this is explicitly stated in the records of Southeast Asian kingdoms. In part this is because so much of what must have been a considerable literature and extensive administrative records have disappeared. Climate, the fragility of the treated palm leaf principally used as a writing medium in Southeast Asia, poor storage facilities that allowed the ravages of mildew and insects, and the destruction of war, all have contributed to the dearth of written sources in Southeast Asia compared to China. All that remains, apart from all-important inscriptions on stone or metal, are those texts that were regularly recopied. These were mainly religious texts, the copying of which generated spiritual merit, various technical treatises on such subjects as agriculture, astrology and law, and court chronicles. In few of these, even the last, can be found any references, however, to political or even economic relations with China.

The reason why even the court chronicles of Southeast Asian kingdoms say next to nothing about China does not, however, indicate China's unimportance for Southeast Asian rulers, though for most, China probably did not loom large. More significant is the kind of text we are dealing with. Court chronicles in the Theravada Buddhist kingdoms of mainland Southeast Asia were not composed as objective historical records. On the contrary, they formed part of the royal regalia of legitimation. They recorded the ruler's genealogy, his marriage alliances and his meritorious deeds, all of which were intended to reinforce his right to rule in the eyes of his subjects.

Given this purpose, it is not surprising that there is little mention of tributary missions to China. No mention was made of China because to have done so would neither have enhanced a king's glory, nor reinforced the Southeast Asian (Hindu/Buddhist) worldview. By contrast, the records kept by the Chinese of embassies received from even the smallest and most remote Southeast Asian principalities did reinforce the Chinese worldview by magnifying the virtue and might of the emperor as ruling 'all under Heaven'. It was for this reason that tribute missions were minutely recorded and their importance consistently exaggerated by Chinese court officials (who even falsified accounts and mistranslated documents to make their point).

Expansion of contacts: trade and religion

In 280 CE the northern Jin dynasty reunified China, though their victory was short-lived. A number of Southeast Asian kingdoms, including Funan and Champa (known to the Chinese as Lin-yi), took the opportunity to establish official relations with the new regime. Over the next disturbed century, however, very few embassies were recorded from Southeast Asia, though it might have been expected that the loss of central Asian trade routes would once again have stimulated Chinese interest in the Nanyang. What did generate renewed interest and contacts in the fifth and sixth centuries was the growth of Buddhism as a religion, both in China and in Southeast Asia, mainly in the Mon areas of southern Burma and Thailand, in the Malay peninsula, and in Indonesia (in both southern Sumatra and central Java).

Trade was often disrupted during this period by war and rebellion in either China or Southeast Asia. Along the coast of central Vietnam, the Cham attempted to extend their domains, while further south Funan was already a declining power. Progress was steadily being made,

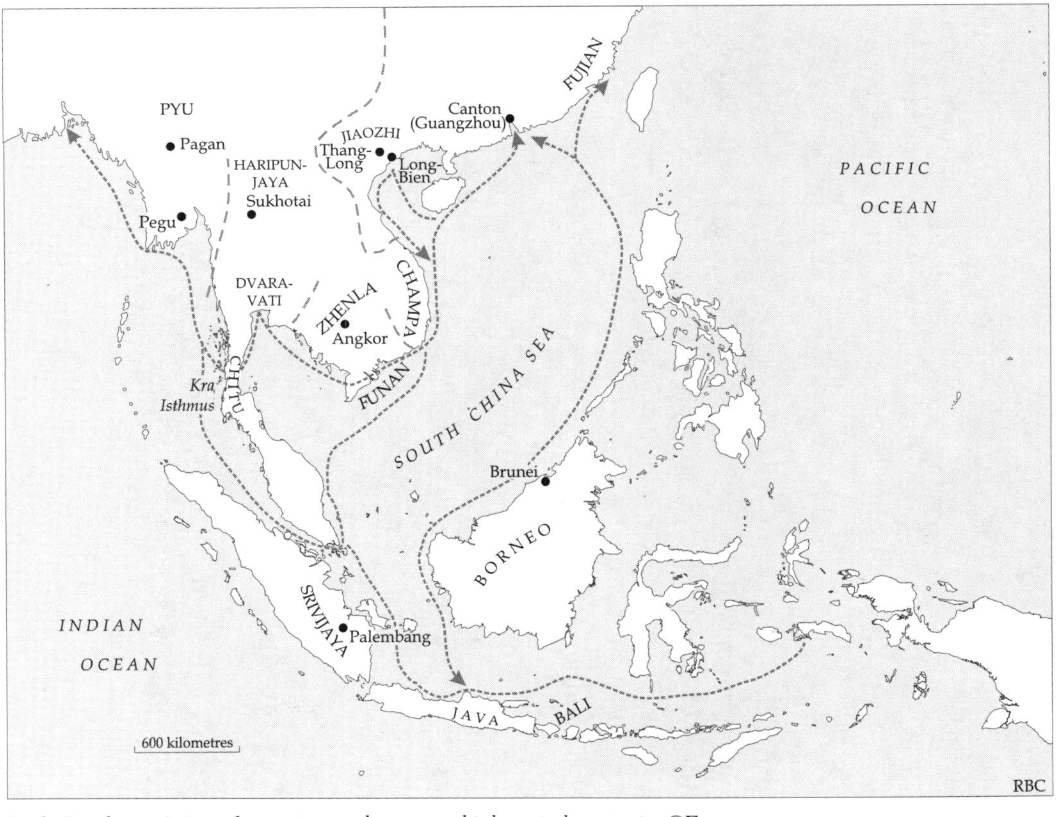

Early Southeast Asia and maritime trade routes, third to ninth centuries CE.

however, in the technology of boat building and navigation. We know that larger trading vessels based on Indian prototypes were being constructed by the Cham and Funanese at this time, if not yet along the Chinese coast. It would appear, too, that Indian and Southeast Asian seamen were learning more about the winds and currents of the South China Sea, using the southwest and northeast monsoons to cross open water rather than hugging the coast. We also know that these ships carried a new group of travellers making the long voyage between China and India. These were ardent Buddhist pilgrims, seeking or bringing back knowledge of this new religion.

Buddhism came to China both by land through central Asia (then from Afghanistan to Xinjiang almost entirely Buddhist) to northern China and by sea from India, Sri Lanka and Buddhist parts of Southeast Asia to southern Chinese ports. Buddhism appealed to the Chinese both on an intellectual level through its metaphysical psychology and its pragmatic approach to spiritual fulfilment, and on a popular level through its magical powers and its promise of reincarnation. The first few centuries CE were a period of great intellectual excitement in the Buddhist world, as new schools of the Mahayana, and later the Tantricism of the Vajrayana, contended with earlier interpretations. Chinese Buddhists were eager to learn of these developments and to study the texts in which they were expounded. It was in order to pursue their studies, and to collect both texts and relics, that Chinese Buddhist pilgrims set out for India.

How many Chinese Buddhists made this long pilgrimage, and how many failed in the attempt, we do not know. We do have important accounts left by a handful of those who returned to acclaim and honour. The first of these Chinese pilgrims whom we know to have sailed via Southeast Asia was Fa-xian in 413, on his return on a Malay-crewed ship that crossed directly from Java to Canton. Others followed, not just Chinese, but Indian and Southeast Asian Buddhists as well. Increasingly embassies from Southeast Asian kingdoms included Buddhist items (texts, relics and the paraphernalia of worship) among their gifts. As Buddhism became widely established in China, so demand grew for such products as aromatic resins and woods used to make incense, dyes and medicinal substances.

Buddhism, in other words, provided both a new area of common interest and a stimulus to trade between China and Southeast Asia. Prior to this, Chinese and Southeast Asians had had little in common. Their worldviews, as outlined above, were far apart. For a while, however, until the Chinese evolved their own forms of Buddhism and the religion declined in the land of its origin, Buddhist pilgrimage added a significant cultural dimension to relations between China and some, at least, of the countries of the Southern Ocean.

Trade, however, still remained the primary concern. For almost three hundred years, until China was again unified under the Sui dynasty in 589 CE, non-Chinese dynasties ruled north China. Though these dynasties did much to promote Buddhism, tens of thousands of Chinese families fled south to the Yangze region and beyond to escape their reach. This permanently shifted the balance of population and reinforced the Chinese character of the coastal provinces south to Guangdong. Southern dynasties centred on Nanjing tried unsuccessfully to recapture lost territory in the north, often to the neglect of still only lightly sinicised regions west of Canton. Jiao-zhi (northern Vietnam) in particular remained a frontier area, a prey to the ambitions of independent-minded governors and raids by Cham fleets sailing up from the central coast of Vietnam. Disruption to trade was at times serious, until in 446 a Sino–Vietnamese expedition decisively defeated the Cham, ushering in more than a century of peaceful relations.

An analysis of fifth and sixth century diplomatic missions from Southeast Asia reveals a clear correlation between tribute and trade on the one hand, and conditions in China on the other.[4] During times of political unrest, central government control over the coastal provinces was weak, and so was demand for luxury products. As lawlessness and piracy increased, foreign vessels were reluctant to call at Chinese ports. When central authority was reimposed, as it was under the Liang dynasty from 502 to 557 CE, Southeast Asian kingdoms quickly responded. Official missions arrived to establish the diplomatic conditions essential for trade promotion and protection.

From the seventh to the tenth centuries China was unified under the Sui and Tang dynasties. Under the Sui, the demand for luxury products from Southeast Asia was artificially stimulated by the extravagance of the court. As supplies were limited, prices rose. The Chinese response was twofold: to seek to control by aggressive use of force those regions within striking range of Chinese fleets and armies; and to use diplomacy to promote trade with kingdoms further afield. In 605, a Chinese army sacked and looted the Cham capital, while five years later a Chinese fleet raided Liu-qiu (the Ryukyu islands).

In 607, the first official Chinese embassy for more than three centuries departed in a substantial fleet for the Southern Ocean. Its goal was to make contact with the new kingdom of Chitu that had arisen on the Malay peninsula with the decline of Funan. The mission was entirely successful, for the king of Chitu needed little urging to promote trade with China. Two tribute missions were dispatched in successive years to establish the necessary protocol, and missions from smaller kingdoms in the region soon followed, including from as far away as east Java (or Bali).

The Tang dynasty that seized power from the Sui in 618 was of mixed Chinese and Turkish descent and created an empire that extended deep into central Asia. It was remarkably open to external cultural influences, particularly to Buddhism.[5] Foreign merchants, missionaries and adventurers flocked to the Tang capital of Changan, which became the most cosmopolitan and populous city in the world. Most came overland along the Silk Road through central Asia, but two other land routes were also travelled: one from India via Tibet and Nepal; the other from Burma via Yunnan.

The confident and outward-looking Tang dynasty encouraged official foreign relations as a means at first of managing foreign trade, though in time limitations on private trade were relaxed. The early

Tang emperors were powerful enough to demand that relations even with the empires of the Uighurs and the Turks should conform to the tributary system. An elaborate ceremonial was developed for escorting envoys to the capital, welcoming them, and preparing them for the official audience and banquet in the imperial presence. Frequent kowtowing was expected, consisting of three kneelings and nine prostrations touching the forehead to the ground, symbolising submission to the Son of Heaven.

The early Tang could demand such submission, before the dynasty was weakened by rebellion in the mid-eighth century. Even thereafter the formalities were preserved, as was the status distinction between Chinese and barbarians. Yet judged on the basis of civilisation this distinction was becoming harder to maintain. Neighbouring kingdoms, including Korea and Japan, developed high cultures that borrowed much from the Tang. In Southeast Asia new and powerful kingdoms arose. In Cambodia the Khmer kingdom of Angkor replaced Zhenla; in southern Sumatra the new power of Srivijaya extended its control over the Melaka and Sunda Straits and adjacent coasts; while in Java the Sailendras created a powerful inland kingdom. All provided examples of high culture (the temples of Angkor, the Borobudur in Java) that were different from, but hardly inferior to that of China.

Tang policy with respect to official contact and trade with Southeast Asia was benign. The two principal ports for the Nanyang trade continued to be Canton and Long-bien near modern Hai-phong. These were connected by inland routes north to the Tang capital, via the Grand Canal that had been much improved to accommodate the increased movement of goods and people. From these southern ports Tang envoys voyaged abroad, and to them foreign missions came—initially from Champa and Zhenla, then from further afield from kingdoms on the Malay Peninsula, Sumatra and Java.

Diplomatic missions even arrived from India and Sri Lanka, indicating the importance of Indians, Persians, and Arabs in the expansion of Indian Ocean trade. Their well constructed and seaworthy ships sailed around the Malay Peninsula, and on to south China. This eliminated the land portage across the Kra Isthmus, and so diminished the wealth and importance of the principalities dependent upon it. By contrast, increasing use of this new sea route between India and China provided the opportunity for Srivijaya, strategically situated as it was astride the Melaka Strait, to wax wealthy. Srivijayan warships patrolled the strait, forcing all shipping to put in to Srivijayan ports, where they were taxed and allowed to proceed.

Despite records of 'tribute' missions from India, it is clear that much of the Southern Ocean trade, particularly by Persians and Arabs, was not covered by any formal recognition of the pre-eminence of the Son of Heaven. For the pragmatic Chinese of the Tang period, it was more important to stimulate trade than to insist on formalities, though this did not in any way lessen Chinese conviction as to the centrality and superiority of the Middle Kingdom.

The burgeoning trade with both Southeast Asia and the Indian Ocean brought large numbers of foreign merchants to Canton and Long-bien, where they were permitted to organise and administer their own communities. This provided increased opportunities for unscrupulous officials to indulge in graft and corruption. In 684, a delegation of foreign merchants was so mistreated by the governor of Canton that a '*K'un-lun* man' (referring to someone from Southeast Asia) killed the governor and several other officials, using a sword smuggled in the sleeve of his robe.[6]

This dramatic event ushered in a period of improved administration and increased trade, until rebellion shook the Tang dynasty. Demand for goods slumped and, in the absence of central administrative controls, corruption again grew apace. By 758 foreign merchants at Canton had had enough. Persian and Arab traders (but apparently not Southeast Asians) pillaged and burned the port, and sailed away. Merchants who stayed were targets for extortion by local rebels, and then had their goods and property confiscated for allegedly supporting rebellion when imperial power was restored.

Malay trading vessel, bas-relief, Borobodur, Java, ninth century.

For the next century trade was intermittent, as reflected by the greatly reduced number of missions from Southeast Asia. The final blow came in 879 when Canton was sacked by Chinese rebels and many foreign merchants were killed. By then the Tang was in terminal decline. After 906 China was again divided with separate short-lived 'dynasties' in the north and south. Not until 960 was it reunited under the Song.

The special case of Vietnam

Northern Vietnam in the form of the Chinese province of Jiao-zhi had long been the interface between China and Southeast Asia. The centre of Chinese power was at Long-bien. From there Chinese officials, with the variable support of a Sino–Vietnamese landed elite, administered a territory stretching south to the shifting frontier with Champa, a distance over which Chinese cultural influence and administrative control gradually diminished. A Sino–Vietnamese elite might hold power, but the peasants they ruled were Vietnamese, and the province developed a tradition of strong local rule. In the words of Keith Taylor:

> Giao [Jiao-zhi] possessed a political momentum of its own, independent of the empire. In fact, it was when the empire was in the deepest trouble that the south prospered most. Whenever the imperial court was strong enough to dominate the region . . . rebellion and political instability ensued. When the court was weak, local forces arose, and stability followed.[7]

These 'local forces' would eventually become sufficiently strong to gain Vietnam its independence. In the meantime, however, Jiao-zhi, despite its predominantly non-Chinese population, remained within the empire. The cultural frontier was fixed along with the political frontier between the Vietnamese and the Cham; or in Chinese terminology, between inner and outer barbarians. While the Vietnamese were forced to live under imperial domination and were expected to adopt Chinese culture, the Cham sent tribute missions as an independent polity and were under no such pressure.

For a brief period in the 540s, the rebellion of Ly Bi established Vietnamese independence. Ly was of Chinese descent, but his principal support came from native Vietnamese. The rebellion was suppressed by imperial forces, but for the rest of the sixth century, until China was reunified in 589, Jiao-zhi retained a high degree of autonomy under the rule of powerful Sino–Vietnamese families owing only nominal allegiance to their Chinese overlords. Buddhism became well established, and the economy flourished as Long-bien temporarily eclipsed Canton as the principal terminus for the Nanyang trade.

The collapse of the Tang provided an opportunity for the independent-minded Sino–Vietnamese elite in Jiao-zhi to break free of imperial control. During the years of political and military turmoil that marked the early tenth century, Jiao-zhi became, to all intents and purposes, an autonomous province. Finally in 966, six years after the founding of the Song dynasty, Dinh Bo Linh proclaimed his independence. Exhausted after years of warfare, and aware that Bo Linh commanded a powerful army, the Song court accepted the de facto independence of Vietnam. Bo Linh was astute enough to follow diplomatic protocol by requesting conferral of Chinese titles. His son, in whose name official communications with the Song court were conducted, was confirmed as 'Peaceful Sea Military Governor' with the additional title of 'An-nam [Peaceful South] Protector General'. Bo Linh himself was granted the curious title 'King of Jiao-zhi Prefecture'.

These claims and titles tell us much about relations between China and Vietnam, and the worldview both shared. By proclaiming himself emperor, Bo Linh was asserting independence from China, but not thereby equality with the Son of Heaven. He was well aware both that this would be quite unacceptable to the Chinese, and that Vietnam could not escape being part of the Chinese world order. This was made evident in the edict conferring his title, where Bo Linh's relationship to the Song emperor was described as that of an obedient son to a benevolent father.[8] By describing Bo Linh as King of Jiao-zhi Prefecture, the Song court was on the one hand accepting his status as on a par with other rulers of independent kingdoms, while on the other hand reminding him that his territory remained, in some sense, part of the empire. In other words, it left open the possibility (or threat) of returning Jiao-zhi to imperial administration. The titles conferred on Bo Linh's son defined the role a Vietnamese ruler was expected to perform within the Chinese world order. He was to accept Chinese suzerainty and keep the peace on the empire's frontiers. (Subsequently the title conferred on the Vietnamese ruler was King of An-nam, though for his own people he was always emperor of Dai Viet.)

To reiterate: for the Chinese the ruler of Vietnam was a king, like any other ruler of kingdoms that presented tribute to the Son of Heaven. For the Vietnamese, in their dealings with China, this was accepted. The emperor of Vietnam designated himself 'king' in his official correspondence with the Chinese court. But because the Vietnamese shared the Chinese worldview, the ruler of Vietnam laid claim to the same cosmic relationship with Heaven and Earth as did the Son of Heaven, and the same relationship of hierarchical superiority to surrounding, less cultured peoples. In his official dealings with the Khmer and Cham and Lao, therefore, the Vietnamese ruler designated himself as emperor.[9] Only by such a device could Vietnam establish an acceptable bilateral relations regime with China, while at the same time expressing its own international relations culture in its dealings with its Southeast Asian neighbours.

The attitudes towards its neighbours that Vietnam adopted as part of its culture of international relations carried with them implications for the extension of Vietnamese power that, not surprisingly, were remarkably similar to Chinese views. Strategically, moreover, Vietnamese expansion to the south (the Truong Son mountains effectively hemmed in the Vietnamese to the west) was undertaken—as was China's southwards expansion—with an eye always on its vulnerable northern frontier. What the steppe peoples were to China in security terms, China was to Vietnam.

Throughout the Song period, Chinese attention was focused on *its* northern frontier where the steppe peoples posed a constant threat. This preoccupation, and the Song policy of avoiding unnecessary armed conflict, enabled the Vietnamese to consolidate their independence. They did so by following a dual strategy in their relations with China, combining military strength with status recognition of Chinese superiority. It was a pattern consistently applied over the centuries that not only kept China at bay for most of the time, but also allowed the Vietnamese to engage their traditional enemies, the Cham, and to pursue their long 'march to the south' (*nam tien*) that over the next seven centuries would leave them in control of all coastal Vietnam, to the Mekong delta and beyond.

Southeast Asia and the Song

During the first millennium CE China was never a naval power. The Chinese continued to be predominantly an inland people, intent on guarding their frontiers against security threats that came from the north and west. Apart from expeditions by sea to punish neighbouring Korea and Champa, the only significant naval operations during the Tang period were to control piracy. The Chinese were learning much about the sea, however. Whereas early trade, as we have seen, was conducted largely in foreign vessels, during the Tang Chinese began building their own merchant ships and sailing them to the Southern Ocean. Their models were the larger and more seaworthy vessels sailed directly to Chinese ports by Malay, Persian, Indian and Arab merchants. The Song continued this tradition of boat building. When the dynasty lost control of northern China, it needed to construct a substantial navy to defend its new capital on the Yangze River. The impetus this gave to Chinese maritime trade particularly affected Southeast Asia, not least through the growth of Chinese merchant communities in the region.

Meanwhile the political face of Southeast Asia was changing as new kingdoms arose. To the south of Dai Viet, the Cham were still powerful. In Cambodia the kingdom of Angkor was in the ascendant. In southern Thailand, the Mon kingdom of Dvaravati was in diplomatic contact with China, but not, apparently, the other two Mon kingdoms of Thaton in southern Burma and Haripunjaya in northern Thailand. In northern Burma, the Burmese had founded the kingdom of Pagan. Srivijaya still controlled the Malay peninsula and Sumatra, though its power declined after its capital was sacked in 1025 by the Tamil Cholas of south India. Java was evolving from a land-based polity into a kingdom with significant maritime interests that posed an increasing challenge to the declining power of Srivijaya. All of these, but for the more remote Mon kingdoms and with the addition of small principalities in the Philippines and Borneo, continued to send tributary missions to Song China during the eleventh and twelfth centuries.

Song China developed an efficient and extensive bureaucracy, recruited by examination based on the new orthodoxy of neo-Confucianism, to administer its expanding economy. While overland trade remained important (exchanging Chinese tea and silk for horses and jade), maritime commerce developed rapidly. Larger ships were able to carry bulk goods, particularly ceramics, along with tea, silks, fine handicrafts and copper cash in return for pearls, pepper and other spices, sugar, and aromatics such as benzoin and camphor. New ports opened up on the Yangze River and the Fujian coast where communities of foreign, mainly Muslim merchants congregated. All trade was still bureaucratically regulated, but Chinese merchants were freer to conduct their commerce and accumulate wealth than they had previously been.

The Song further elaborated the tributary system, especially its ceremonial aspects, as the weakened dynasty tried desperately to preserve the supremacy of the Son of Heaven. A precise ceremonial was developed for the reception of northern barbarian envoys, some of whom represented kingdoms as powerful as the Song itself. Chinese superiority could only be demonstrated by insisting on strict rules of conduct for foreign embassies (including the size of missions, and what trade could be conducted), combined with grandiose ceremonial receptions designed to impress. These formalities were then applied to all envoys, including those from Southeast Asia.

The weakness of the northern Song permitted only rhetorical assertion of Chinese superiority, through insistence that any country wishing to enter into relations with China could only do so on China's terms, as a vassal of the Son of Heaven.[10] For the court mandarins, all means of reinforcing the Chinese worldview strengthened their own influence. If lofty isolation was the price to pay, its ideological and moral value nevertheless outweighed any material benefit to be gained from trade over tribute. If the Tang had revelled in the opportunities offered by more open intercourse with the rest of the world, the Song were more wary.

With the defeat of Song armies in northern China, and the fall in 1126 CE of the Song capital of Kaifeng to the Jurchen Jin empire, the Song court fled south to Hangzhou. The new capital, however, was vulnerable to attack from the sea and so for the first time a Chinese dynasty had to build a permanent sea-going navy. Many warships at first were converted and armed merchantmen, sailed by experienced merchant seamen, but in time the Southern Song constructed its own superior vessels with improved naval technology and weaponry.

The Southern Song navy was primarily a defensive force, protecting the mouth of the Yangze River and the capital from northern attack, and coastal shipping from the depredations of Korean and Japanese pirates. It was not used offensively to project Chinese power into the Nanyang. That was left to the succeeding dynasty. Given the cost of defence and its reduced land and salt tax base, the Southern Song dynasty looked to overseas trade to provide an additional source of revenue. Private trade seems initially to have diminished following the loss of northern China, but soon picked up again as Muslim traders returned to southern ports.

With China again divided, however, tribute missions to the Southern Song fell away, especially from more far-flung regions. Despite the importance of seaborne trade, the dynasty did little to extend relations with Southeast Asia, though Suryavarman II, builder of the great temple of Angkor Wat, did dispatch Cambodia's first diplomatic mission to China. Regular missions also arrived from Dai Viet (Vietnam), Champa and Srivijaya, because it was in their interests to maintain good relations with China. For Dai Viet, the Southern Song still represented the threatening proximity of Chinese power; for Champa, China was a powerful arbitrator to whom to appeal in the face of Vietnamese or Cambodian aggression; while for Srivijaya, Chinese markets were essential for the entrepôt trade that was its lifeblood.

Conclusion

The Hindu–Buddhist worldviews of Southeast Asian polities that evolved during the first millennium CE were very different from that of Confucian China. Both, however, included elements that were sufficiently compatible to form the basis for functional bilateral relations regimes that tacitly accepted the Chinese world order. Contact increased, especially during the Tang dynasty, through more open trade and a common interest in Buddhism. But Buddhism in China was never able to modify the Chinese world order centred on the worship of Heaven and the cult of the emperor, which continued to shape China's culture of international relations.

Chinese power did not weigh heavily on Southeast Asia during this time. The kingdom of Nanzhao in Yunnan remained an independent buffer, and Vietnam broke free of the empire after the collapse of the Tang dynasty. China posed only a minimal strategic threat, therefore, to Southeast Asia, except for Vietnam, whose independence rested on acceptance of a tributary relationship that conformed more closely to Chinese demands than did the bilateral relations regimes other Southeast Asian kingdoms worked out with China.

Trade continued to be central to China–Southeast Asia relations. During the Tang, much of the trade between China and Southeast Asia was still in the hands of non-Chinese (including Southeast Asian) merchants and shipping, but by the time of the Song a significant shift was underway. Chinese ship building came of age and more of the Nanyang trade was carried in Chinese vessels. Just as communities of foreign merchants congregated in Chinese ports, so Chinese merchants began to form semi-permanent communities in Southeast Asian trading ports. Over time, due principally to official Chinese attitudes towards overseas Chinese, these communities grew in size, to the point where they came to constitute a permanent, complicating factor in relations between Southeast Asia and China.

4 MONGOL EXPANSIONISM

中國

Chinese attention during the Southern Song was always directed north, and with good reason. The Song policy of using the Mongols to oppose the Jurchen ended in disaster, however, when the Mongols swept into northern China. By 1236 Mongol armies were ready to thrust south of the Yangze, though it was not until the accession to power of Khubilai Khan in 1260 that the Mongol conquest of the Southern Song was pressed to its conclusion. Six years earlier, the kingdom of Dali, successor to Nanzhao in the region of Yunnan, had fallen to the Mongols and been incorporated within the Chinese empire. Hangzhou was captured in 1276, and Canton, whence the Song court had fled, succumbed the following year. Two years later, destruction of what remained of the Song fleet gave the Mongols total control over an expanded Chinese empire.

This was not the end of Mongol expansionism. The next target was Southeast Asia. The incorporation of Yunnan into the empire provided a base for operations against mainland Southeast Asian kingdoms. Burma and Vietnam both suffered invasions that were Mongol led but comprised mainly Chinese troops. Elements of the Song navy captured by the invading Mongols formed the core of the war fleets that projected Mongol power into maritime Southeast Asia. In attacking Southeast Asia, however, Mongol forces encountered determined resistance. The lesson learned was that armies from China could be defeated on home territory where local forces had the advantage, but that the tributary relationship thereafter needed to be re-established as a security measure.

Mongol conquests

The impact of the Mongol conquest of China on the face of it threatened the very basis of the Chinese worldview. This was the first time that the entire Chinese cultural area had fallen under barbarian rule. Mongol military might had proved superior to Chinese virtue (*de*). The Chinese response was to sinicise their conquerors. The Mongols were incorporated into Chinese history as a Chinese dynasty, the Yuan. In this capacity, Mongol rule for almost a century had a far-reaching impact on China's relations with Southeast Asia: it extended Chinese control in the southwest over a region that topographically was more part of Southeast Asia than of China, populated overwhelmingly by non-Chinese peoples; it projected Mongol/Chinese sea power aggressively into Southeast Asia for the first time; and it demonstrated in both these ways the potential implications for other countries of China's imperial view of the world.[1] Let us look at each of these.

In terms of geography, environment, population and culture, Yunnan was, and in many ways still is, a northern extension of mainland Southeast Asia. Much of the area is a high plateau, falling away to the south and east. Much, too, is mountainous. Through high, narrow valleys flow the tributaries of the great rivers that water southern China and mainland Southeast Asia, none navigable on their upper reaches. But despite the difficult terrain, merchants and pilgrims established regular access routes from China, through Yunnan, and down into Burma. This was the so-called southern silk route, never a fraction as important as the northern route through Central Asia, but a conduit nevertheless for exchange between China and India.

Who the early inhabitants of Yunnan were, we do not know, but they were unrelated to the northern Chinese. Very limited Chinese settlement may go back to the late fourth century BCE in the vicinity of Kunming, and parts of Yunnan were claimed by the Han dynasty. These were officially listed as Chinese prefectures, but administered by local rulers who, as inner barbarians, sent tribute to the Han court. The Chinese presence was thus minimal, and during the three centuries of division before the Sui reunified the empire, the whole region reverted to local rule.[2]

Yunnan well illustrates the process of Chinese colonisation, and the extension of Chinese imperial power. It also illustrates how relations between Han Chinese and 'southwestern barbarians' were conducted. Often adventurous individual Chinese traders were the first to make contact with tribal peoples. Trade was mainly in forest products, deer antlers, hides and skins, resins and aromatic woods, in exchange for iron and salt. Once trade became established, or traders regularly passed through tribal territory, protection would be the excuse for administrative intervention. Tribal chiefs would be persuaded to acknowledge nominal (from their point of view) Chinese suzerainty in exchange for official recognition, gifts and titles. They thereby became part of the Chinese world, their territory incorporated within the empire as a frontier commandery or prefecture. This provided tribal peoples with the priceless opportunity (from the Chinese viewpoint) to become civilised; that is, to become culturally assimilated, a process encouraged both by Chinese migration and settlement, and by intermarriage, for Chinese men were seldom reluctant to take non-Chinese brides.

This extension of Chinese influence took place in the context of population pressure and migration. From Chinese sources it is difficult to trace population movements because the names assigned to tribal groups change. Broadly speaking, however, population movements into what is now southern China came from two directions: from the east, as Chinese displaced Yue peoples inland from the south China coastal provinces; and from Sichuan to the north. Tribal peoples, in turn, were forced either to move into more marginal mountainous country, or to migrate further west and south.

Ironically, it was the Tang policy of consolidating minor kingdoms by favouring specific tribal chiefs over their rivals that resulted in formation of the first substantial indigenous kingdom in Yunnan. In the early eighth century, the southernmost of six principalities or *zhao* in the vicinity of the Er-hai lake gained ascendancy over the others and established its capital at Dali. At first the kings of Nanzhao accepted their status as inner barbarians within the Tang empire. Tribute was offered and respects paid. But in 750, when king Ko-lo-feng failed to obtain imperial redress for the extortions of Chinese officials, he took his own revenge. A Nanzhao army occupied Tang territory to the east, then convincingly defeated two Chinese armies sent to punish him. Rebellion in China then intervened to distract Tang attention, and Nanzhao was left to consolidate its independence. At its greatest extent, Nanzhao comprised all of Yunnan, western Guizhou, southern Sichuan and as far south as northern Laos and Thailand and northeastern Burma.[3]

The independence of Nanzhao, and its successor kingdom of Dali, lasted six centuries before being snuffed out with relatively little resistance. At first Nanzhao was a powerful regional kingdom, invading Burma from 757 to 763 CE, Sichuan several times between 829 and 873, and Jiao-zhi (northern Vietnam, but then part of China) between 861 and 866. None of these invasions succeeded in significantly increasing the territory of Nanzhao. Central Sichuan would have been the most valuable prize, and control over the Red River delta would have given Nanzhao access to the sea. Both were vital for the Tang to defend, which they did. Nor was Nanzhao able to control upper Burma where its victory over, and destruction of, the Pyu kingdom only opened the way for the Burmans to become the dominant ethnic group, and to establish the kingdom of Pagan.

By the end of the tenth century, an independent Vietnam and independent Nanzhao seemed to define the limits of Chinese expansion into Southeast Asia. Both had been subjected not only to extensive sinicisation, but also to substantial Chinese settlement. Many of these settlers had intermarried with the local population, however, and owed little allegiance to their homeland. Both Vietnam and Nanzhao accepted tributary status in their dealings with China, a relationship that under the Song—when Nanzhao had contracted to form the kingdom of Dali—settled into comfortable mutual non-aggression.

There were important differences between Dali and Vietnam, however, that go some way towards explaining why only the latter retained its independence in the face of Mongol expansionism. For one thing, Vietnam was administered on the Chinese model, while Dali was a looser, Southeast Asian *mandala*. Also in Vietnam the Sino–Vietnamese ruling elite, with the backing of a relatively ethnically homogeneous Muong/Viet peasantry, were determined to defend Vietnamese independence. In Dali, the ruling elite was non-Chinese (probably belonging to a tribal people known as the Lolo) and ruled over a highly ethnically diverse population with less clearly defined loyalties. In such circumstances, Chinese settlers, especially locally powerful families, retained their cultural allegiance to what for them was their own superior civilisation. Another reason was that for three hundred years before the Mongols invaded, Vietnam had faced a more uncertain, more competitive, and more strategically sensitive political and economic environment than had Dali. Trade, both tributary and non-tributary with China and commercially with other parts of Southeast Asia, was always more important than it was for landlocked Dali. Moreover, while Vietnam faced a security threat from Champa to the south as well as from China, Dali encountered no such southern threat and tended, as a result, to become more complacent and inward-looking. In short, Dali was much less prepared than was Vietnam to counter Mongol invasion.

Once the Mongols had seized control of Yunnan, they set about administering it as a Chinese province, under Mongol direction. As many Mongols were then Muslim, Islam was propagated and widely embraced, so that even today Yunnan has the second largest Muslim population (after Xinjiang) of any province of China. Given both the topography and ethnic diversity of Yunnan, it was relatively easy, through a policy essentially of divide and rule imposed by military garrisons, to maintain Chinese domination. Steady, if slow, migration that has continued up to the present day swung the balance of population over time in favour of the Chinese, and assisted in the process of sinicisation.

The conquest of Yunnan altered forever the relationship between China and Southeast Asia. Strategically it projected Chinese power to the south and west into direct contact with kingdoms and peoples with whom they had previously had little or no intercourse at all. These included the Burmese, the Tai of Sukhothai and Lan Na, and the Lao of Luang Phrabang, then known as Meuang Sua. Under threat of military invasion, all were brought within the Chinese tributary system, thus initiating lasting diplomatic and political relations.

At the same time, new trade routes were opened up from Yunnan into Burma and the Tai kingdoms along which Yunnanese merchants led their hardy mountain ponies. The Venetian traveller, Marco Polo, may also have passed this way. While overland trade never matched sea trade in importance, it was significant for the countries involved and for Yunnan itself, for alternative routes east were long and difficult. As the wealth of mainland Southeast Asian kingdoms grew, so too did trading opportunities with Yunnan, though the full potential for trade between the two regions still remains to be realised with the improved communications envisaged for the twenty-first century.

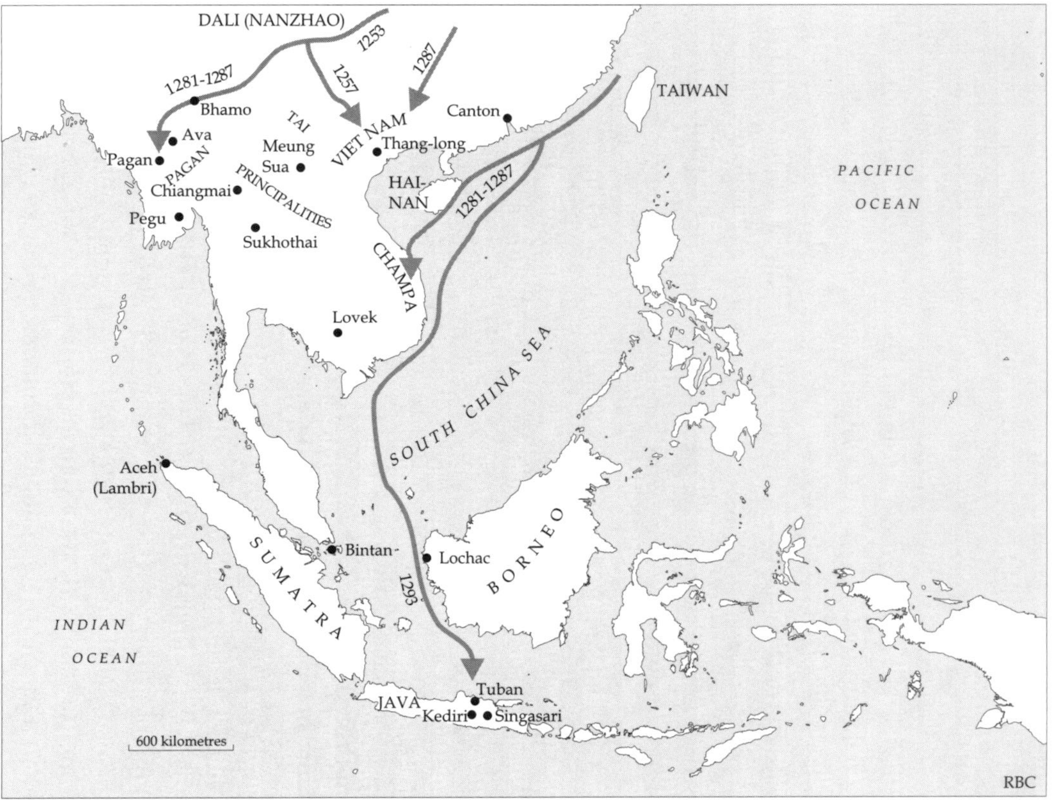

Mongol invasions of Southeast Asia, late thirteenth century CE.

The projection of Mongol power

The Mongols had conquered Yunnan as part of a grand strategy to outflank the Southern Song, rather than to extend the Chinese empire into Southeast Asia. The danger posed to the independent kingdoms of Southeast Asia was soon apparent, however. Using Yunnan as a base the Mongols intended to sweep south and east through northern Vietnam to threaten Canton. When in 1257 permission for their forces to pass through Vietnamese territory was refused, a Mongol army mounted a swift invasion. The Vietnamese capital of Thang-long (modern Hanoi), was seized and sacked, but the Vietnamese resorted to guerrilla warfare, and as climate and disease took their toll, the Mongols were forced to withdraw. Southern Song resistance continued for another twenty years. Vietnam's punishment was to come later.[4]

On his succession to power in 1260 as both emperor of China and Khan of Khans, Khubilai determined to bolster his legitimacy through enforcing the submission of tributary states, by conquest if necessary. Though still engaged in subduing the Southern Song, Khubilai notified all kingdoms tributary (in theory) to China that a new dynasty had received the mandate of Heaven, and called not just for appropriate tribute to be offered, but for submission in person by the ruler. Particular attention was paid to Vietnam. In 1267, Khubilai demanded not only the Vietnamese king's personal submission, and that his sons should reside in Beijing as hostages, but also that a population census be carried out to serve as the basis for taxation and military *corvée* (forced labour owed to a feudal lord), and that a Mongol governor be appointed. For the Vietnamese these conditions were quite unacceptable, for they amounted to de facto loss of Vietnamese independence. The Vietnamese parried these demands, while continuing to send the usual tribute missions; but they were playing a dangerous game. States that proved uncooperative, as did Japan, could expect retaliation. Mongol fleets invaded Japan in 1274 and again in 1281, both times with disastrous results, thanks to the 'divine wind' (*kamikaze*) that sank so many Mongol ships.

The next Mongol invasion by land was directed not at Vietnam, however, but at Burma. The first Yuan envoys despatched to King Narathihapate of Pagan (reigned 1256–87) came from the Mongol governor of Yunnan. They must have been received by the Burmese with some surprise. Only twice before had the court of Pagan dispatched what were probably goodwill missions to China (to the Song in 1004 and 1106). It is not recorded what either brought, so we have no idea whether the Burmese intention was to stimulate trade or propagate Buddhism. The Song knew nothing of Pagan, except that it was a large kingdom. Burmese gifts were nevertheless recorded as tribute, and Pagan took its place as an outer barbarian state whose rulers had given due recognition to the Son of Heaven. So when the Yuan dynasty took power, Pagan was informed that tribute was due. This the Burmese (no doubt interpreting 'tribute' in the Southeast Asian sense of the word) refused to provide, though eventually a Burmese mission did accompany the Mongol envoys back to Beijing, ostensibly to worship a tooth of the Buddha, but more likely to gain time and information about this new and aggressive Chinese dynasty.

Khubilai personally received the Burmese mission, and sent his personal emissary back with it to demand that the Burmese king present himself in person to pay hommage to the Great Khan. King Narathihapate was so incensed at the haughty attitude of the Chinese envoys, who apparently were reluctant to remove their shoes in his presence, that he ordered the execution of the entire Chinese mission. Word was slow to reach Beijing of this atrocity, and Khubilai's attention was directed elsewhere. But when the Burmese were presumptuous enough to invade a former vassal principality that had submitted to China, Khubilai ordered an invasion to punish this further insolence. An army was amassed in Chongqing, then the Mongol administrative centre for Yunnan, and in 1277 descended on Burma. Narathihapate fled Pagan, earning himself the sobriquet in the Burmese chronicles of 'the king who fled the Chinese'. Chinese and Burmese accounts differ on the outcome of the invasion. The Chinese claimed a victory when the Mongol cavalry stampeded the Burmese elephant corps in a great battle east of Bhamo, but the invaders were forced to retire without achieving any of their aims: the Burmese were not defeated, nor was their capital taken; King Narathihapate was not punished, nor was tribute forthcoming.[5]

For these reasons another invasion was ordered in 1287, led this time by Khubilai's grandson, Esen Temür. Once again the Mongol/Chinese force met stiff resistance. Meanwhile Pagan was plunged into political crisis. King Narathihapate was poisoned by one of his sons, while another seized the throne and offered to pay tribute to China. This was apparently enough to convince the invaders to withdraw before reaching Pagan. The impact on Burma had been devastating, but since the Pagan dynasty continued for almost another eighty years, the Mongol invasions alone can not be held responsible for its collapse. Pagan was not destroyed, and while the Mongols were not militarily defeated, climate and environment took their toll and the two invasions were hardly worth their cost.

The next land invasions of mainland Southeast Asia took place in 1285, and between 1287 and 1289, both directed against Vietnam. Both, however, were linked to Khubilai's attempts to punish Champa as well. King Jaya Indravarman VI had been reluctant to accede to Khubilai's demands that Champa send a tributary mission to the Yuan court, led by the king in person. Like the Vietnamese, the Cham played for time. To punish Cham procrastination, and to avenge claimed ill treatment of his envoys, Khubilai ordered an attack on Champa by sea. In 1281 a fleet of one hundred ships bearing 5000 men under the command of Sogetu, one of Khubilai's leading generals, sailed from Canton and landed in the vicinity of the Cham capital at Vijaya.

The Cham response was similar to the Vietnamese. The elderly Cham king abandoned his capital and retreated into the mountains, while the crown prince resorted to spirited guerrilla warfare. So fierce was Cham resistance that the Mongols decided to send a relieving force overland through Vietnam. But again the Vietnamese objected. This was not out of solidarity with the Cham, but because Mongol conquest and occupation of Champa would have left Vietnam exposed to attack on two fronts. The furious Mongol response came in 1285 when a Mongol-led Chinese force from Yunnan invaded Vietnam and took Thang-long. As before, the Vietnamese mounted a sustained guerrilla resistance under the inspired leadership of Tran Hung Dao, and again heat and disease took their toll on the invaders. A Vietnamese counterattack was successful. Remnants of the invading force, retreating towards Yunnan, were ambushed in the mountains. Meanwhile an attempt by Sogetu to relieve the battered Mongol army ended in his own death.

A second invasion was immediately ordered, this time from Guangxi. A Mongol/Chinese army crossed into Vietnamese territory in 1287 and, for the third time, seized the capital. But again the Vietnamese resorted to guerrilla warfare. The Mongol cavalry was useless on the Red River flood plain, and the Chinese infantry were again ravaged by heat and disease. The following year, as the invaders ran short of supplies, the Vietnamese won a great naval victory. Four hundred Chinese junks were destroyed as they tried to manoeuvre in shallow and confined Vietnamese coastal waters. The Mongol army was again forced to retreat, suffering heavy losses on the way. Prudently, both Champa and Vietnam thereupon dispatched lavish tribute missions to the Yuan court to re-establish tributary relations, though neither king attended in person.

So ended the Mongol attempt to extend their Chinese empire into mainland Southeast Asia. Cambodia was never subject to the same pressure. Having initially detained Khubilai's envoys, the Cambodian king, Jayavarman VIII, also sent tribute for fear that the Mongol army in Champa might cross to the valley of the Mekong and march south. Further west, the Tai/Khmer principality of Lopburi, which had declared its independence from Angkor, sent its first tribute mission to the Yuan court in 1280. Others followed until 1299, though Lopburi seems to have retained its independence into the 1340s before being incorporated into the expanding Siamese kingdom of Ayutthaya. In return, Chinese envoys were sent to Southeast Asian capitals, a famous example being Zhou Daguan's visit to Angkor in 1296–97.

The final Mongol thrust into Southeast Asia by sea was even more daring, but just as unproductive. In 1289 Khubilai sent personal envoys to Java to demand that King Kertanegara of Singhasari, in the east of the island, should acknowledge Chinese suzerainty. Java had sent three missions to the Song, in 992, 1109 and 1131. What the last two brought was not recorded, but it seems clear from the list of valuable goods presented by the first mission that its principal purpose was trade. The Javanese asked for horses, saddles and weapons, which the Chinese gave in return, along with 'very rich' gifts of gold and silk.[6] It was one thing to enter into diplomatic relations in order to trade, however, but quite another to accept subject status. The Mongol envoys returned home 'with disfigured faces', which probably meant that their noses had been sliced off.

Such an insult cried for vengeance. In 1293 Khubilai dispatched a war fleet to Java to punish Kertanegara. This was the first great projection of Chinese sea power into maritime Southeast Asia. In the meantime, however, events in Java had moved on. Kertanegara and several of his loyal followers were assassinated by a disgruntled vassal, who promptly declared himself king. Soon after, the Mongol armada reached Tuban, a port on the north central Javanese coast that had once sent its own tribute/trade missions to China. The arrival of this substantial force presented Prince Vijaya, Kertanegara's son-in-law and designated heir, with a golden opportunity. In return for accepting Chinese suzerainty, he sought Mongol assistance in defeating the usurper. The Mongol commander agreed and the usurper was duly crushed. Vijaya then turned on his allies, picking off scattered contingents of the Mongol force until the Mongol position became untenable and the fleet was forced to withdraw.[7]

Prince Vijaya established a new dynasty and a new capital at Majapahit, the name by which this Hindu kingdom became known. Thus, the Mongol intervention again failed to achieve what it had set out to do. It had, however, played a crucial enabling role in Javanese history. Majapahit was a powerful kingdom, comprising as its core East Java, Madura and Bali, but with important trading interests that extended its influence, if not its political control, across much of the Indonesian archipelago, including Brunei and the Borneo coast. Official relations between Majapahit and China remained sporadic, but were resuscitated by the early Ming dynasty (between 1369 and 1382). Trading relations were more important until Majapahit declined in the early sixteenth century.

Although the Yuan dynasty drew a distinction between tributary and private trade, and encouraged the former, private trade was relatively free. Chinese merchants sailed to Southeast Asia and returned with lucrative cargoes. Substantial profit margins lured wealthy families into the Nanyang trade. New trade networks were established, sailed by larger and more seaworthy ocean-going junks. These linked Chinese coastal towns with ports in Southeast Asia where resident Chinese communities developed new and sophisticated regional trading networks and strategies.

Mongol intervention also had significant repercussions on mainland Southeast Asia. Yuan relations with much of this region (excluding Vietnam, Champa and Cambodia) were through the governor of Yunnan. It would seem at first glance that the founding of the first Tai kingdoms was in some way related to the Mongol conquest of Yunnan in 1253. Yet there was no sudden massive migration of population: the Tai peoples had been slowly on the move for centuries. Nor is it likely, as some have surmised, that the Mongol example suddenly stimulated Tai energy and imagination: other examples of organised kingdoms had long been available (not least in Yunnan.) The rise of the Tai kingdoms is better explained by the steady decline in Khmer power after the reign of Jayavarman VII (reigned 1177–1215?), and the disunity of the Mon, than by such tenuous linkages. A power vacuum existed in central mainland Southeast Asia, and the Tai filled it.

Several small Tai principalities (*meuang*) had come into existence as early as the first half of the thirteenth century in what is now southern China (Chiang Hung), in northern Thailand (Chiang Saen) and as far south as Sukhothai, in northeastern Burma on the Shan plateau, and as far west as Assam. It seems likely that these principalities accepted Mongol hegemony in return for a free hand in their struggle against the Mon and Khmer. By the second half of the century, charismatic rulers were able to weld together larger kingdoms. King Ramkhamhaeng (reigned 1279?–1298?) expanded Sukhothai to become a powerful Tai kingdom comprising most of central Thailand and stretching east as far as Viang Chan, south down the Kra Isthmus to Ligor, and west to Pegu. To the north King Mangrai conquered the former Mon kingdom of Haripunjaya (1281) to form the kingdom of Lan Na. In 1292 he established his new capital at Chiang Mai.

The only threat to expanding Tai power came in 1287 when the Mongols invaded Pagan for the second time. The three most powerful northern Tai princes came together the same year to conclude a pact to oppose any Mongol invasion of their territories. When Chiang Hung fell to Yuan forces in 1292, Mangrai came to the aid of its ruler and retook the city. Four years later the city again twice changed hands. A major Mongol campaign in 1301 turned out to be a complete disaster, and only emboldened the Tai to raid further north into Chinese territory. At length diplomacy won the day. King Ramkhamhaeng of Sukhothai had sent his first tribute mission to Beijing in 1292, in response to the arrival of a Chinese mission ten years earlier inviting Sukhothai to acknowledge Chinese suzerainty. The delay may have reflected Siamese resistance to this, and the mission, when it was despatched, may have been a shrewd insurance measure, given events in Burma and Java, against possible Mongol intervention (which, as we know, was requested by Lopburi). This first

Siamese embassy was followed by several more as the value of Sino–Siamese trade became evident. One mission may even have been led by the king himself. Among the valuable presents Ramkhamhaeng is said to have received were a number of Chinese potters who established ceramic kilns at Sukhothai and Sawankhalok. Lan Na did not send its first tribute mission to Beijing until 1312, followed by six more to 1347, by which time the Yuan dynasty was already in decline.

Implications for Southeast Asia

The impact and significance of these momentous events, covering the second half of the thirteenth century, for relations between China and the countries of Southeast Asia were considerable. The importance of the extension of Chinese power south from Sichuan into Yunnan has already been noted. It opened up a whole new area for Chinese migration and settlement, not just in Yunnan, but also in the largely non-Chinese populated provinces of Guangxi and Guizhou. This placed intolerable pressure on minority groups who had either to retreat deeper into the mountains or submit to Chinese administration, assimilation and exploitation. A trickle of minority peoples south out of southern China into northern Laos, Burma and Thailand continues to this day.

Overland invasion of Burma and Vietnam taught the kingdoms of mainland Southeast Asia the very real threat of Chinese armed intervention. I say 'Chinese' and not 'Mongol' because although these armies were Mongol-led and included contingents of Mongol cavalry, they comprised mainly Chinese troops. Moreover, they came from China in the name of a ruler who proclaimed himself emperor of China. So though these invasions can be seen as a continuation of aggressive and expansionist policies pursued by Mongol rulers, for the peoples of Southeast Asia they were projections of Chinese power.

In turning their attention to Southeast Asia, the Mongols enjoyed a strategic advantage not available to most Chinese dynasties: they did not fear attack on the empire's northern frontiers. This may not have been evident, however, to Southeast Asian rulers and their advisers. Moreover, the failure of invasions of Burma and Vietnam to secure their military objectives suggests two things: one is that despite their formidable military might, the Mongols overreached themselves; and the second is that they were entirely ignorant of conditions of warfare in these countries, both in terms of climate and environment, and with respect to the sustained opposition they were likely to encounter.

Ruling elites in Southeast Asia probably drew other conclusions. They had, after all, fought Chinese armies to a standstill, but only after suffering terrible devastation. Moreover, successful defence of territory was no guarantee that another invasion would not follow, as it did for the Vietnamese. The best way to avoid that was to acknowledge Chinese suzerainty and the superiority of the Son of Heaven. The way to ensure security, in short, was to send a tribute mission, and thereby participate in the Chinese world order. Investiture might be as a vassal king of the Chinese emperor, but for the royal courts of Southeast Asia this was recognition that also reinforced political legitimacy.

One thing worth remarking on, in assessing the response of Southeast Asian kingdoms to the Mongol threat, is the lack of concerted action. Apart from the brief alliance between the Tai kings of Sukhothai, Lan Na and Phayao in response to the Mongol invasion of Burma, the countries of mainland Southeast Asia did not conclude any defensive pact or treaty. No attempt was made to form an anti-Chinese coalition. A suggestion by Champa to conclude an alliance with Dai Viet was rebuffed, and hatreds ran too deep between Champa and Cambodia after a series of wars and the mutual sack of each others' capitals. Ruling elites were indeed more likely to take advantage of the predicament of other kingdoms than to come to their aid.

This response has more to do with *mandala* relations and the workings of karma than with a failure of nerve or diplomacy. The kingdoms of Southeast Asia, both mainland and maritime, were in frequent communication with each other. Their trading contacts provided useful sources of information about conditions elsewhere, political as well as economic. Powerful kings sought queens from distant kingdoms as evidence of their prestige and power. One of Kertanegara's principal queens, for example, was a Cham princess.[8] There was apparently little, therefore, to prevent the formation of some kind of coalition in order to present a unified opposition to Chinese power. Yet this never happened. Balance-of-power thinking is European, not Southeast Asian. For Southeast Asian rulers there was another, surer way to ensure the security of their realms, and that was by acquiescing in the Chinese world order, humiliating though this might occasionally be.

The events of the second half of the thirteenth century proved, however, that the Chinese world order also had its downside for those on the receiving end. In dispatching envoys to all those states listed in Chinese records as tributaries to the Middle Kingdom, Khubilai Khan was responding as previous Chinese emperors had done when founding new dynasties. He sought thereby to exalt himself as Son of Heaven through reinforcing the Chinese world order. The ritual presentation of homage and tribute constituted public and formal endorsement of the hierarchical relationships that comprised that order. Failure to respond risked imperial vengeance. Thus for mainland Southeast Asian kingdoms in particular, reunification of the Middle Kingdom under a new dynasty ushered in a dangerous period of threatened intervention.

For the maritime kingdoms, the lessons were somewhat different. The projection of Chinese sea power was worrying, for China evidently had the means to construct a powerful navy (as the Ming were again to demonstrate). But the Yuan navy was a patchwork force including elements of both the Song and Korean navies. For a land-based people, the Mongols had taken to the sea with remarkable alacrity, but they had done so with insufficient preparation and planning, in a knee-jerk response to the treatment of their envoys. The armada dispatched against Japan was substantial, but the fleet that sailed for Java was insufficient to defeat a powerful kingdom. The Javanese could take pride in the way they had, through tactical deception and martial ability, defeated the invaders. They had not had to rely upon divine protection, as had the Japanese, but had simply used their own guile and fighting skills. For the Javanese, therefore, a danger lay in underestimating the Chinese threat.

Changing worldviews

The Yuan dynasty enjoyed only a century of power, the last few years of which were a period of decline. This was a crucial time in the history of Southeast Asia, for it saw the consolidation of new kingdoms that would endure well into the sixteenth century, when they were first visited by Europeans, and in most cases well beyond. More importantly, it saw the rise of new religions (Theravada Buddhism in mainland Southeast Asia; Islam in the Malay world) that continue both to characterise and divide the region. Theravada Buddhism was already well established in Burma when, in the thirteenth and fourteenth centuries, it was adopted by the Siamese and Lao, and replaced both Hinduism and Mahayana Buddhism in Cambodia. Its worldview shared much with Hinduism, particularly belief in karma (though the Buddhist notion focused more on intention than on action: what one thinks is as important for Buddhists as what one does). Theravada Buddhism placed more emphasis on impermanence and individual effort. Like Confucianism, it endorsed social hierarchy, but for very different reasons that allowed more scope for individual initiative in the face of social conformity. Most importantly for China–Southeast Asian relations, however, Theravada Buddhism endorsed the Indian *mandala* relationship between polities, with its emphasis on contingency and flexibility.

Theravada Buddhist kings took particular pains to structure their kingdoms as microcosmic replicas of the divine macrocosm. At the centre stood the palace, earthly equivalent of the divine abode of the gods on Mount Meru. A king's right to rule derived both from his superior personal karma, and from possession of the symbols of power housed in the palace (including notably a potent Buddhist image that served as the palladium of the dynasty or the kingdom). Kings thus ruled over competing centres of power, each claiming superior divine status, to be demonstrated, as circumstances permitted, through conquest leading to expansion of the *mandala*. This was a world of fluid power, shifting relationships, and flexible responses, ready to adapt as occasion demanded.[9]

Islam, as it seeped through Indonesia, carried by Muslim merchants and missionaries, brought with it an entirely different worldview, one that was essentially incompatible with the earlier Hinduism and Buddhism of maritime Southeast Asia. For most of the Malay world, Islam was at first but a thin veneer acquired through the statement of belief in Allah and Muhammad, his Prophet, that is required of all Muslims (those who submit to God's will). But Islam brought with it some potentially subversive ideas. One was that all Muslims are equal before God, as symbolised by the *ummat* (the people of God) at prayer in the mosque.[10] This was never enough to shake the foundations of Malay social hierarchy, for Islam also taught obedience and submission, which could without too much difficulty be transferred from God to man, but it did make it more difficult to accept pretensions to superiority by non-Muslims.

As a revealed religion, Islam itself engendered a sense of superiority through the exclusivity that comes from possession of divine truth. It was a characteristic of Christianity, too, that marked both Europeans, and subsequently Filipinos. As revealed religions, both Islam and Christianity tended to be less tolerant of other beliefs than either Buddhism or Hinduism, less prepared to make room for them in a comprehensive worldview. Beyond the *ummat* stood the unbelievers, and they included most Chinese. The space this opened up between Malays/Indonesians and overseas Chinese has hardly been bridged to this day, for the only way to close it is through conversion.

The Islamic worldview influenced relations between China and the Muslim Malay/Indonesian world in significant ways. Acceptance of Islam drew the region into an alternative international order, one that looked to sultan or caliph as *primus inter pares* among Muslim rulers, designated by Allah to preside over the congregation of believers. Such a worldview allowed no cosmic dimension for the Son of Heaven. Indeed, the very concept was blasphemous, as it was for Christianity. Chinese power might be respected, to the point where the rulers of minor Muslim states were prepared to perform the kowtow before Chinese emperors, but the cosmic basis of the Chinese world order could never be accommodated by Islam. With the conversion of the Malay/Indonesian world to Islam, intellectual compromise with the Chinese world order was rendered virtually impossible. While this had little effect on trade relations, it did in time alter the context in which official relations were conducted—not for the Chinese for whom all official missions were taken as tributary recognition of the exemplary virtue of the Son of Heaven, but for Malays and Indonesians for whom diplomatic relations were undertaken for entirely pragmatic reasons.

Conclusion

The Mongol invasions extended the frontiers of the Chinese empire to include Yunnan, but their armies failed to incorporate either Burma or Vietnam, and their war fleets failed to subdue either Japan or Java. The lesson learned, once the aggressive phase of the dynasty subsided and it became increasingly Chinese, was that nominal acceptance of China's hegemonic dominance within a sinocentric world order was as satisfying to Chinese pride as world empire, and was far less costly.

As for the kingdoms of Southeast Asia, they had proved themselves tough and resilient in defence of their territories. Symbolic submission was one thing, subjugation was another. Trade with China continued for—under whatever dynasty—it was too important to Southeast Asian rulers for them to quibble over China's terms. The Chinese world order thus remained in place, even as important parts of Southeast Asia were adopting new ways of understanding the world that—particularly in the case of Islam—introduced potentially incompatible elements that threatened to complicate any future bilateral relations regimes worked out between Muslim Southeast Asian powers and the Middle Kingdom.

5
SEA POWER, TRIBUTE AND TRADE

In 1368 the Ming replaced the Yuan dynasty, thereby returning China to Han Chinese rule. The new dynasty was very conscious of the need to expunge all barbarian influence, which it undertook to do in time-honoured Chinese fashion by seeking precedents in the past. Texts were combed, especially from the former great Chinese dynasties of the Han and Tang, in order to determine the proper way of conduct, in government and in foreign relations. What resulted was a systematic restructuring of institutions based on traditions dating back to the Zhou dynasty (and projected back even further to legendary times), administered by a bureaucracy trained in neo-Confucian orthodoxy. Scholar officials determined the elaborate formalities of state ceremonies whose purpose was to reassert the supremacy of the Son of Heaven and the Chinese world order. All aspects of foreign relations—exchange of envoys, the reception of diplomatic missions, regulation of trade, even extradition procedures—were systematised.

In the year of his triumph, Hongwu (reigned 1368–1398), the first Ming emperor, dispatched envoys to all tributary states informing them of the change of dynasty and summoning their rulers to acknowledge the new Son of Heaven. In return they were offered formal investiture and lavish gifts. Among the first to arrive was Emperor Tran Du Tong of Vietnam (reigned 1341–1369), King of Annam to the Chinese, who was received with due ceremony. He was followed by ambassadors from several other Southeast Asian kingdoms: Champa, Cambodia, Ayutthaya (which had replaced Sukhothai in central Thailand), Majapahit, and several coastal principalities in Java, Sumatra and Borneo.

Hongwu modelled himself on the Confucian ideal of a benevolent ruler, while at the same time proclaiming Ming power and superiority. This is made abundantly clear in edicts and letters he dispatched to subordinate rulers. As Hongwu reminded the Vietnamese king: 'In the highest place comes acceptance of the way of Heaven; in the next, respect for China . . .'[1] As Son of Heaven, the emperor desired what Heaven desired, and that was 'untroubled harmony.' To that end, vassal states were required to respect China's superior status and maintain peaceful relations with each other. In the event that they did not, they could expect to be admonished by the emperor, or even punished by a Chinese military force.

For his part, the emperor committed himself to treating all peoples justly and impartially. Hongwu assured his tributaries that: 'Every land on which the sun and moon shine I look on with the same benevolence.'[2] Nor would China abuse her superior power by taking aggressive action. Neighbouring kingdoms need have no fear. Their security was assured simply by accepting Heaven's way and the emperor's commands. Hongwu even listed (in 1395) those countries, by direction, that China pledged not to attack without provocation. These included, to the south, all the countries of Southeast Asia, beginning with Vietnam. The list specifically excluded the nomad peoples to the north and northwest.

Despite these reassurances and their high moral tone, however, the Chinese conception of tributary relations and how to enforce them had changed.[3] This was thanks to the Mongols. Whereas the Tang and Song dynasties had, for the most part, relied upon the power of virtue (*de*) to convince barbarians to acknowledge Chinese suzerainty and superiority, the Yuan had relied much more on 'majesty' (*wei*), and military force, to extend the empire and subdue foreign powers. As barbarians themselves, the Mongols could claim little virtue, in Chinese eyes at least, and their loss of the mandate of Heaven only confirmed this. The Ming, by contrast, claimed great virtue; but they did not forget the lesson of the Yuan: where foreign relations were concerned, they saw 'no real contradiction' between virtue and force, providing the force was applied by a virtuous ruler.[4]

The tributary system

Under the Ming, imperial authority was extended to include all relations between Chinese and barbarians, including trade relations. Private overseas trade by Chinese merchants was prohibited and Chinese were forbidden to voyage abroad. The only officially sanctioned trade was by merchants from countries that acknowledged Chinese suzerainty, and then only when they accompanied actual tribute missions. Such trade attracted only a minimal 6 per cent tax, a clear indication that the dynasty did not count on trade as a major source of revenue. Three ports only were designated to receive tribute missions, depending on where they came from. The port for missions from Southeast Asia was Canton, though the envoys of some inland kingdoms arrived via Kunming.

The whole tributary system was also placed on a more formal footing. Regulations were issued specifying how tribute was to be offered and how frequently. 'Near countries' on China's borders, such as Vietnam, were required to send tribute every three years. 'Distant countries', which included all of Southeast Asia beyond Champa, were required to send tribute only 'infrequently'. Tribute did not need to be lavish, Hongwu told Vietnam, and should not be a burden: the intention was what counted. The symbolism of ritual submission took precedence over economic benefit.[5]

An elaborate ceremonial was put in place, based on historical precedent. Court officials greeted the envoys, and prepared them for the emperor's banquet at which a tributary memorial was presented, along with 'local produce', the more exotic the better. Envoys were instructed how to behave and when to kowtow. Less important banquets followed until it was time to leave the capital, escorted by an appropriate official. Even more revealing of the Chinese view of the world were the equally detailed instructions on how Chinese envoys were to be received by foreign courts, especially when bearing an imperial edict or seal of office for the investiture of the ruler as a Chinese vassal.

More Chinese envoys travelled abroad during the early Ming than at any other time in the history of relations between China and Southeast Asia. Five were despatched to Ayutthaya by Hongwu, for example, and nine by Yongle. They came to instruct as well as inform, to let Southeast Asian courts know exactly what was expected of them. Their demeanor was both superior and patronising, as was the message they carried. The ritual for the reception of Chinese envoys reflected in large part the ritual for the reception of tributary missions in China. Some Southeast Asian kingdoms went to great lengths to impress visiting Chinese envoys, for this was an opportunity for reciprocal demonstrations of royal power and wealth. Great reverence would be shown to an imperial edict or letter, but in Siam, for example, the envoy was led into the royal presence barefooted and was required to prostrate himself three times before the king. Even during the early Ming, however, more embassies were sent to China from Southeast Asia than were received from China. In fact, more missions were dispatched from Cambodia in the first fifty years of the Ming than were sent throughout the rest of the Angkor period (802–1431).

The new Ming restrictions applying to trade reduced both its volume and value. In response, Southeast Asian principalities and some larger kingdoms attempted to increase trade by dispatching missions more frequently. Srivijaya, for example, sent six missions in the space of seven years, while Siam and Cambodia also markedly increased the number of tribute missions. Some private merchants attempted to disguise trade in the form of bogus official missions, but Ming officials applied strict criteria for verifying the authenticity of embassies and issued warnings against such ventures.

Southeast Asian rulers were not averse to the official trade regime imposed by the Ming, for it reduced competition from private traders. Private Chinese merchants, by contrast, especially those from coastal Fujian who had been engaged in free trade with the Nanyang over the previous two centuries, were most unhappy, and immediately set about circumventing the new restrictions. Many resorted to smuggling, which increased dramatically, encouraging piracy in its wake. Others sought to cooperate closely with official tributary missions, even going so far, as in Ayutthaya, as effectively to manage tributary trade to the joint benefit of both court and merchants. In a few cases ethnic Chinese actually led official missions (from Java in the 1430s and 1440s, and from Siam in 1478 and 1481).[6]

Despite the increase in smuggling and in the frequency of tribute missions, the total volume of trade between Southeast Asia and China declined in the last decades of the fourteenth century. This had a serious impact, especially on smaller Malay trading settlements, and indirectly provoked political disturbances. Thus attempts by south Sumatran ports, such as Malayu, to gain Chinese recognition as independent polities, indirectly provoked their conquest by Javanese Majapahit. Another effect was to increase the resident Chinese population in Southeast Asia, as merchants feared reprisals if they returned to China. Some merchant families in China fled abroad for fear of prosecution or persecution. In order to maintain their commercial buying networks, Chinese merchant communities in Southeast Asia redirected trade towards the muslim West, while waiting for the situation in China to ameliorate.

Chinese foreign policy under the Ming, as reflected in the new regulations on tribute and trade, obviously cannot be understood purely in economic or commercial terms. The first Ming emperor was not interested in generating wealth through tribute or trade. But he was interested in reimposing a Chinese world order, in which China was universally accorded supreme status as the Middle Kingdom, and all countries acknowledged the power of the emperor's virtue. Limitations on foreign travel and trade were designed to impose imperial control over all Chinese, and to minimise contacts between Chinese and non-Chinese that might cause friction. Stipulations on tribute were designed to place foreign relations on a formal footing, regulated by prescribed ritual (*li*).

It should be noted that because China stood at the centre of the world, and because the emperor enjoyed the mandate of Heaven, any friction that arose in foreign relations was necessarily due to the failure of vassal kingdoms to act in accordance with Chinese expectations. In such cases punishment might be necessary—always because China had been provoked, and always to restore the peace that China desired—on China's terms. Given the Chinese conceptions of hierarchy and harmony, it was always possible to justify aggressive policies in high moral terms when it was in China's interest to do so. An example of this self-serving approach from Hongwu's reign was the reimposition of Chinese domination over the non-Chinese people of Yunnan, who in the later Yuan period had regained much of their former independence.

Ming expansionism

There were good reasons for Ming concern that the southern frontier should remain peaceful. Unlike the Yuan, the Ming again faced a hostile coalition of Mongols and Turks on the grasslands to the north and west. Hongwu did not want any unrest in the south, either in Yunnan or in Vietnam. In 1380, the decision was taken to reincorporate

Yunnan into the empire, on the pretext that the presence in Kunming of a Mongol prince posed a threat to the dynasty. A force of almost a quarter of a million men took first Kunming, then Dali, but it was another three years before the region was declared 'pacified', and then only after considerable loss of life. Principalities ruled by non-Chinese were overthrown in both Yunnan and Guizhou and either made to acknowledge Chinese suzerainty through payment of an annual tribute, or brought under direct Chinese administration. In 1388, the first of three invasions was launched against the Tai principality of Luchuan, southwest of Dali, an area never previously claimed by any Chinese dynasty. The independence of Vietnam was not threatened during Hongwu's reign, though it was required, as a Chinese vassal state, to supply rice to Ming forces in Guizhou.

The Chinese invasion and conquest of Dali extended the southern frontier of the empire, while Chinese migration into the region reinforced Chinese control. Yet these actions were rationalised not in strategic or security terms, but as punishment for refusing to acknowledge Chinese suzerainty and for 'obstructing culture'.[7] Emperor Hongwu's proclamation that he had no intention of attacking small barbarian countries in Southeast Asia had proved hollow for the Tai principalities on China's southern frontier, for a pretext had easily been found that they were 'causing trouble'.

Hongwu and his Confucian court did not see themselves as pursuing an aggressive foreign policy. Instead, they saw foreign relations as flowing naturally from a reassertion of Chinese rule within the Middle Kingdom, which brought with it restoration of the cosmological basis of the Chinese world order. The barbarian Yuan had been defeated because, lacking virtue (*de*), they had lost the mandate to rule. The *de* of the new dynasty could not be taken for granted, however. Its real and practical proof lay in acknowledgment of China's superior status at the summit of the hierarchy of powers through homage and tribute, and in the universal extension of peace and harmony beyond China's frontiers—if necessary through the use of force.[8]

The second great Ming emperor, Yongle (reigned 1402–1424), only succeeded in gaining the throne after three years of civil war, as a usurper at the expense of his nephew. This may have been why he was determined to enhance his own status as emperor by bringing all the known world within the Chinese world order, with himself at the centre. Modelling himself on the great conquering emperors of the past, Han Wudi and Tang Taizong, Yongle embarked upon a series of maritime expeditions and military campaigns to extend Chinese influence throughout the Nanyang and into Central Asia.

Yongle's attention was attracted to the Nanyang in part because the conquests of Timur (Tamerlane), the last of the great Mongol conquerors, had severed trade routes to the west through Central Asia. This forced the new emperor to reassess his predecessor's policy towards seaborne trade. But in 1405, Timur died and the empire he had created split apart. The Mongols and Tartars were still both powerful forces, but their disunity provided Yongle with an opportunity to play one off against the other, and so neutralise the Mongol threat to north China. Between 1410 and 1424, Yongle personally led five great, ultimately futile military campaigns deep into the grasslands. To mount these campaigns he moved the Ming capital from Nanjing to Beijing, a mere 60 kilometres from the Great Wall, where it has remained ever since (but for brief interludes). Thus within his own reign did Yongle's attention shift from the sea to the steppes; and there the attention of his successors remained focused.

Yongle's first priority, however, was to project Chinese power south. The Chinese hold on Yunnan was reinforced and extended. Beyond lay a ring of tributary kingdoms designated as 'pacification superintendencies' whose responsibility was to keep the peace along China's frontiers. These included the the Tai principalities of Luchuan and Cheli (Sipsong Phan Na), the Lao kingdom of Lan Xang, the kingdom of Lan Na in northern Thailand, and the kingdom of Ava in Burma, all of whose rulers were designated 'pacification superintendents', with the status of Chinese ministers. All conducted their official relations with China via Yunnan.

None of these 'pacification superintendencies' had ever been administratively part of China. But there was one area that once had been part of the empire, and that was, of course, Vietnam. The Ming attempt to reimpose Chinese rule over Vietnam coincided with its projection of naval power into the Nanyang and beyond, and clearly formed part of a concerted policy both to expand the empire and to strengthen and extend Chinese influence.

In 1400 a powerful Vietnamese mandarin named Ho Quy Ly took advantage of the political turmoil in China to replace the child emperor of Vietnam, last of the Tran dynasty, with his own son and to proclaim a new dynasty. Once the Yongle Emperor's victory was assured, tribute was sent to the new Son of Heaven, who graciously recognised the new Vietnamese dynasty. However, in response to appeals by supplicants claiming to be members of the Tran royal family, Yongle saw an opportunity to reassert Chinese control over Vietnam, and seized it.

The pretexts given for the Ming invasion of Vietnam in 1406 focused on the crimes committed by Ho Quy Ly and the need to punish them in order to protect the Vietnamese people. Forgotten were the reassurances of Hongwu that Vietnam need not fear Chinese attack. As always, aggressive Chinese action was given moral justification by placing all the blame on Vietnam. Twenty crimes were listed, the most serious of which were that the Vietnamese had murdered the legitimate Tran ruler and his family, and assassinated the Chinese-backed Tran pretender; that they had deceived the Chinese about the Ho usurpation; that they had insulted China by sending a criminal as an envoy; that they had encroached on Chinese territory; and that they had attacked Champa, a vassal of China, and annexed some of its territory.[9] In other words, Ho Quy Ly had disrupted the peace and order that China desired to maintain on its southern frontier. All Yongle intended in invading Vietnam, so he claimed, was to restore the legitimate Tran dynasty and so restore harmony and well-being to the country and the region. Despite assuring the Vietnamese that they were all his children, the force that Yongle dispatched carried out a massive slaughter. Vietnamese resistance was fierce and tens of thousands were killed before the Vietnamese capital was taken and Ho Quy Ly captured.[10]

The Ming hardly had the intention of restoring independent Tran rule, for Vietnam was immediately incorporated into the Chinese empire as a province under the old name of Jiao-zhi, with all the paraphernalia of Chinese administration soon in place. The justification for this was that Vietnam had previously been a province of China. During its four centuries of independence China had 'been engaged with many things' and so had been prevented from reasserting control.[11] An annual tribute was imposed of silk, lacquerwork, aromatic woods and kingfisher feathers, and taxes levied. Private overseas trade was banned, as elsewhere in the empire, and the Vietnamese economy was subordinated to that of China.

The annexation of Vietnam constituted the second major southern extension of Chinese power south, after Yunnan. Had it been successful, the shape of relations between China and Southeast Asia would today be very different. As it was, however, the 'peaceful south' (Annam) was never pacified. Vietnamese resistance continued, waiting only for the right political circumstances to expel the invaders. In the meantime, the Yongle Emperor turned from the land to the sea as a means of projecting Chinese power.

The Ming voyages

Between 1405 and 1433, a remarkable series of seven great maritime expeditions were mounted, all but the last on the orders of the Yongle Emperor. Apart from materially contributing to the prestige and prosperity of the Middle Kingdom, the impact of these voyages was felt for

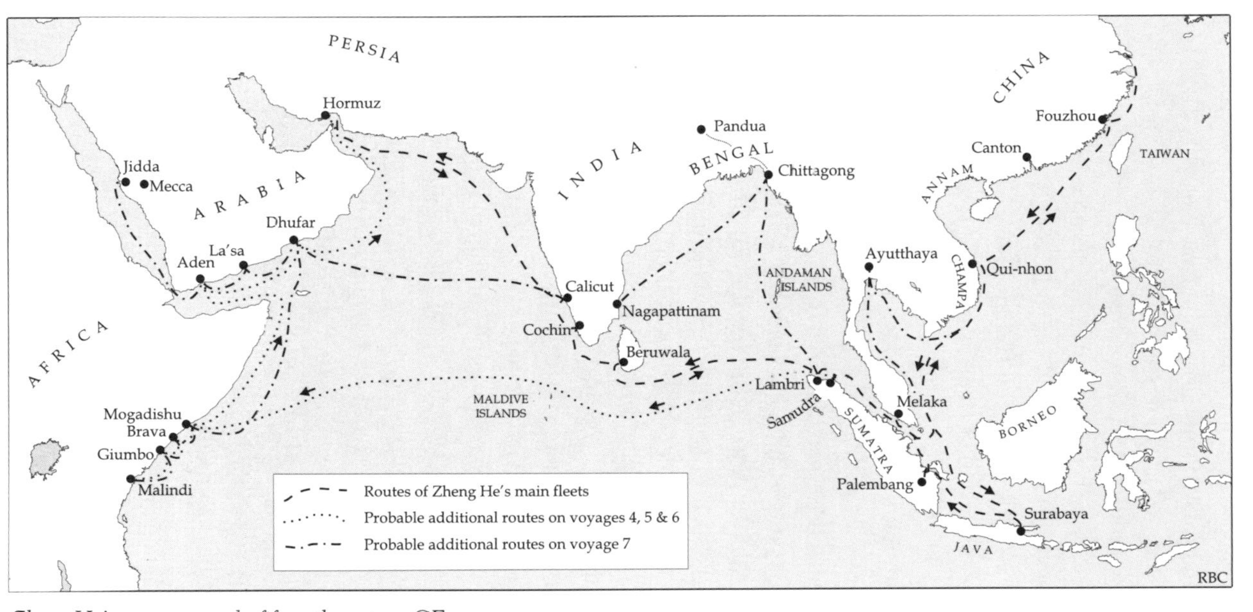

Zheng He's voyages, early fifteenth century CE.

years far beyond China's shores. Just the bare outline of these seven voyages is impressive enough.[12] The first expedition of 1405–07 comprised 317 ships, 62 of them so-called 'treasure ships', great five-masted ocean-going junks up to 120 metres (400 feet) in length and 50 metres (160 feet) wide, with up to nine masts, four decks, and watertight bulkheads. They were thus several times larger than the largest Portuguese caravelles that sailed into the Indian Ocean a century later, and represented the pinnacle of fifteenth-century maritime technology. At its height, Yongle's navy counted 250 of these vessels of seven different kinds, the largest capable of carrying 500 men, along with over 3000 warships provisioned by 400 armed supply vessels.

The first fleet carried 27 870 men, including officers, soldiers, seamen, interpreters, medical orderlies, various artisans skilled in boat repair and maintenance, and numerous officials in charge of everything from rationing stores and purchasing supplies, to valuing and keeping meticulous accounts of the treasure, gifts and trade goods exchanged. This expedition, like subsequent ones, was under the overall command of the grand imperial eunuch, Admiral Zheng He, a Muslim from Yunnan who had gained imperial favour for his military prowess. The fleet visited at least ten countries, as far as Cochin and Calicut on the Malibar coast of southern India, where it stayed for about four months awaiting a change in the monsoon winds before the return voyage.

The next two voyages took place in 1407–09 and 1409–11. Both again went to Calicut, though the third also visited Sri Lanka. The fourth voyage, from 1413 to 1415, went beyond India for the first time, as far as Hormuz at the mouth of the Persian Gulf. It comprised 63 ships carrying 28 560 men. The fifth expedition of 1417–19 sailed even further, down the coast of Africa as far as Malindi, just north of Mombasa. No record survives of the complement of ships and men on this or the sixth expedition (1421–22), which reached Aden and the Somali ports of Mogadishu and Brava. On all these voyages, elements of the fleet were directed to other ports of call, including the Andaman

Reconstruction of Ming 'treasure ship' compared to Columbus's St Maria, *fifteenth century. (Jan Adkins from Louise E. Levathes,* When China Ruled the Seas, *Simon and Schuster, New York, 1994.)*

and Nicobar Islands and Bengal. The furthest of these subsidiary voyages was to Mecca, the most distant place to send an envoy to the Ming court.

The sixth expedition was the last despatched by the Yongle emperor. After it came a break of ten years, during which there was steady retraction of Chinese sea power and presence overseas. Laden with honours, Admiral Zheng He was named 'Defender' of Nanjing and given responsibilities ashore. Then, in 1430, the Xuande emperor, perhaps in emulation of Yongle, ordered Zheng He, at the age of fifty-nine, to undertake one last voyage. This lasted from 1431 to 1433. More than 100 large ships transported 27 550 men to twenty destinations, though not all were visited by the main fleet. Zheng He died in 1435 at Nanjing, where his tomb can still be seen. In the course of his seven voyages he had personally visited thirty-seven countries as the foremost ambassador of his age.

These Ming voyages have attracted considerable scholarly interest, as much for their unexploited potential as for their importance for the history of Chinese foreign relations and diplomacy. Nowhere in the Ming records is the purpose of these great expeditions explicitly stated. Scholars have debated the reasons why they were dispatched, why they were on such a vast scale, why they ended so abruptly, and why they were all but forgotten subsequently. That these expeditions—or at least the first one or two—were dispatched to seek out Yongle's young nephew (and pretender to the throne) can probably be dismissed. Personal aggrandisement and Yongle's need to bolster his political legitimacy by ensuring that a steady stream of foreign ambassadors came to pay him homage in his new capital at Beijing almost certainly played a part. Another possible reason may have been that closure of overland trade routes convinced Yongle of the need to compensate by controlling maritime routes. There is evidence that imports of goods from both Southeast and South Asia fell short of demand during the Hongwu period, and Yongle required a steady supply of luxuries. Moreover, as the emperor was personally interested in fostering diplomatic relations with Southeast Asia and the Western Ocean, he may have wanted more information about them.

These reasons, even combined, are still not entirely convincing. Even though Chinese demand for overseas products had grown substantially since the days of the Tang and Song, this could presumably have been met by encouraging more private traders to come to Chinese ports. For the Ming, however, maritime trade had to accompany tribute, not just to ensure official control over greedy merchants, but to enforce acceptance of the Chinese world order.

The size of the Ming fleets was designed to overawe and bring submission through recognition of the superiority of Chinese civilisation and power. Ideally, power was not to be used in an aggressive way. Ritualised submission was sufficient to satisfy the Ming court that surrounding kingdoms accepted the Chinese world order and its status hierarchy. To explain how this worked, Zheng He carried with him thousands of copies of Chinese texts to be distributed to local rulers for their edification.

There was, in other words, a powerful ideological purpose behind the Ming voyages. They were designed to convince the known world to accept their designated place within the Chinese world order. At the centre stood the Son of Heaven, whose cosmic role was to ensure through the power of his virtue (*de*) the universal peace and harmony essential to human welfare. This universal ambition had to include all those countries whose merchants traded at Chinese ports—Arabs, Persians and Indians, as well as Malays, Thai and Cham. By continuing on from India to Hormuz and Mecca, Zheng He, good Muslim that he was, brought the world known to China within the Chinese world order.

Early Ming rhetoric makes abundantly clear the intention of the dynasty to reestablish the Chinese 'imperial order'. The lofty tolerance, the benevolence and impartiality, masked a reality with regard to power that the Ming were determined should be well understood. Power had always formed a crucial dimension of the hierarchical Chinese world order. China stood at the centre of the world, not just because of its superior civilisation and the virtue of the emperor, but because of its imperial power—to command, enforce, and punish if necessary. Zheng He's kid gloves of diplomacy only partially masked his capacity to enforce the order he represented. The very size of his fleet and the soldiers at his command were designed to amaze and overwhelm, to coerce through fear.

Although the voyages were designed to bring even far countries in the Western Ocean, including India itself, within the Chinese world order, their impact on Southeast Asia was especially great. Each fleet had to wait for up to four months in a port on the north Javanese or east Sumatran coast, or at Melaka, in order to catch the east–west monsoon, more than enough time to become well informed about local politics and economic opportunities and, in particular, the activities of overseas Chinese.

The ambiguity of official Chinese relations with overseas Chinese is well illustrated by the case of Srivijaya, centred on Palembang in southern Sumatra. Srivijaya was by then a declining power, recently reduced to the status of a dependency of the Javanese kingdom of Majapahit. But Palembang remained a major Chinese trading centre with a large resident Chinese population. As strong local government collapsed, Chinese traders elected their own leader who obtained the blessing of the Ming court. Peaceful transit for merchant shipping through the vital Melaka Strait was thereby assured. When in 1405 a Chinese pirate, Chen Zuyi, seized control of Palembang, Zheng He attacked and defeated him. Seventeen ships were sunk or seized, and more than 5000 of Chen's men killed in a series of engagements over three months. Chen was sent in chains to China, where he was beheaded. One message from these events was clear: force would be used to ensure peaceful conditions for legitimate trade. Another was less evident: the interests of China took precedence over those of Chinese overseas.

Force was also used to ensure respect for China's imperial order. In 1411 Zheng He returned from his third voyage via Beruwala, on the west coast of Sri Lanka. There the local Sinhalese ruler rashly refused to acknowledge Chinese suzerainty. Conflict arose and several battles were fought, resulting in a decisive Chinese victory. The king, his family, and several leading officials were carried off as captives to Beijing. There Yongle demonstrated his benevolence by releasing them and permitting them to return to Sri Lanka, once they had rendered him homage.

On his fourth voyage, Zheng He executed an imperial command to depose a usurper who had seized control of Samudra on the northeast coast of Sumatra, and restore the rightful ruler to his throne. The usurper's forces were defeated, and he himself was taken as a prisoner to China, along with his wife and child. This time the sentence was death, for the Chinese-sanctioned order had been disturbed. The message was again clear. China reserved the right to intervene in local affairs, and Chinese power would be used where Chinese interests were at stake. China's readiness to use force thus stood as a warning to any ruler in Southeast Asia who might disturb the existing order.

Later Ming–Southeast Asia relations

The reign of the Yongle Emperor was by any account a remarkable one. By the time he died in 1424, the dynasty was at the height of its power, the empire was prosperous and at peace (though the Mongol threat remained), and China enjoyed diplomatic relations with sixty-seven overseas kingdoms and principalities. Indeed, Chinese sea power reached further beyond her frontiers than ever before or since, to dominate not only the Nanyang, but also much of the Indian Ocean as far west as the African coast. Under Chinese naval protection, seaborne trade flourished, bringing wealth not only to the tribute ports of southern China, but throughout the empire wherever goods for export were produced or imports traded.

Yet as we have seen, even during the Yongle Emperor's reign, Chinese attention had again shifted north. This was due to both external and internal factors. Externally, Turks and Mongols continued to pose a threat to the security of the empire. Internally, scholar officials succeeded in contesting the power of the court eunuchs. The great voyages were criticised for their cost and extravagance, and those associated with them lost influence. Finances were required for the army and for building the new capital with its imposing Forbidden City.

Zheng He's voyages were not the only cost involved in Yongle's southern strategy. Vietnamese resistance had continued since 1406, and substantial Chinese reinforcements had had to be dispatched. The most effective resistance centred on the mountains west of Thanhhoa, where a member of the local landed gentry named Le Loi led a motley band, with the support of the Muong, a non-sinicised people close to the ancestral Vietnamese. Other loyalists joined him, and in 1418 Le Loi launched his campaign to drive out the Chinese. At first he had little success. An attempt to gain Lao support was subverted by the Chinese and Le Loi was almost captured. His opportunity came in 1424 with the death of Yongle.

Over the next year Le Loi seized all the region from the frontier of Champa to north of Nghe-an, but for isolated Chinese garrisons in district centres. By the end of 1426, much of the Red River delta was in his hands. Massive Chinese reinforcements were not enough to stem the Vietnamese advance, and in early in 1428, after yet another significant Vietnamese victory, a face-saving peace was concluded. Remaining Chinese forces were permitted to withdraw without further attack. Le Loi was left to found the Le dynasty, grudgingly recognised by the Ming court in 1431 after appropriate tributary submission. The Xuande emperor loftily proclaimed: 'I am specially sending envoys with a seal and am ordering that [Le Loi] temporarily take charge of the affairs of the country (*guo*) of Annam and govern the people of the country.'[13] No longer was Vietnam a Chinese province.

The Ming invasion of Vietnam had given the Vietnamese another national hero. Once again the lesson was learned: Chinese occupation could be defeated by refusing to surrender, mounting a guerrilla resistance, and fighting a protracted war relying on popular support. It was a recipe that served the Vietnamese well into the twentieth century. But a further step was necessary. After defeating Chinese armies on Vietnamese soil, peace had to concluded in the only face-saving way that was acceptable to the Chinese—that is, by restoring the hierarchical tributary relationship. At this the Vietnamese were adept. Vietnamese officials, good Confucian mandarins that they were, knew exactly the right form of address to use in humbly requesting imperial favour. And the Chinese, pragmatic about a lost cause, graciously responded by permitting Le Loi to rule his country as a nominal Chinese vassal. Thus was the security of Vietnam ensured.

China's relations with other kingdoms in Southeast Asia were much more friendly. Numerous embassies were exchanged following the Zheng He voyages as even minor principalities sought to benefit from trading relations with China. One was Melaka whose independence was expressly underwritten by Yongle. Melaka was founded around 1400 by a truant prince from south Sumatra, named Parameshvara. The port was strategically situated to control the Melaka Strait, but sat on the fringes of the empires of both Majapahit and Ayutthaya, and was claimed by both. When Melaka was visited in 1403 by a Chinese envoy, Parameshvara appealed for Chinese recognition and protection. A tributary mission was dispatched; Zheng He visited Melaka in 1409; and Parameshvara went in person to make his submission to Yongle in 1411.

China took a particular interest in Melaka, both because of its importance as a trading emporium, and because of its strategic location. In 1405 Melaka was accorded the significant honour of being the recipient of the first of four inscriptions Yongle personally addressed to foreign rulers. In it the emperor graciously acknowledged Parameshvara's desire to be part of the Chinese world order, and to benefit from its cosmically ordained harmony.[14]

The king of Brunei was another minor potentate who personally led a tribute mission to China. His reward was Chinese endorsement for Brunei's independence. Yongle magnanimously freed Brunei of any obligation to pay tribute to the declining power of Majapahit. A royal inscription presented to the Brunei sultan demonstrated, however, the essentially condescending Chinese view of its vassal status. In all, seven kings made the long trip to the Chinese capital, all from minor principalities (including three from Melaka and two from Brunei).

For the Melakan ruler, the benefits of Chinese protection were immediate and tangible. Ayutthaya had attempted to impose its own suzerainty over Melaka by confiscating the imperial seal Yongle had bestowed on Parameshvara. Zheng He's voyage of 1407, and again that of 1419, visited Ayutthaya to warn the Siamese king not to infringe

China's suzerainty over Melaka. The example of Ho Quy Ly was explicitly cited, and the warning was enough to thwart Siamese attempts to control the straits. An even stronger warning to the Javanese to settle their civil war, and to pay compensation in gold for executing Chinese envoys, also made reference to the fate of Annam.

For Southeast Asia, China had previously been as a great but distant power, one that might take upon itself to offer admonition or arbitration, but which seldom aggressively interfered in regional affairs. The voyages of Zheng He brought Chinese power much closer. Small kingdoms like Melaka and Brunei, that feared being absorbed by powerful neighbouring *mandalas*, eagerly sought protection. Medium polities such as Champa and Cambodia, worried about pressures from neighbours, looked to China to maintain the status quo. Larger kingdoms such as Vietnam or Ayutthaya, expansionist themselves, resisted intervention, while promoting trade with China.

The effectiveness of China as arbitrator and protector depended on its capacity to respond to an appeal from a tributary. After the Vietnamese invaded Lan Xang in 1479, Lao envoys requested Chinese assistance. The matter was investigated, and blame placed squarely on the Vietnamese. China admonished Vietnam, and demanded withdrawal of its forces on pain of punishment, though by then the Vietnamese had already retreated. Two years later, reports that Vietnam was again planning to invade Lan Xang elicited a strongly worded warning. Meanwhile a Lao request for Chinese forces from Yunnan to assist them in avenging the Vietnamese invasion was turned down. The Lao were told that the Chinese emperor regarded both Lao and Vietnamese as his 'children', and that he desired only to end their enmity, for 'this is China's way'. Instead of troops, Chinese envoys were dispatched to both sides in order to 'instruct' them how to maintain good relations and to care for their people.[15]

Eighty years later, when Burmese armies marched east into the Tai world, Ming power was on the wane and Chinese admonitions carried less weight. Even so, the possibility of calling upon China as arbitrator remained and was resorted to on occasions, just as small powers might call upon the United Nations, with similarly nugatory effect.

Conclusion

We cannot be certain how the countries of Southeast Asia responded to this early fifteenth-century projection of Chinese power into the region, for as usual we have no Southeast Asian source materials. All we have to go on are the Ming records, written as they were from a markedly sinocentric point of view. One thing is obvious, however, just from the frequency of missions sent to China, and that is that trade was the primary motive. If trade was important for China, despite official restrictions, it was the lifeblood of small Southeast Asian kingdoms. Where it was a royal semi-monopoly, as in Ayutthaya, profit from trade contributed a substantial proportion of court revenue. After Yongle abolished restrictions on the frequency of missions, Champa sent envoys almost every year, while Ayutthaya on several occasions dispatched two missions in a year, in an effort to maintain the level of trade in the absence of private commerce. For the smaller port principalities, trade was their major source of revenue. After 1435, when embassies from Siam and Champa were again limited to one every three years (a rule subsequently also applied to Java), only illegal channels were available, which had the effect of concentrating trade in the hands of Chinese smuggling networks.

A second point to note is that only the rulers of small and vulnerable principalities led missions to the Ming court in person. No king of Champa or Cambodia, let alone Ayutthaya or Majapahit, ever paid homage to the Son of Heaven. That Chinese emperors preferred to accept the homage of kings in person is evident from the lavish way the minor rulers of Melaka and Brunei were received in Beijing, for the submission of a king enhanced the status of the emperor. Rulers of more powerful Southeast Asian kingdoms must have been aware of this, but rejected all inducements to pay homage in person. Moreover, apart from Vietnam, the kingdoms even of mainland Southeast Asia did not place China alone at the apex of the international hierarchy. In the seventeenth century, for example, Siam accorded similar recognition to ambassadors from Mughal India and Persia as they did to envoys from China.[16] India was always an alternative pole of attraction (and status) for Buddhist kingdoms, for the same reason that Mecca was for Muslim polities. Thus for all their acceptance of the Chinese world order, Southeast Asian kingdoms never saw themselves as committed to that order alone. Their foreign relations cultures, while hierarchical, recognised several potentially competing centres of power, and made allowance for shifting power relationships.

The Ming voyages confirmed that China was indeed the regional hegemon, with a capacity to project its naval power well beyond its maritime frontiers. But the voyages themselves were more about affirming the status of an ambitious emperor and reinforcing the Chinese world order than about imposing political or military domination. When Ming armies did invade Vietnam, they were driven back, and the tributary relationship was re-established. Security rested, as always, on determined defence plus acceptance of the moral obligations implicit in the Chinese world order, for both vassal and hegemon.

6
ENTER THE EUROPEANS

From the mid-fifteenth to the mid-seventeenth centuries has been called the 'age of commerce' in Southeast Asia.[1] Part of the initial impetus for this period of increased trade and prosperity came from Admiral Zheng He's voyages, which established conditions for regular maritime trade. The seizure of Melaka by the Portuguese in 1511 marked the violent arrival of Europeans in Southeast Asia, though their activities at first had little effect on trading relations between China and the Nanyang. More important from the point of view of both China and Southeast Asia was the lifting, in 1567, of the Ming ban on private overseas trade. Even the arrival of the Dutch did not at first disrupt trade patterns. As the Dutch grip strengthened, however, they were able to impose a monopoly over most of the spice trade, notably from the Maluku islands, with critical effects on indigenous commerce. The so-called junk trade between the Nanyang and China continued, however, until it was progressively eclipsed by European shipping between the late eighteenth and mid-nineteenth centuries.

More importantly for this study, throughout the period from the heyday of the Ming through the resurgence of Chinese power during the early Qing, official relations between China and foreigners, whether Southeast Asian or European, continued to be conducted in accordance with the 'tributary system'—that is, in terms of the Chinese world order. Envoys from European powers—the Portuguese in Melaka and Macau, the Spanish in Manila, the Dutch in Batavia (Jakarta)—were required to meet the same formalities as envoys from 'tributary' kingdoms in Southeast Asia. As the Europeans were in no position to challenge Chinese power until the nineteenth century, they had no alternative but to acquiesce. Not until the famous British embassy of Lord Macartney in 1793 did a European envoy refuse to perform the kowtow of 'three kneelings and nine prostrations' that in Chinese eyes signified submission to the emperor, and so served to reinforce the Chinese view of the world and their own place in it.

Tribute and trade

After the voyages of Zheng He, Ming foreign relations settled into what one scholar has characterised as a 'defensive, passive, and bureaucratic mode'.[2] Official justification for the retreat from Yongle's expansionist attempt to assert Chinese superiority and power was couched in the rhetoric of the traditional Chinese worldview, combined with pragmatic economic and political considerations. Court mandarins argued that the exemplary moral virtue of the emperor and the superiority of Chinese culture were sufficient to ensure barbarian submission without the costly use of force. If this did not work, barbarians could always be played off against each other. In any case, as trade was believed to be more important for barbarians than for self-sufficient China, they would continue to behave as required.

During this period policies towards Southeast Asia reflected those developed to deal with Central Asia, where instead of welcoming trade, as the Tang had done, the Ming tried to circumscribe it. After the expeditions of Zheng He, the dynasty no longer looked upon the distant world beyond China's frontiers as a source of tribute and knowledge. Some of the records of Zheng He's voyages were actually destroyed; others were filed away and forgotten. From the mid-fifteenth to the mid-sixteenth centuries, official China became progressively more isolationist and inward-looking.

No attempt was made to maintain even a reduced naval presence in Southeast Asian waters, let alone in the Indian Ocean. As a result, the number of tribute embassies rapidly declined. The last mission from Bengal arrived in 1438 and from Sri Lanka in 1459. Embassies from Southeast Asia, including Champa, Cambodia, and Melaka, continued with reduced frequency. No mission arrived from Sulu after 1421, from Brunei after 1426, or from Samudra-Pasai in Sumatra after 1435. In their place an extensive Southeast Asian shipping network supplied the China trade.

This regional trade network comprised two parts: a western route linking Champa to ports on the Malay peninsula and northern Java (Surabaya, Gresik and Tuban); and an eastern route linking the Ryukyu islands (Liu-qiu), the Philippines (Luzon), Sulu and Borneo (Brunei).[3] Most of the inter-island trade was in Indonesian vessels, but the China connection from Champa or Siam and the Ryukyus was sailed by Chinese. The earlier Java network was coordinated by long-established Chinese communities on the north Java coast, while the later Ryukyu network was controlled by merchants from Fujian. Trade goods came from as far away as the Sunda islands and Timor, including sandalwood, tortoise-shell, shark fins, pepper, and spices. They reached China either illegally or as tribute trade accompanying official missions from those countries that continued to dispatch embassies on a regular basis: every year from Vietnam, every two years from the Ryukyus, and every three years from some more distant kingdoms, such as Ayutthaya, though some sent missions more frequently.

The tribute trade from Southeast Asia entered China through Canton (Guangzhou), while embassies from the Ryukyus arrived at Quanzhou in Fujian province. (A third port of entry at Ningbo was used by Japan.) Despite the greater frequency of Ryukyu embassies, almost one a year from 1435 to 1475, Canton was able more or less to monopolise the Nanyang trade. Fujian merchants who had previously been successful in developing new trade routes were thus particularly disadvantaged by the ban on private trade. Some took to smuggling, with the connivance of local gentry and officials. Some moved to Canton, or to the Ryukyus in order to profit from the tributary trade. Others, as we have seen, migrated to one of the Chinese settlements already established in Southeast Asia.[4]

Two things should be noted about Chinese trade and settlement in Southeast Asia at this time. The first is that the number of Chinese involved in the trading networks supplying the Java and Ryukyu tributary trade, and the actual number of settlements, both increased, though most Chinese communities numbered in the hundreds, rather than the thousands. Though Melaka dominated peninsula Malaya, there were substantial Chinese settlements at Pattani and smaller ones at places like Pahang and Kelantan, and on the north Java coast at Semarang and Cirebon. The Chinese presence in Cambodia and Siam also increased, and there is evidence of Chinese in the Philippines. In every community intermarriage occurred and many resident Chinese adopted elements of local culture. Others, however, retained a more traditional Chinese lifestyle, particularly where family ties with home villages remained strong. Many Chinese in coastal Java, Sumatra and Malaya, it should be recalled, were already Muslims and may actually have assisted in the Islamisation of Indonesia.

The second point is that these Chinese communities played no part at all in the foreign policy of the Ming dynasty, even though Chinese merchants often accompanied official Southeast Asian embassies. From the point of view of the Ming court, Chinese living outside the frontiers of China were living beyond the pale of Chinese civilisation, and by so doing were failing to fulfil their duty to the emperor. At no time were these communities used as a means of exerting Chinese influence on Southeast Asian rulers, even though in places they performed politically sensitive tasks, such as tax collection. From the point of view of local rulers, Chinese were tolerated along with other semi-permanent merchant communities, and were not seen as a threat to the political order. Indeed they were encouraged, for it was above all the China trade and how this was organised that determined the prosperity of Southeast Asian port cities.[5]

Towards the end of the fifteenth century, illegal Chinese trade increased, especially along the Fujian coast, to which officials, eager for exotic goods, turned a blind eye. Chinese ships sailed to Luzon, Brunei, Ayutthaya, the north Java coast and Melaka, while coastal trade continued with Vietnam and Champa. Ming attempts to suppress this illegal trade led merchants to band together and arm their vessels. Smugglers thus became pirates in official eyes, no better than, and often confused with, the Japanese pirates (*wako*) who plagued the China coast. In retaliation, China first restricted, then in 1560 banned, all direct trade with Japan. Sophisticated trade networks developed in response to official suppression, in which Chinese, Southeast Asian, and by then early European traders were involved. The 'pirate' problem persisted, however, until the Ming legalised private trade in 1567, after which it quickly disappeared.

China, Southeast Asia, the Portuguese, and the Dutch

The Portuguese capture of Melaka in 1511 did little to change trading patterns, though Chinese as well as Malay vessels at first tended to avoid a port where Muslims were unwelcome. In time, however, the Portuguese presence, particularly the activities of private Portuguese merchants, began to stimulate a competitive demand for Southeast

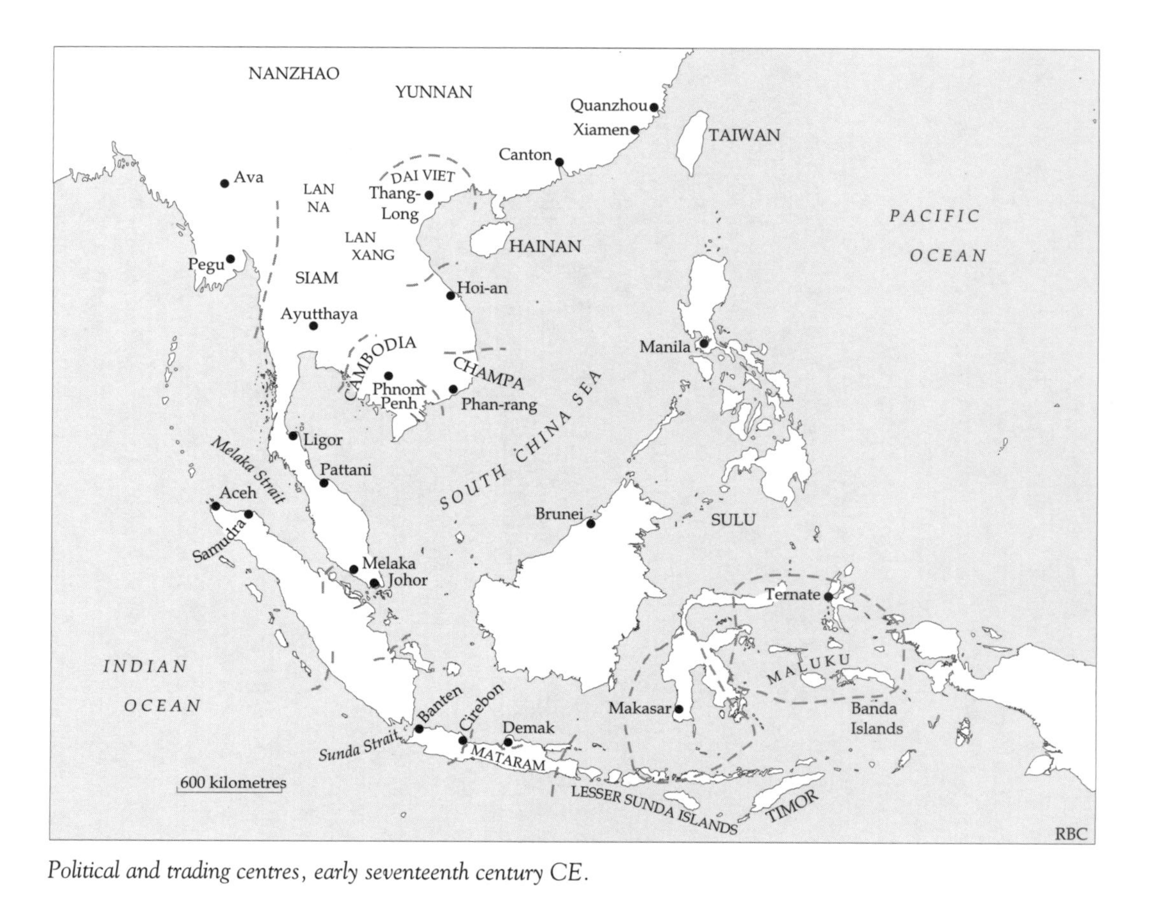

Political and trading centres, early seventeenth century CE.

Asian products, most importantly spices. The Portuguese were not slow to realise that enticing profits were to be made from trading directly with China. The first Portuguese vessel to reach the coast of China arrived in 1517 and was allowed to proceed to Canton, while a second soon after sailed north to Fujian. The meeting of Ming bureaucracy and Iberian arrogance led almost inevitably to misunderstanding and conflict, however. For the Ming, the newcomers were as difficult to deal with as the Japanese, for like the Japanese they indulged in both insolent behaviour and piracy. From 1521 to 1554, by imperial order, trade with the Portuguese was banned.

After the ban was lifted, the Portuguese were permitted, in 1557, to establish a trading outpost at Macau, for which they paid an annual rent. Attempts to send an official embassy to Beijing were, however, unsuccessful and not until a new dynasty was in power was a European mission received at the Chinese court. Under the Ming, all official contacts with merchants and envoys from the Nanyang, among whom Europeans were numbered, were dealt with at Canton. After the Portuguese, Spanish envoys arrived from Manila in 1575, followed by the Dutch in 1604, though neither obtained permission to trade, thanks in large part to Portuguese machinations. The profitable trade that sprang up between China and the Philippines thus remained entirely in the hands of Chinese merchants from Fujian.

The Portuguese seizure of Melaka posed something of a challenge to the Ming in their official dealings with Southeast Asia, for the deposed ruler immediately appealed to China for assistance in driving out the invaders and re-establishing the ruling dynasty. But if the sultan was expecting China to dispatch another powerful fleet, he was disappointed. Late Ming China had neither the means nor the will to enforce its own world order, even for the sake of a loyal tributary. Melaka was far from Beijing, and Ming attention was focused on the northern grasslands.

In their relations with tributaries in Southeast Asia, the later Ming relied more on words of high principle than on deeds of intervention. Aggression by one tributary against another was frowned upon, for that destroyed the peace and harmony the Chinese world order was supposed to uphold. By the time a tributary kingdom appealed for protection in the face of invasion, however, it was usually too late to prevent it. Faced with a fait accompli, the Chinese bureaucracy could do little more than investigate the situation, a process that might take so long that the crisis resolved itself. It was, of course, in China's interest to prevent the rise of an expansionist power that might pose a security threat to the Middle Kingdom, but it was immaterial whether some Tai principality, such as Chiang Mai, was tributary to Ayutthaya or Burma—so long as the victor maintained properly respectful relations with China.

As for Southeast Asian rulers, they seem to have seen appeal to China as a last resort. The second half of the sixteenth century was a period of conflict and struggle throughout much of mainland Southeast Asia. By 1547, King Tabinshwehti, founder of the Toungu dynasty, succeeded in unifying Burma after two centuries of division. Buoyed by his success, Tabinshwehti proclaimed himself a *chakravartin* or world conqueror, one whose karma predestined him to be a universal ruler, at least of the Buddhist Theravada world. His pretensions were challenged, however, by both King Chakkraphat of Ayutthaya and by King Xetthathirat of Lan Xang, both of whom made similar claims. When the Siamese became embroiled in a succession dispute, Tabinshwehti took the opportunity to invade southern Thailand, while a Cambodian force pillaged and plundered further east. Yet none of the four Siamese tribute missions sent between 1554 and 1560 appealed for Chinese assistance or arbitration.

Conflict continued throughout the turbulent second half of the sixteenth century, but the Ming took no initiative to arbitrate an end to the fighting. No envoys were dispatched to Pegu to demand restraint on the part of the Burmese. Nor did the Tai kingdoms, mostly on the receiving end of Burmese aggression, appeal to China to intervene. Even reports reaching Beijing from Yunnan that Burma had 'annexed' a number of small Tai principalities formerly tributary to China failed to provoke a response.

Succession disputes were another source of civil conflict and social disorder. These particularly interested the Chinese, for it was Chinese policy to endorse only legitimate lines of succession. Usurpers were not tolerated, for their actions went against the moral law of Heaven. Yet it was often easier to endorse a properly submissive usurper who appeared to have a good hold on power than to restore a discredited legitimate line. When, in 1541, the Vietnamese usurper, Mac Dang Dung, offered not only his abject submission, but also five mountainous frontier districts in response to a threatened Chinese invasion in support of the deposed—but in Chinese eyes still legitimate—Le dynasty, the deal was graciously accepted.

The period from the 1580s to the fall of Beijing to the Manchus in 1644 was one of decadence, rebellion and final collapse of the Ming dynasty. The court fell under the control of powerful eunuchs who took no interest in relations with Southeast Asia. Apart from regular embassies from Vietnam and Champa, tribute missions from other polities (Cambodia, Siam, Java) were irregular. The last embassy from Burma arrived in 1567 and from the Philippines (Luzon) in 1576. Yet this was a crucial period in Southeast Asia, for it saw the arrival and consolidation of power of the Dutch East India Company (VOC), followed later by the English and French.

The first Dutch vessels to reach Southeast Asia arrived on the Java coast in 1596. In 1602 the Dutch East India Company obtained a monopoly on all Dutch trade with Asia, and set about excluding its European rivals. First the Portuguese were driven out of the Maluku islands (1605), then the English were excluded from the Banda islands (1623). This left the principal spice (cloves, nutmeg and mace) producing region of Indonesia entirely in Dutch hands. In 1640 the Dutch drove the Portuguese from Sri Lanka and, the following year, they took Melaka, leaving East Timor as the only Portuguese toehold in the Nanyang.

As in the case of the Portuguese, early Dutch contacts with China moved rapidly from mutual incomprehension, to frustration, to armed conflict. After Dutch requests to trade were refused (1604, 1607), force was used. A Dutch flotilla first unsuccessfully attacked Macau in 1622, then was driven from the Pescadores islands, and finally established a fort on Taiwan. From there the Dutch opened regular trading relations with Japan, though the China trade continued to elude them.

If China took little interest in these developments, wracked as it was by internal rebellion, Southeast Asian rulers and their courts certainly did. It did not take regional political elites long to realise that Europeans were greedy and ruthless in their pursuit of trade; that they were prepared to intervene in local politics; and that their superior military technology was a two-edged benefit—it could be used by Southeast Asian rulers, and it could be used against them. With the arrival of the Dutch, something else was evident: there were different kinds of Europeans, and they did not like each other. One kind could therefore be played off against another.

In both Burma and Cambodia in the first half of the seventeenth century, Portuguese and Spanish freebooters attempted unsuccessfully to seize political power. With its capital at Batavia, the VOC established a maritime commercial empire capable of bringing political pressure to bear throughout the Indonesian archipelago. European mercenaries served in both the Burmese and Siamese armies, while European arms merchants plied their trade to anyone who would buy. When civil war broke out in 1627 between the Trinh in the north and the Nguyen in the south of Vietnam, the Dutch supported and sold arms to the north, while the Portuguese did the same for the south.

Arms and precious metals were about the only European goods of value in regional trade. European manufactured goods, including woollen cloth and linen, were not in demand. Arms were mostly purchased by ruling elites, while silver and gold were in high demand from Asian merchants. Silver, in particular, fuelled European trade with

China, almost all of it from the Americas. As the price for silver in China was substantially higher than in Europe, vast amounts flowed around the world to meet the insatiable demand for Chinese silk, porcelain, and tea. The famous Acapulco galleon that arrived twice yearly in Manila directly from Mexico brought silver to exchange for Chinese products transported there by Chinese merchants.

As the lucrative galleon trade attracted more and more Chinese, their numbers at Manila rose rapidly. Even though the Chinese presence depended entirely on the continued flow of Spanish silver, the outnumbered Spanish saw the Chinese as a threat. In 1603, fearing an uprising, the Spanish turned on the Chinese community and in an appalling massacre killed as many as 23 000. In the aftermath of this tragic event, two things became apparent. The first was that the Ming government would, or could, do nothing to protect Chinese settlers in Southeast Asia. The second was that Europeans had become dependent on the Chinese, not just as middlemen importing food and other consumer goods, but also artisans and labourers, whose industry was essential for the economic life of European-administered ports. The Spanish authorities were forced to re-admit Chinese settlers, though they no longer permitted Chinese to live within the walls of the Spanish town. Within a few years the Chinese population of Manila again numbered several thousand. Five more pogroms occurred in the seventeenth and eighteenth centuries, and yet each time the Chinese returned, lured by the prospects of profit and a more comfortable life.

The Qing

In 1644 Beijing fell to the Manchus, a sinicised confederation of warrior tribes from the northeastern steppes of Manchuria, who had already proclaimed their Qing ('pure') dynasty eight years before. The turmoil that accompanied the change of dynasty spilled over into

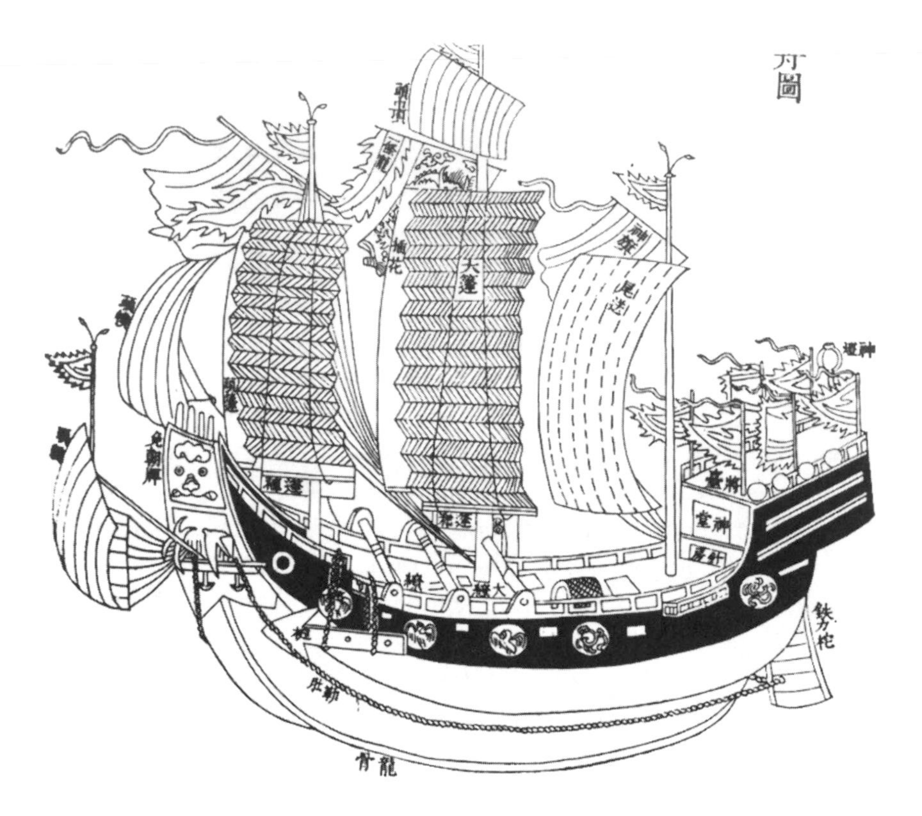

Chinese ocean-going junk, eighteenth century.

Burma. Following the defeat in 1659 of the last Ming armies, the young Ming pretender and a few hundred retainers sought asylum in the Burmese capital of Ava. In the meantime, thousands of leaderless Chinese soldiers and 'bandits' ravaged much of upper Burma, at a time when Burma was also at war with Siam in the south. As the Burmese king seemed incapable of dealing with the crisis, his brother deposed him in a palace coup. The Ming prince was handed over to an invading Manchu army, to be put to death. No tribute at this time was either demanded or offered, and in fact the first Burmese tribute mission to the Qing was not dispatched until 1750, in a hopeless bid for Chinese support to prevent the collapse of the Toungu dynasty.

The Qing conquest of Taiwan had an indirect impact on Southeast Asia. For centuries there had been limited Chinese settlement on the island, mainly by pirates and criminals fleeing justice. Japanese pirates and some Spanish merchants also used the island, but most of the inhabitants were Austronesian-speaking tribal peoples. In 1624, after being driven from the Pescadores, the Dutch expelled the Spanish and established a number of trading posts. When the Ming loyalist, Zheng Chenggong (known to Europeans as Koxinga), lost control of the Fujian coast to the Manchu, he seized Taiwan from the Dutch, and established it as a powerful base for anti-Manchu naval operations.

The Qing response was slow in coming. When in 1673 anti-Manchu forces on Taiwan joined in support of a revolt by three Chinese generals, the Qing forcibly removed the entire coastal population of Zhejiang, Fujian and Guangdong provinces 10 kilometres inland, and laid waste the deserted towns and villages. Already in 1661 a ban had been placed on all foreign trade, reminiscent of the one enforced by the Ming. Depopulation of the Chinese coast destroyed what little Nanyang trade remained. In 1683, with the support of a Dutch fleet, Qing forces finally occupied Taiwan and placed it under the provincial administration of Fujian.

The defeat of Koxinga had unforeseen repercussions in Vietnam. In 1679 3000 Ming loyalist soldiers aboard a fleet of fifty junks sought asylum in central Vietnam. Fearing Qing displeasure, the Nguyen ruler sent them south to settle the borderlands in the Mekong delta contested by the Vietnamese and the Khmer. Half settled at Bien-hoa, the rest at My-tho. Within twenty years both were incorporated as provinces in the Nguyen domains. Ten years later the Chinese community at Ha-tien also gave its allegiance to the Nguyen. Thus was Chinese settlement instrumental in extending Vietnamese control over what is now southern Vietnam.

The catalogue of Qing conquests in Mongolia, Xinjiang and Tibet is enough to establish that, like several earlier dynasties (Tang, Yuan, Ming), it was expansionist in its determination to bring non-Chinese peoples under Chinese rule. Outer barbarians were thereby converted to inner barbarians and given the opportunity to adopt elements of superior Chinese culture, be subject to the benevolence of the Son of Heaven, and be part of and benefit from the Chinese moral/political order. In other words, the justification for Qing imperialism was, like that of previous dynasties, couched in terms of the Chinese worldview. This did not differ radically from the 'white man's burden' justification given for nineteenth century European imperialism—and the outcome for subject peoples turned out to be very similar.

Later invasions to 'punish' Burma and Vietnam were repulsed (see below), leaving China's southern frontiers much as they were. The Qing conquest of Taiwan, however, extended the empire some 300 kilometres west to within 400 kilometres of the principal Philippines island of Luzon. Taiwan thus provided China with both a trading base and an offshore bastion whose value in terms both of defence and offence would not become fully evident until three centuries later. In the meantime, Taiwan provided new opportunities for Chinese colonisation.

The early Qing emperors followed the precedent of the Ming, whose ceremonial diplomacy they adopted. Tributary countries were informed that a new dynasty ruled under Heaven and were invited to return the imperial seals given them by the Ming. The Qing published their own *Collected Statutes*, stipulating how tribute should be presented and how accompanying trade should be conducted. Tributary missions were not to number more than 100 persons, only twenty of whom were permitted to proceed to Beijing from the place of entry. No more than three ships were permitted to enter port, each with a maximum of 100 men. No additional accompanying ships were allowed to dock, nor was any vessel not accompanying an official tributary mission. All foreign communications had to be forwarded to the appropriate authorities in Beijing.[6]

Tribute, as opposed to trade items, was to consist only of the local products of the country. Detailed instructions were issued on how emissaries were to be received and conducted to and from the capital. Trade accompanying tribute was strictly regulated. Goods could be exchanged only in a specially organised market close to the government Residence for Tributary Envoys, under official surveillance. Members of the mission not proceeding to the capital were permitted to trade locally, but not to purchase implements of war or, curiously, books on history. Departing ships were forbidden to transport shipbuilding materials, food over and above what was needed for the voyage, or any Chinese passengers.

The elaborate ceremonial for the formal presentation of tribute took place in the imposing surroundings of the Forbidden City in Beijing. We can gain some idea of how impressive these ceremonies were from the accounts of European envoys allowed to present tribute in the seventeenth century (Portuguese, Dutch, and from the Vatican). No such accounts record the impressions of Southeast Asian envoys, but one has only to walk the way they must have taken into the outer courtyards of the Forbidden City to imagine the scene they encountered.

The foreign delegation would be assembled before dawn by attentive Chinese officials, who conducted them to the Tiananmen (Gate of Heavenly Peace). From there they approached the Forbidden City proper, guarded by the soaring Wumen (Gate of the Meridian) with its imperial yellow roof tiles. By the time the envoys passed through into the first courtyard, over marble bridges, and through a side gate beside the Taihemen (Gate of Supreme Harmony), they would see before them the serried ranks of officials drawn up in the vast 200 metre square courtyard before the Hall of Supreme Harmony.

There they waited, awed by the magnificence of silken banners and embroidered robes, until the booming of a great bell and the cracking of whips announced the arrival of the emperor. Officials in order of precedence made their triple obeisance before the envoys in turn were called upon to perform the 'three kneelings and nine prostrations', foreheads to the ground, before the Son of Heaven, all in time to instructions shouted by the Master of Ceremonies. If they were lucky they might be conducted close enough actually to see the emperor on his throne, even to exchange a word of ceremonial greeting as he terminated the audience.[7]

One can imagine the impact of such a ceremony on royal envoys from even the most powerful Southeast Asian kingdoms, who had travelled for days from city to city just to reach the Chinese capital. And one can imagine what stories they would have told on their return of the population and wealth of the Middle Kingdom. Little wonder, therefore, that the countries of Southeast Asia within easy reach of China quickly resumed their tributary relationship with the new dynasty. Yet the response was uneven. Vietnam and Siam sent embassies every three years, but none arrived from Laos (Luang Phrabang) until 1730 or from Burma until 1750. The Sultan of Sulu sent his first mission in 1726. No missions arrived from port cities previously listed as tributaries in Java, Sumatra and the Malay Peninsula that had fallen under European control. Even so, in some Qing texts these former tributaries continued to be listed (along with Champa, by then all but absorbed by Vietnam, and Brunei, which had declined to the point of insignificance.)

Private trade continued, however, with many parts of Southeast Asia outside the tributary system, especially after restrictions were lifted in 1684. By this time, the great majority of trade between China and Southeast Asia was in Chinese hands, organised by networks of Chinese merchants resident throughout the region and shipped in Chinese junks. The principal ports involved in this trade came to be categorised as 'non-tributary trading countries'. They included notably Java (Dutch Batavia), Luzon (Spanish Manila), Aceh in Sumatra, and several ports on the Malay Peninsula, including Johore and Siamese

Pattani. Cambodia fell into the same category, once its status had been reduced to a vassal jointly of Siam and Vietnam.

Much of the information available to the Chinese court on European activities in Southeast Asia came from Chinese merchants. The repeal of the Qing prohibition on overseas trade stimulated a new wave of Chinese migration into the region. Many went to peninsula Siam and the Malay sultanates to mine tin and grow pepper, but increasing numbers were attracted to territories under European administration. There they met with a mixed reception. We have seen the fate of the Chinese in the Philippines. In Java, Chinese settlement increased substantially, so that by 1739 there were as many as 15 000 Chinese living in and around Batavia alone.[8] Such were their numbers that the Dutch grew fearful, and planned to ship some off to Sri Lanka. Believing they were to be drowned at sea, many Chinese rose in rebellion. Thousands were massacred, as the rebellion spilled over into the territory of Mataram and the VOC intervened.

The Qing entered into direct contact with countries of the 'Western Ocean' through agreeing to receive official missions from Portugal (1670, 1678) and Holland (1656, 1667, 1686). All sought increased trading rights, for which they were prepared to perform the full kowtow as prescribed by Chinese ceremonial, and even to accept nominal tributary status. All, however, were unsuccessful. The only European power with which the Qing deigned to enter into negotiations leading to a treaty was Russia (in 1689). The Treaty of Nerchinsk was designed, however, at least as far as the Chinese were concerned, to keep yet another Central Asian foe at arm's length, and to control trade. The treaty was concluded, in other words, in the context of Qing policy towards Central Asia.

The rise of Dutch power in Southeast Asia in the eighteenth century was at first of little consequence to China. The Qing court felt no need to accommodate the demands of Dutch envoys because Holland, despite its monopoly of trade to Europe, did not threaten Chinese trading interests. Throughout the eighteenth century, the

China trade remained firmly in the hands of Chinese merchants, whose extensive trading networks and busy fleets supplied all the imports China needed, in return for what seemed to be an insatiable regional demand for Chinese silk, porcelain and tea. And given the availability of these products, the Dutch did not feel the need to press the issue of direct trade with China.

The Qing were unclear as to the whereabouts of Holland, but they knew that though the Dutch ruled Java, they 'governed at a distance.'[9] These 'red-haired barbarians' were nonetheless treated as a Southeast Asian power, whose relations with the Middle Kingdom fitted into the existing tributary pattern for Nanyang countries. This was never understood by European envoys, who saw only the bureaucratic restrictions that stood in the way of profitable trade. Thus while the relations between China and Southeast Asia that had developed in the course of a millennium came to constitute a set of bilateral relations regimes compatible with the worldviews of both parties, no such regimes evolved between European powers and China.

The preparedness of early European envoys to the Qing court to perform all the ceremonial required of them only reinforced Chinese belief that they had accepted the same tributary relationship as other countries of the Nanyang. Embassies that for the Europeans had been manifest failures were highly satisfactory for the Chinese, for they confirmed that even the most distant peoples were prepared to acknowledge the overlordship of the Son of Heaven. Thus were the universal pretensions of Chinese worldview reinforced. In particular, the proper hierarchy constituting the Chinese world order was maintained, and harmony preserved, for no conflict resulted. The envoys were cared for, laden with presents, and left. It did not matter what they really wanted or thought. The ritual they performed signified submission, and that was the only reality that mattered for the Chinese.

By the end of the eighteenth century, however, Qing power had already begun to wane. Two attempts to 'punish' obstreperous tributaries, Burma from 1766 to 1769 and Vietnam in 1789, both ended in bruising defeat. Both attempts can be seen, therefore, as portents of Qing weakness, though this is hardly how they were interpreted in Beijing.

In 1752, Alaungp'aya, the third great unifier in Burmese history, had founded the Shwebo dynasty. It was his second son, Hsinbyushin, however, who consolidated and extended his father's conquests. In 1767, the Siamese capital of Ayutthaya was taken and sacked. It was not this aggression against a loyal tributary that provoked Chinese intervention, however, but simultaneous Burmese attempts to reinforce their control over the Shan principalities along the vaguely defined frontier with Yunnan, plus a dispute over trade. An attempt by a Burmese embassy to negotiate a settlement was unsuccessful as the Chinese decided to punish Hsinbyushin for disrupting peace in the region.

No fewer than four Chinese armies invaded Burmese territory to attack Ava, but they were unfamiliar with the terrain, poorly coordinated, and constantly harassed by the Burmese. Burmese stockades held out against Chinese attack, and at length hunger and the climate took their toll. The Chinese generals sued for peace, to which the Burmese agreed. An agreement was signed that permitted remaining Chinese forces to withdraw, reopened trade, and committed Burma to sending missions once every decade to Beijing. Hsinbyushin was furious that the invaders had been allowed to escape. Not until after his death in 1776 did a Burmese mission eventually leave for Beijing to obtain investiture for his more pacific successor. A properly submissive relationship was thus restored, at least in Chinese eyes.

In 1789 it was the turn of the Vietnamese. Between 1773 and 1787, the great Tayson rebellion finally brought an end to the moribund Le dynasty by destroying the regimes of both the Nguyen in the south, and the Trinh in the north. These events were closely followed in southern China, and when jealousy divided the three Tayson brothers, the opportunity presented itself to reassert Chinese hegemony on the pretext of restoring peace and order. A large Chinese army easily occupied Thang-long (Hanoi), nominally to protect the last Le emperor.

The youngest of the Tayson brothers, the brilliant military commander Nguyen Hue, thereupon gathered his forces and marched rapidly north. During the new year celebrations of 1789, having proclaimed himself emperor of a new dynasty, Nguyen Hue routed the Chinese army of occupation. Immediately he did what victorious Vietnamese generals before him had done—humbly requested Chinese recognition, thereby restoring Chinese status and superiority. The request was graciously acceded to, and insignia bestowed. Whereas Vietnamese tribute missions had averaged less than one every four years over the previous 120 years, embassies arrived every year from 1789 to 1793. Once again the Vietnamese had defended their independence through force of arms, and ensured their security through re-inscribing in the Chinese world order.[10]

For the countries of Southeast Asia, Qing weakness was not apparent. China remained the dominant economic power, and the Chinese world order still prevailed. Kings continued to seek investiture in order to obtain trading rights, goods and markets only China could provide. Where succession was in the male line, investiture was a formality; but Beijing remained cautious about recognising anyone suspected of being a usurper, and reluctant to provide any material assistance. It took King Taksin of Siam six years and three diplomatic missions to convince the Qing court that, although Chinese on his father's side, he had a right to his throne, during which time the Chinese brushed aside his requests for iron and weapons. Only after he had decisively defeated the Burmese, and his claim to the throne was secure, did the Qianlong emperor deign to recognise Taksin as king of Siam, and again receive Siamese tribute missions.

Challenges to the Chinese world order

Apart from the Russians, only two eighteenth-century European missions were received at the Qing court before the famous embassy of Lord Macartney arrived in 1793. Both were from Portugal—one in 1727, the other in 1753. Neither dented the tributary system, even though each established a small precedent. On the first, the ambassador succeeded in presenting his credentials in person, rather than through the intermediary of Chinese officials. On the second, protests that this was not a tributary mission were apparently acknowledged, but not recorded. This was not an accidental omission. Chinese bureaucrats regularly wrote reports that envoys had performed exactly as Chinese protocol demanded, even when they had not. They even redrafted correspondence from foreign rulers that did not sound sufficiently submissive. This preserved Chinese convictions about their place in the world, but at the expense of distorting what the world was really like.

The Macartney embassy provided the first official contact between a British king and a Chinese emperor. By the second half of the eighteenth century, Dutch power had declined and Britain was the rising hegemonic European power. Of these developments the Qing court seems to have been largely unaware. In the meantime, however, European knowledge of China had improved, mainly through the writings of Jesuits serving at the Qing court. At any rate, the Macartney mission was the first to attempt to impress upon the Chinese that it represented not a tributary barbarian kingdom, but an empire of equivalent standing and status as that of the Qing. Lord Macartney insisted in handing over his letter from George III to the emperor in person, and refused to perform the kowtow as demeaning both to himself and to his king and country.

Even so, the Qing court managed to preserve the Chinese world order. Lord Macartney was allowed to present his letter on one knee, in the rather informal setting of a great tent in the grounds of the summer palace at Chengde. Ceremonial protocol had been breached, but not at the centre of the Chinese world in Beijing. Despite the breach, the Macartney embassy was described as a tributary mission, both on the banners accompanying it and in the official Qing records. All attempts by Macartney to enter into meaningful negotiations were blocked. In his first edict addressed to George III, the Qianlong emperor commended the 'respectful humility' of the British monarch, but rejected as 'utterly unreasonable' the request for a British representative to be resident in Beijing. Qianlong continued:

> Our dynasty's majestic virtue has penetrated into every country under Heaven, and Kings of nations have offered their costly tribute by land and sea. As your Ambassador can see for himself, we possess all things. I set no value on objects strange or ingenious, and have no use for your country's manufactures . . .[11]

Qianlong's second edict, rejecting any liberalisation of trade, made the point that the Chinese capital was 'the hub and centre about which all quarters of the globe revolve', and so was hardly the place for the conduct of trade. All private trade would continue to be conducted at Canton; no new ports would be opened; and no 'British barbarian merchants' would be permitted to establish a 'factory' on Chinese soil.[12]

Here the matter rested. The Chinese world order remained intact, at least as far as the court was concerned. A Dutch mission following hard on the heels of Macartney was the last time a European envoy kowtowed before a Chinese emperor. In 1816, a second British embassy was summarily dismissed when it became clear that the envoy, Lord Amherst, would refuse to conform to Chinese ceremonial—at a time when Britain, following victory in the Napoleonic wars, was the most powerful imperial power in the world.

In the following years, European nations strengthened their grip on the Nanyang. Singapore was founded as a British settlement in 1819, after the return of Batavia to the Dutch. Five years later, the First Anglo–Burmese war gave Britain control of the Arakan and Tenasserim coasts of Burma, in addition to the Straits Settlements in Malaya. At the same time, direct Dutch rule in Java was extended and reinforced, interrupted only by the Java War of 1825–1830, the last great paroxysm of traditional Javanese resistance. Elsewhere in the archipelago, the Dutch increasingly made their presence felt. Southeast Asian and Chinese maritime trading networks continued to operate, but increasingly the region was drawn into an expanding global economy dominated by European powers, from which China still remained largely insulated.

The First Opium War of 1839–42 should have shaken Chinese complacency to the core. Ostensibly a response to Chinese attempts to curtail the lucrative British opium trade, it was also the outcome of mounting misunderstanding, anger and frustration on both sides. The lesson drawn by the Qing court, however, had more to do with the disgraceful behaviour of Western barbarians than with what the impunity with which British warships could bombard Chinese ports revealed about the weakness of Chinese naval defences.

Other countries saw the implications more clearly. European nations benefited from the opening up of four more port cities for international trade (in addition to Canton) along the China coast, but were jealous of the concession in 1842 of the island of Hong Kong to Britain. These 'treaty ports' extended rather than replaced the 'Canton system'. France and America quickly signed similar treaties, followed by other Western powers. To each China magnanimously and impartially extended the same privileges as she had to Britain (the most-favoured-nation provision). Not until territorial concessions were later sought were China's sovereignty and territorial integrity seriously threatened.

In the early 1850s, a series of anti-dynastic rebellions broke out in China that were only put down with great difficulty and with some Western assistance. The Taiping rebellion was finally crushed in 1864, but the devastation led thousands to seek new opportunities abroad. Suppression of a Muslim rebellion in Yunnan, and the last great Miao (Hmong) uprising sent rebels fleeing south to pillage the northern border regions of Vietnam, Laos and Burma. In the 1880s, Siam sent several military expeditions into northern Laos to clear the area of marauding Chinese, who penetrated as far south as Viang Chan. Hmong refugees, meanwhile, settled quietly in the secluded mountains and began to grow the only cash crop they could—opium.

Peasant rebellion shook Qing complacency much more deeply than had Western pressure and incursions, because it threw into question the dynasty's right to the mandate of Heaven. In the middle of it all, Britain and France contrived a Second Opium War (1856–58) to obtain further trade concessions. China promptly agreed to open ten more treaty ports, four on the Yangze River upstream to Wuhan; but not until an Anglo–French force had marched on Beijing and sacked and burned the summer palace did the court at last agree to accept permanent Western embassies in Beijing.

A significant outcome of the Second Opium War for Southeast Asia was that the Qing court rescinded its ban on the movement of Chinese overseas. The first shipment of Chinese contract labourers had departed Xiamen (Amoy) on a French vessel as early as 1845. Thereafter, this 'coolie trade' developed rapidly. Large numbers of Chinese were transported as far afield as Cuba and Chile, but most went to Southeast Asia to work the mines and plantations, or to take up commercial farming of crops such as pepper, gambier and sugar. In Siam, they built canals to drain new rice land in the Chao Phraya delta. Many fled the aftermath of rebellion; others were lured by hopes for a better life. Most were transported in European ships, though Chinese junks were also engaged in the trade.

In Southeast Asia the wars and rebellions that shook the Qing dynasty were followed closely by political elites. Vietnam (so-called after China recognised the Nguyen dynasty that came to power after the Tayson were defeated in 1802), Siam, Luang Phrabang, and Burma all responded to news of the death of the Taokuang emperor in 1850 by dispatching embassies to China. Despite some delay, missions from all four were recorded as arriving in 1853, though the Lao delegation never actually reached Beijing. These were the last tribute missions sent by Siam and Luang Phrabang. Burma sent one more in 1875, while Vietnam sent its last mission in 1883 in a desperate appeal for Chinese assistance against the French.[13] All were received in the traditional way, as if nothing had changed since the accession of the Qing dynasty more than two centuries before.

After Burma was annexed by Britain, and Vietnam by France, only Siam retained its independence as a buffer state between the expanding British Indian and French Indochinese empires. It is instructive, therefore, to follow the course of Chinese–Siamese relations during the declining years of the Qing dynasty to gauge the only independent Southeast Asian reaction to Chinese weakness and European dominance.

In 1862, Chinese envoys to Siam chided King Mongkut for neglecting to send regular tribute missions. The Siamese, however, were well aware of the outcome of the opium wars and why they had been fought. More specifically, they were aware of the shift in the balance of power in the region. The junk trade between Siam and China, so valuable still in the early nineteenth century, had all but collapsed and Britain had become Siam's principal trading partner. Mongkut understood better than any of his fellow monarchs in mainland Southeast Asia how Europeans viewed the world. It would not help Siam to be seen as a tributary of China.

What the court wanted was continued friendship with China (especially in view of the large numbers of Chinese in Bangkok), but on the same basis as the Western powers. Since how to obtain this seemed impossibly difficult, Mongkut made excuses and played for time. Not so his son. As soon as Chulalongkorn came to the throne, he sent a mission to China offering to resume diplomatic relations, but only on a basis of formal equality. This was rejected by Beijing, which in 1875 and again in 1878 demanded dispatch of a Siamese tribute mission. The Siamese again procrastinated, but in 1882 Chulalongkorn finally notified the Qing court that Siam repudiated any tributary obligation to China.[14]

The Siamese decision was taken for a variety of reasons that principally had to do with Siam's evolving national identity, and the regional power configuration. One issue was security. The seizure by France of southern Vietnam (Cochinchina), and imposition of a protectorate over Cambodia (until then tributary to Bangkok) in 1863, had convinced Mongkut that only Britain, as the most powerful nation in the region, could protect Siam from further French incursions. From then on, until the rise of Japan in the late 1930s, friendship with Britain remained a keystone of Siamese foreign policy, despite British seizure of territory in Burma and Malaya formerly tributary to Bangkok.

This security dimension becomes more evident when Chulalongkorn's break with China in 1882 is compared with the response of Emperor Tu Duc of Vietnam to French encroachments. Despite signing a treaty with France in 1874 accepting French protection, five years later the Vietnamese emperor requested China to fulfil her obligations as suzerain power by suppressing Chinese bandits—known as the Black Flags—in the border area. The real threat, however, came from France, and as the Siamese well understood, any appeal to China to protect Vietnam from France would be useless. For this reason Bangkok had already turned elsewhere for powerful friends. But the Siamese could more easily do this because they conceived the world as in perpetual flux, with new centres of power arising from time to time. The Vietnamese, ambivalent though their relationship was with China, found it more difficult to free themselves from their commitment to the Chinese world order, for that order also constituted their own view of the world.

Security was also a Chinese concern. When a small French military force seized Hanoi in April 1882, China reacted with vigour. Chinese troops entered Vietnam while a Chinese naval force moved into Vietnamese waters even before Vietnam sent a last desperate appeal for assistance. In May 1883, the Black Flags ambushed and killed the French commander of the Hanoi garrison, and France went on the offensive. Meanwhile, the old Vietnamese emperor, Tu Duc, had died and the court was in turmoil. The French occupied Hue and advanced into Tonking where they were opposed by combined Vietnamese and Black Flag forces. Negotiations proved fruitless as France was determined to take control of Vietnam while the Qing court continued to insist that Vietnam remained tributary to China.

August 1884 saw the outbreak of the undeclared Sino-French war. French naval vessels bombarded Fuzhou and attacked Taiwan. In Vietnam, however, Chinese forces drove the French out of Lang-son, and France agreed to negotiations. These resulted in the Treaty of Tianjin signed in June 1885, which recognised Vietnam as a protectorate of France. Vietnam's relations with foreign powers, including China, would henceforth be conducted through the French Ministry of Foreign Affairs.

Thus was this closest of all tributary relationships in Southeast Asia brought to a close, a decade before Japanese invasion did the same for Korea. In 1886 Britain annexed Upper Burma, and in 1893 Siam ceded the Lao territories to France. China had lost all her protective ring of tributary states, and instead faced European imperial powers on her northern (Russia) and southern (Britain and France) borders, not to mention an aggressive Japan to the east. Not only was the Chinese world order at an end, but by being forced to define national boundaries within which it would exist as a nation-state and beyond which it would have no further claim, China was drawn inexorably into the Western world order.

Much of the impetus for the French conquest of northern Vietnam and the British occupation of Upper Burma came from a belief that their possession would open up opportunities for trade with the interior of China. At first it was hoped to use the Salween, Mekong and Red Rivers as access routes, and when these proved unnavigable, railways were planned. Only the line from Hanoi to Kunming was built, however, and the volume and value of trade never lived up to expectations.

The arrival of European powers on China's southern frontiers worried Beijing. For the first time a serious security threat existed along previously peaceful, if poorly defined frontiers with cooperative tributary states. European intentions were unclear and European demands unreasonable. Clearly defined borders had to be marked out in areas inhabited by non-Chinese over whom Chinese jurisdiction was questionable. Negotiations over just where the frontier should lie were longer and more involved in the case of Burma than for Vietnam, where an agreed division of administrative responsibility already existed. Laos proved more contentious for the French, but an agreement was signed in 1895. An initial Anglo–Chinese agreement on Burma actually recognised a degree of continuing Chinese suzerainty, but this was eliminated in the 1894 and 1897 treaties defining the Burma–China border. These agreements still left some issues unresolved, however, and as late as 1947 Nationalist China laid claim to a portion of Burmese territory. The communists, of course, viewed all such treaties with imperialist powers as unequal, and thus needing to be renegotiated.

The late Qing and overseas Chinese in Southeast Asia

The lifting of restrictions on travel did not just legalise the coolie trade, it changed the whole relationship between the Nanyang Chinese and Qing officialdom. For as long as overseas Chinese were considered as truant subjects, and so little better than criminals, any

Chinese coastal trading junk.

who returned to China were at the mercy of local officials. Even merchants who had stayed away longer than their permits allowed were forced to bribe officials on their return. The new policy not only encouraged more overseas Chinese to visit China, it opened up avenues of communication that provided higher Qing officials with a much better knowledge of the activities and achievements of Chinese settlers in Southeast Asia. Just as the traditional relationship between China and the countries of Southeast Asia was collapsing, therefore, China discovered new interests in the Nanyang.

Chinese resident in, or migrating to, Southeast Asia were quick to take advantage of the commercial opportunities made available by the growing European presence. Reformers in China hoped to tap into the expertise of overseas Chinese entrepreneurs who had learned how to operate in the world of international capitalism, invite them back to China, and so use their knowledge to assist China's modernisation. As the extent of the wealth of overseas Chinese capitalists became evident, Qing officials began to see them also as a source of investment in China. In 1893, an imperial edict gave overseas Chinese and their families the right to return to and leave China at any time, in pursuit of their business. In 1909, the Qing proclaimed the principle of *jus sanguinis* as the basis for Chinese nationality: anyone whose father was Chinese, no matter where born, was a Chinese citizen. Thus were the Chinese of Southeast Asia reclaimed for China.

It was abuses in the coolie trade that first alerted Qing officials to the need to protect Chinese going abroad, and led to the establishment of permanent overseas Chinese missions. In 1877, sixteen years after China was forced to accept foreign embassies in Beijing, the first Chinese legation was established in London. The first consul-general for the Nanyang Chinese was appointed the following year, based in Singapore. In 1886, a Qing Commission of Inquiry visited the Philippines, the Straits Settlements, Burma, Java, and even Australia to gain information about Chinese communities overseas. As a result, vice-consulates were opened in Penang and later in Manila (1899). Disagreement over the status of Chinese in Indonesia (for the Dutch all were Dutch subjects, not Chinese citizens) delayed establishment of a consulate in Batavia until 1910. No Chinese consulate was established in French Indochina until well after the fall of the dynasty.

Singapore was the strategic base for China's new 'forward policy' to open up relations with the Nanyang Chinese. It was from there that Qing representatives travelled throughout the region, raising funds through the sale of imperial honours, seeking talented Chinese to assist in China's modernisation, and urging wealthy Chinese to invest in China. Nanyang Chinese wealth poured into railways in particular, but also into shipping, commerce, industry and agriculture. Very large investors were rewarded with mandarin rank.

The City of Fouzhou in 1884.

The colonial powers, Britain, France and Holland, were not entirely at ease over the rapid development of Qing relations with the Nanyang Chinese. The consulates in Singapore and Penang, in particular, were effective in developing networks of contacts with overseas Chinese throughout the region. As Nanyang communities increasingly accepted direction from Qing representatives in areas such as education and cultural norms, colonial powers feared they were losing the loyalty of 'their' Chinese.

The rapidly increasing numbers of Chinese in Southeast Asia also caused concern. In Indonesia the number of Chinese more than doubled between 1860 and 1905, from an estimated 221 000 to 563 000.[15] The increase was particularly marked in Sumatra, where thousands of coolies were brought in to work the tobacco and rubber plantations. It was in Malaya, however, that the increase in the number of Chinese immigrants was greatest, and where they came to constitute the highest percentage of the total population. In the Straits Settlements of Penang, Malacca (Melaka) and Singapore, the Chinese population increased from just over 96 000 in 1860 to over 370 000 in 1911. By then 550 000 more lived in the Malay states, mainly in the tin mining areas of Perak and Selangor.

In Burma no accurate figures were available prior to the 1911 census, when Chinese numbered 122 000. Most were concentrated in Rangoon and Upper Burma, where several thousand Chinese were engaged in the flourishing overland trade with Yunnan. Migration of Chinese to northern and central Vietnam (Tongking and Annam) was strictly controlled by the Nguyen emperors until the 1880s, but encouraged by the French in Cochinchina and Cambodia, where they made up over 3 per cent of the population. The 1921 census registered 156 000 Chinese in Cochinchina, 39 000 in the rest of Vietnam, and 91 000 in Cambodia. In Siam the estimated 300 000 Chinese and Sino–Thai in 1850 had increased to nearly 800 000 by 1910, approaching 10 per cent of the population. Increased Chinese migration in the 1920s and 1930s pushed all these figures considerably higher.

Conclusion

At first the European presence in Southeast Asia only minimally disrupted trading patterns between China and the Nanyang, and the Qing could treat European diplomatic missions arriving in Canton in the same way as they did seaborne tributary missions from Southeast Asia. Even as Qing power waned and European, especially British, power grew, the Qing court clung desperately to the crumbling façade of the Chinese world order. When finally it collapsed, the only alternative was for China to adapt to the Western world system. By that time all of Southeast Asia, with the exception of Siam, had been colonised—and Siam had long since repudiated its tributary relationship with China.

Just as China's relations with Southeast Asia atrophied at the official level, however, Chinese migration increased dramatically. The economic success of the overseas Chinese attracted both the Qing court and its political opponents, and both used them as avenues of influence in the Nanyang. The Qing Nationality Law and the swelling tide of Chinese nationalism caused considerable disquiet among colonial administrators and indigenous elites alike in Southeast Asia. But China remained far too weak to challenge European power in its own treaty ports, let alone beyond its shores. The late nineteenth century thus marked the nadir in two millennia of relations between China and Southeast Asia.

7 THE CHANGING WORLD ORDER

The tenacity with which the Qing regime, even in terminal decline, clung to the façade of its tributary system of foreign relations was a matter for wonder at the time. For China, however, adopting a new international relations culture as demanded by the Western powers was not a matter simply of conducting diplomacy in a different way. What was at stake was the whole cosmic, hierarchical and moral underpinning of the Chinese world order, with the emperor as its pivot. The Qing regime could not relinquish its conception of how foreign relations should be conducted without placing its own legitimacy in question, for the two were facets of a single worldview.

It is well to be clear about the nature of the alternative world order that China was being forced to join. Inter-state relations in an age of strident nationalism and imperial competition existed in an essentially anarchic environment in which power was the real determinant of status. States might, in principle, be equally sovereign, but they were not equally powerful and might assured right, despite international law. With arrogance and insensitivity, European nations had carved up the world into competing empires, and seemed intent on carving up China too. No wonder the regime struggled desperately to avoid such a fate by clinging for as long as possible to its own world order, and to the strategic protection afforded by the ring of tributary states along its borders.

It is ironic to think that had the Qing regime been stronger, it might more easily have become a player in this world of competing empires. Its own phase of (Manchu) imperial expansion had drawn to a close over a century earlier, however, and Japan rather than China learned the lesson that the Western world order was in reality an arena of aggressively competitive empires. In the 1890s, when Britain, France and Holland were ruthlessly bringing the last autonomous parts of Burma, Indochina and Indonesia under their control, Japan set out to create its own empire, at the expense of its nearest neighbours, Korea and China.

Even after China's humiliating defeat by Japan in the Sino–Japanese War of 1895, however, the Meiji restoration in Japan and the success of Japanese modernisation still provided an attractive model for Chinese reformers. But the ruling elite was divided in China, and the reform movement of 1898 was nipped in the bud. Suppression of the Boxer uprising (1898–1901) by a combined Western and Japanese force again demonstrated Qing weakness. Only the support of Western powers that profited from China's infirmity prevented the collapse of the dynasty. In 1905 the core of the old order was fatally undermined by the abolition of the Confucian examination system. Even so, a new flurry of reform was too little too late.

In the end, the Qing dynasty was blown away by the revolution of 1911–12. But the transition to a modern nation-state was not easy. Deep-seated traditional beliefs persisted about how Chinese society should be governed, and about China's relations with the rest of the world. Where China stood at the time, vis-à-vis the major powers—its own powerlessness, its humiliation—was implicitly contrasted with where it should stand—given its size, its culture and its history, and the respect all Chinese felt that these deserved. All subsequent Chinese foreign policy has had the overriding goal of restoring China to its 'rightful' place in the world.

For Republican China two immediate challenges stood out: to create a new political order, and to preserve the empire's unity and territorial integrity. But new political institutions were weak and unstable, and China fragmented into warlord fiefdoms. Not until 1923 was a Nationalist government proclaimed in Canton, with Sun Yatsen as president and Chiang Kaishek (Jiang Jieshi) as military commander. Given lukewarm support from the West, Sun had turned to the Soviet Union for both political and military assistance. Soviet agents had assisted in organising Sun's Nationalist Party, the Guomindang (GMD). On instructions from the Comintern (Communist International), the Chinese Communist Party (CCP), founded in 1921, supported the new government while simultaneously strengthening its own position. When Sun died in March 1925, Chiang proclaimed himself president of the Republic of China. The following year, Chiang embarked upon his 'northern expedition', which finally succeeded in reuniting the country.

Foreign intervention continued, however, particularly on the part of Japan. So too did the foreign concessions flaunting their extraterritorial disdain for Chinese jurisdiction. The West threw its support behind Chiang after he broke with the communists in 1927, and set out to destroy them. But Chiang's action divided Nationalists and communists who engaged in an implacable struggle that took two decades of conflict and war to resolve.

Nationalism and politics among the overseas Chinese

Throughout these tumultuous years, relations between China and Southeast Asia were practically non-existent on a nation-to-nation basis. Only Siam was in a position to accord recognition to the new Nationalist government, yet it failed to do so. As for European colonial administrations, any interests they might have had in opening up a dialogue with China or in expanding trade were subordinated to those of their metropolitan governments. All matters that concerned China and Southeast Asia were referred to European capitals. Paradoxically, however, as official relations atrophied, unofficial relations—primarily between political movements in China and overseas Chinese—blossomed as never before (or since the establishment of the People's Republic of China in 1949).

Just as Southeast Asian elites saw their voices silenced by colonial domination (nowhere more cruelly than in the Philippines, whose revolution against Spain led only to annexation by the United States), overseas Chinese in these countries began to be stirred by Chinese nationalism. This was actively encouraged by Guomindang agents dispatched to Southeast Asia to raise money for the party, and to remind overseas Chinese that their primary loyalty was still to China. In 1926, the newly established Overseas Chinese Affairs Commission of the GMD spelled out its objectives. These were essentially to ensure that overseas Chinese enjoyed equal rights and treatment in their countries of residence; to assist overseas Chinese to give their children a Chinese education; and to encourage overseas Chinese to set up industries and invest in China. All overseas Chinese, after all, remained citizens of China.

In 1929, the Nationalist government passed a Nationality Law that reiterated Qing policy with respect to overseas Chinese: that is, that all children born of a Chinese father, wherever they lived, were of Chinese nationality. The law encouraged Chinese in the colonial context of Southeast Asia, where they fell into a separate national and racial category, to think of themselves as Chinese, but it created difficulties with respect to dual nationality and exacerbated social tensions with indigenous peoples by encouraging ethnic and cultural exclusivism. The success of Nationalist policy, however, was reflected in the remittances by overseas Chinese. These averaged from $80 to $100 million from the early 1930s, a figure that doubled in 1938 following the outbreak of the Sino–Japanese war.[1]

The GMD was overtly anti-colonial. As its political activity increased, colonial authorities began to be alarmed and to take measures to contain it. Chinese language schools were monitored and Chinese organisations registered and kept under surveillance. Concern was also expressed at the continuing high level of Chinese migration, though little was done to limit it. Chinese political activity in Southeast Asia also alarmed indigenous elites, who looked with suspicion on moves by families of mixed Chinese–indigenous ancestry to reassert their Chineseness. Had indigenous leaders been in a position to respond, their responses might well have been similar to that of Siam, which showed its disapproval of GMD policies by refusing to establish diplomatic relations with Nationalist China (see below). As it was, Chinese nationalism served to stimulate indigenous nationalisms that ominously allowed little room for alien communities.

Nowhere was political organisation more advanced among overseas Chinese than in the British colonies of Malaya and Singapore. As early as 1906, branches of Sun Yatsen's Revolutionary Alliance were formed in Singapore and Kuala Lumpur. With the formation of the GMD in August 1912, sympathisers in Malaya enthusiastically formed their own branches. When local authorities—concerned over anti-imperialist propaganda—demanded membership lists, the organisation went underground. Supporters continued to meet and collect funds for the party, however, and in 1925 British authorities responded by banning the GMD as a subversive organisation.

The British had several concerns. They were worried about anti-colonial, and especially anti-British propaganda associated with the GMD's determination to avenge China's past humiliation; they were worried about GMD control over Chinese education (dozens of Chinese school texts were banned); and they were worried about methods that might be used to force Chinese to donate to the party. But, most of all, they were worried that the Chinese in Malaya would fall under the control of the Chinese government, and so come to constitute 'a state within a state'.[2]

Negotiations between the British and Chinese governments eventually led to a lifting of the ban on the GMD. What was never legal was membership of the predominantly Chinese Malayan Communist Party (MCP). Its appeal and its activities were limited, however, and it took the outbreak of the Sino–Japanese war in 1937 to stimulate recruitment of more Chinese into the MCP. The war galvanised the whole Chinese community in Malaya, as elsewhere in Southeast Asia, and feelings ran high. Large sums of money were collected by the China Relief Fund to assist the Chinese war effort, and boycotts of Japanese goods were organised.

These Chinese political activities, so evidently an expression of Chinese nationalism, may have caused little concern among the rural Malay population, but the Malay political elite was well aware of their implications—particularly in relation to political representation and the vexed question of citizenship for Chinese born in China. But these issues only became pressing in 1946, after the defeat of Japan.

In Burma, the Chinese community was much smaller than the Indian community and attracted less suspicion and hostility than in Malaya. Moreover, it was divided between those Chinese who had arrived by sea and settled in Lower Burma, mainly in Rangoon, and those who had come overland from Yunnan and were concentrated in northern Burma and the Shan states. Among the Yunnanese, political activity was limited, and most support for the GMD came from Chinese in Rangoon.

With the outbreak of the Sino–Japanese war, the need for an alternative supply route for Chinese Nationalist forces became evident. Late in 1937, work began on the Burma Road running from the Burmese frontier to Kunming along an ancient trade route. The road was officially opened just over a year later, to the apprehension of some Burmese who feared it might attract Japanese reprisals, or encourage an accelerated influx of Chinese into northern Burma.

It was along the Burma Road that Chinese forces were to enter Burma in March 1942, three months after the Japanese invasion. By then British troops were in full retreat, and the Chinese, after initial resistance, could do little but retreat as well. When a Japanese flanking movement into Shan state threatened to close the Burma Road, the Chinese withdrawal became a rout. Rather than pursuing the retreating Chinese, however, the Japanese turned their attention to India. Not until 1945 was the Burma Road reopened, too late to make any difference to the war effort in China.

In Indonesia, Dutch policy deliberately created a divide between Chinese and Indonesians. Until 1900, Chinese could only live in the Chinese quarter of a city, and were not allowed to own land. They did, however, enjoy certain economic advantages that they made the most of. Most Chinese in Indonesia were very much aware of their identity as Chinese, and eagerly welcomed the Revolution of 1911. When the Dutch took exception to the hoisting of the Republican flag, riots ensued which were forcibly suppressed, for although political activity was less restricted than in Indochina, the Dutch were determined not to permit China to gain undue influence over the Indonesian Chinese community.

Dutch attempts to win the loyalty of Indonesian Chinese by giving them separate representation on the advisory Volksraad, or parliament, set up in 1918, failed, however, to weaken Chinese nationalist sentiment. Guomindang representatives paid frequent visits to Indonesia, while Chinese consuls arrived to register all Chinese born in China. (At the time, annual Chinese immigration into Indonesia rose as high as 43 000 in 1921 for an interwar average of over 28 000.)[3] Chinese in Indonesia were incensed by the aggression of Japan after 1931. Boycotts against Japanese goods were organised, as in Malaya, and large amounts were contributed to Chinese relief funds and through purchase of Government of China bonds. As elsewhere, such activities tended to stimulate indigenous nationalism, though there was minimal cooperation between Indonesians and Chinese.

In no colony in Southeast Asia had relations between European authorities and Chinese settlers been worse than in the Philippines under Spanish rule. The history of those relations in the seventeenth and eighteenth centuries is a sad litany of prejudice, discrimination, oppression, and recurrent pogroms. Large numbers of Chinese were periodically massacred and expelled, and migration was strictly controlled. Even so, Chinese and Filipinos freely intermarried and a large, well-integrated Sino–Filipino *mestizo* community grew up. Perhaps not surprisingly, members of this community took the lead in the revolution against Spain, which was also supported by many Chinese.

Chinese were better treated by the American administration, though exclusion laws limiting migration remained in place. A Chinese consul-general was appointed to Manila, and branches of the Guomindang established. Political events in China were followed with interest, the split between the GMD and the CCP giving rise to a left-wing group in Manila. Funds were raised for relief in China and boycotts organised of Japanese goods.

In Indochina the situation was rather different from that in other Southeast Asian colonies. The Chinese communities in Vietnam, Cambodia and Laos were divided for administrative purposes into five *congrégations* (Cantonese, Teochiu, Hokkien, Hakka and Hainanese) responsible for managing their own social and cultural affairs (schools, temples, etc.). Chinese were taxed at different rates from indigenous Vietnamese, Cambodians, Lao and hilltribe minorities. While some Chinese took up agriculture and fishing (in northern Vietnam), most were employed in industry and commerce, especially the rice trade. Over the two decades prior to 1935, roughly a third of all Indochinese trade was with China, virtually all of it in the hands of Chinese. In 1935, the French finally permitted Nationalist Chinese consulates to be established in Saigon and Hanoi, in the hope of stimulating greater French participation in trade with China.

The importance of Chinese nationalism for Vietnam lay not so much in the effect it had on Chinese living there (as in Malaya and Indonesia), but on the revolutionary model it provided for Vietnamese nationalism—revolutionary because the French authorities banned all political activity outside Cochinchina. At first, after the failure of the 1898 Reform Movement in China, Vietnamese nationalists looked to Japan for inspiration. The secret 'Eastern Travel' society smuggled young Vietnamese through China to study in Japan, until they were expelled in 1909 under the terms of a financial agreement with France. With the success of the 1911 Revolution, China became the preferred model and the principal refuge for Vietnamese nationalists, and several young Vietnamese gained entry to Nationalist Chinese military academies.

The success of the GMD in unifying China stimulated the founding, in 1927, of the Vietnamese Nationalist Party, known from its Vietnamese name as the VNQDD. As an illegal political party, the VNQDD was forced to operate clandestinely. Like the GMD, it was organised on Leninist democratic centralist lines in small cells, but was soon infiltrated by the French secret police. In February 1930, the VNQDD instigated an abortive uprising by Vietnamese troops stationed at a French military garrison in northern Vietnam. In the repression that followed, many of its young leaders were arrested and guillotined; others fled to China. This left the way open for the better organised Indochina Communist Party (ICP).

The ICP had its roots in the cooperation that existed prior to 1927 between Chinese Nationalists and communists. Among the Comintern agents sent to Canton at this time was Nguyen Ai Quoc, better known under his later alias as Ho Chi Minh. For two years, from mid-1925 to mid-1927, Ho worked closely with members of the Chinese Communist Party. He then left China, only to return to Hong Kong in 1930 with the task of unifying disparate Vietnamese communist organisations to form the ICP.

Relations between the revolutionary movements in China and Vietnam were practically nonexistent for much of the 1930s, until the CCP completed its 'Long March' to its remote northern base at Yan'an. Communication thereafter was still a problem, but Ho managed to pay a visit in 1938. With the outbreak of war with Japan, communications became even more difficult. Vietnamese and Chinese revolutionaries remained in contact in southern China, however, and it was there Ho Chi Minh returned early in 1941. By that time Chinese Nationalists and communists had agreed to form a united front against the Japanese. Ho and other members of the ICP worked closely with GMD forces in the China–Vietnam border area. In May 1941 Ho and his circle, including Pham Van Dong and Vo Nguyen Giap, formed the Vietnam League for Independence (Viet Nam Doc Lap Dong Minh), commonly known as the Vietminh, to act as a broad front for their independence struggle against French colonialism.

During the war years, Vietminh activists were protected in their bases on the Chinese side of the border by local left-leaning GMD officers. There they built up their organisation and studied communist ideology and guerrilla warfare. Meanwhile in Vietnam the French administration remained in place, under an agreement between Japan and the Vichy government in France. As French military operations made it difficult to establish secure bases in Vietnam, Ho turned to China for help. His intention to seek a closer working relationship with the CCP was thwarted, however, by his arrest and imprisonment for more than a year by GMD authorities.[4]

The Chinese Nationalists, in the meantime, attempted to bring together a number of non-communist revolutionary organisations to form the Vietnam Liberation League (Dong Minh Hoi). This was part of a deliberate attempt 'to resuscitate China's leadership in Asian affairs', and more especially its 'special position' with respect to Vietnam.[5] The Dong Minh Hoi, like the Vietminh, was dedicated to liberating Vietnam from French colonialism, but under Chinese Nationalist, rather than communist, tutelage. Ho Chi Minh was nevertheless released to take part. Evidently he felt it prudent to co-operate with the GMD at this juncture. In the longer term the Dong Minh Hoi would prove to be no match for the Vietminh.

Communist agents were active elsewhere in Southeast Asia during the interwar years, but as agents of the Comintern, not the Chinese Communist Party. The best known and most active (including M. N. Roy, Tan Malaka and Ho Chi Minh) were not Chinese. Many of those drawn to communism in the region were, however, local Chinese attracted by clandestinely circulating propaganda of the CCP. At first, as in Thailand, Chinese activists formed overseas cells of the CCP, but Comintern policy was to promote national communist parties. In Malaya, for example, Chinese constituted most of the membership of the Malayan Communist Party. Its goal was to expel the British and bring about a communist revolution on behalf of the peoples of Malaya, but Malays feared it would reduce Malaya to an overseas dependency of China. In this way, communist Chinese policy towards overseas Chinese in Southeast Asia often tended to exacerbate racial and social tensions.

Sino–Thai relations

Assimilation of the Chinese community in Siam in the nineteenth century encountered fewer of the social or religious constraints and distortions due to colonialism in the rest of Southeast Asia. Nevertheless, as the Chinese population expanded, tensions developed. Several localised Chinese protests were brutally suppressed by Siamese troops, and there was resentment over the economic success of Chinese employed as 'tax farmers' to collect revenue for the government. In the second half of the century, migration of Chinese increased. Still by far the majority were male and most married Siamese wives. The basis was thereby laid for an assimilable Sino–Siamese community.

It was the simultaneous rise of Siamese and Chinese nationalism in the early twentieth century that exacerbated dissension between the two communities. Two developments in particular engendered distrust. One was the 1909 Qing Nationality Law, which continued in force under the Republic and laid the basis for China's claim to the loyalty of Chinese abroad—to the extent that seats were reserved for them in the National Assembly. In 1913 the Siamese passed their own Nationality Act which added nationality through birth in the country (*jus soli*) to nationality through descent in the male line (*jus sanguinis*). 'Chinese' born in Siam were therefore Siamese, and the only Chinese were those born in China. From 1919 to 1937, the latter more than doubled to over 700 000, though the number who could claim Chinese nationality under Chinese law was at least twice that.[6]

The second development was the higher proportion of women among the increasing number of Chinese immigrants, especially after 1920. As a result, Chinese–Siamese intermarriage decreased, and Chinese cultural identity was given greater emphasis, even by assimilated Sino–Siamese. This was similar to what was happening elsewhere in Southeast Asia, especially in Malaya and Indonesia where assimilated, locally born *peranakan* Chinese became more culturally aware of their Chinese roots under the influence of *totok* (China-born) immigrants. Siamese concern over migration levels, however, never translated into effective control measures.

Attempts by the GMD to gain political support among overseas Chinese were resented by the Siamese government, which saw it as interference in Siamese affairs. GMD political activists came to Siam to establish branches of the party and raise funds for its struggle against the warlords. As elsewhere in Southeast Asia, reunification of China became a popular political cause among Siamese Chinese. By 1928, active GMD membership stood at around 20 000[7] and delegates from Siam attended GMD congresses in China. As much as anything, it was fear that the Chinese community would become an extension of the

GMD that led the Siamese authorities to reject attempts by no fewer than three Chinese missions to establish diplomatic relations. Another concern was that conflict between Nationalist and Communist Chinese would be fought out in Siam. All overtures were therefore rejected.

Siamese nationalist discourse had been encouraged by King Rama VI Vajiravudh, who dubbed the Chinese 'the Jews of the East',[8] and was further stimulated by the military coup of 1932. One of the first acts of the military regime was to make communism illegal. Later, the government of General Phibul Songkram enacted a number of measures that, though they applied to all foreign nationals, were deliberately designed to reduce Chinese influence in Thailand. Education in Siamese was made mandatory. Most Chinese schools and newspapers were closed, Chinese were excluded from certain economic pursuits that were reserved for Siamese, new taxes on foreigners were introduced, and remittance of money made illegal. At the same time, naturalisation requirements were tightened, so fewer Chinese could claim Siamese citizenship. In June 1939, the nationalist aspirations of the government were symbolically demonstrated by changing the name of the country to Thailand, and by embracing a pan-Tai ideology to include all Tai-speaking peoples, notably the Lao of Laos and the Shan of Burma, and even potentially the Leu of the Xishuangbanna in southern China.

This anti-Chinese turn greatly agitated the Chinese community in Thailand, but as China and Thailand had no diplomatic relations, there was little the Nationalist government could do. Chiang Kaishek expressed the hope to General Phibul that Chinese citizens in Thailand would be permitted to continue to contribute to the Thai economy. It was an ineffectual intervention, for by this time Thai attitudes to China had become complicated by the rise of Japan as a major Asian power, and by the outbreak of the Sino–Japanese war.

Thai military leaders, particularly General Phibul, were impressed by Japan's success in modernising its economy and building its military power. Japan, they believed, provided the best model for Thailand to follow. Perceptions of the Chinese in Thailand as a disloyal fifth column only tended to reinforce Thai preference for Japan over China. In the League of Nations, Thailand refused to condemn Japan's aggression in Manchuria. The Thai could recognise a rising regional hegemon when they saw one. They were disappointed, therefore, when the 1941 Treaty of Tokyo, concluded under Japanese auspices, awarded Thailand relatively little additional territory after its brief war against French forces in Indochina.

This did not prevent Thailand from concluding an agreement with Japan, after twenty-four hours of symbolic resistance, that permitted the movement of Japanese troops through Thai territory, followed in December 1941 by a formal Thai–Japanese Alliance. Both moves made good sense to a Thai government seeking to protect Thai independence and security. That the best way to do this was through alliance with the dominant power in the region was central to Thai international relations culture. For the Thai, 'the bamboo bends with the wind'. Declarations of war on Britain and the US followed, but not on Nationalist China. Instead Siam recognised, at Japanese urging, the Japanese-sponsored puppet government in Nanjing. Meanwhile the anti-fascist Free Thai movement made contact with the Allies through Chongqing, Chiang Kaishek's wartime capital.

The defeat of Japan left Thailand to face the victorious Allies. Bangkok feared that northern Thailand would be subjected to Chinese occupation, as in Indochina. That this was avoided was a relief to the Thai government and a disappointment to many Thai Chinese. Chinese riots in Bangkok were quelled by the Thai military, to the protestations of Chongqing, which again demanded opening of diplomatic relations. This led finally to a Treaty of Amity in 1946, establishing a Chinese embassy for the first time in Bangkok. It had been almost a century since the last Siamese tributary mission was dispatched to Beijing.

In order to avoid a Soviet veto to its application for United Nations membership, Thailand was also forced to rescind its anti-communist legislation and allow Moscow to establish a legation in Bangkok, its first in Southeast Asia. Briefly thereafter Bangkok became the hub of communist activity in the region for Chinese and Vietnamese agents.[9] Subsequent military governments outlawed communism and transferred diplomatic relations to the Republic of China on Taiwan. Not until 1975, when the US was withdrawing from mainland Southeast Asia and China had become the rising regional hegemon, did Thailand transfer its recognition to Beijing.

The Second World War and its aftermath

Relations between the Nationalist Chinese government in its remote inland wartime capital of Chongqing and the countries of Southeast Asia all but ceased during the years of the Second World War, except, as we have seen, in different ways with Burma and Vietnam. China was far too engaged in its own life and death struggle against Japan to follow closely the dramatic impact of the war in Southeast Asia. Authorities in Chongqing were as unaware of the momentous political changes that had occurred in the region as were officials in London and Washington, let alone in occupied Paris and The Hague.

Though Nationalist forces were relatively ineffective against the Japanese, at least compared to the communists, Nationalist China came out of the war with enhanced international status. This was partly due to effective Chinese diplomacy, and partly to strong support from the United States: Britain and France were less eager to accord China status as a great power with a permanent seat on the newly created United Nations Security Council.

Enhanced Chinese status coincided with the reduced political leverage available to former colonial powers. Throughout British Southeast Asia, independence movements had taken advantage first of the defeat of colonial regimes by the Japanese, then of the power vacuum left by the Japanese surrender, to seize the political initiative and mobilise popular support. Throughout the region, the struggle for independence was underway, a struggle that would absorb all the energies of political elites. Not until independence was achieved would they face the task of forging new relations with what by then would be a very different China.

Nationalist China had little time to enjoy its new international prominence. The defeat of Japan had been in the Pacific, not in China. Though Nationalist armies and communist guerrillas had tied down large numbers of Japanese troops, Japanese forces in China still remained largely intact. Japan's surrender and withdrawal set the stage for China to plunge back into civil war. As Nationalist and communist forces fought for supremacy over the next four years, there was little time to devote to, and little interest in, building relations with emerging independence movements in Southeast Asia. Contacts were primarily with overseas Chinese communities among whom the propaganda war between Nationalists and communists was intense.

Communism was not just a force in China. Throughout Southeast Asia communists had been among the most resolute and courageous opponents of the Japanese. Where nationalist elites had opportunistically taken advantage of the demise of colonial regimes to further their goal of independence, even if this meant cooperating with the Japanese (as in Burma and Indonesia), communists (at least after Germany invaded the Soviet Union) had done all they could to assist the anti-fascist cause. At war's end nowhere—even in Vietnam—could communists claim majority support, but they did wield considerable political, and even military, power. The challenge they posed to social democratic national independence movements was considerable.

In both the Philippines and Burma, the first two former colonies to gain independence, communist movements took up arms against governments to which independence had been ceded without armed struggle. In the Philippines, the Huk rebellion continued into the mid-1950s before being crushed with substantial American assistance. In Burma, despite wartime collaboration with socialists within the Anti-Fascist People's Freedom League (AFPFL), the Burmese Communist Party took the path of armed insurgency aimed at overthrowing the socialist government of Prime Minister U Nu. Though both these insurgencies owed much of their guerrilla strategy to the Chinese Communist Party and the writings of Mao Zedong, neither was beholden in any direct way to the CCP. Their timing may have been due to a Comintern decision, but both arose mainly as a result of wartime disruption and post-war tension, political disappointment, and a naked struggle for power.

In Indonesia, Sukarno and Mohammad Hatta proclaimed independence immediately following the Japanese surrender. Dutch determination to reassert colonial control, however, precipitated a three-year war for independence in which nationalists and communists at first fought side by side. In 1948, a communist attempt to seize control of the independence struggle (the Madiun rebellion) was put down by forces loyal to the nationalist leadership. This had the unforeseen result of gaining American support for Indonesian independence, which came on 27 December 1949, less than three months after the proclamation of the People's Republic of China. In a move designed to establish its neutralist credentials, the new government in Jakarta took the lead in requesting the GMD to terminate all activities in Indonesia, thus clearing the way for diplomatic relations to be established between Jakarta and Beijing in August 1950.[10]

In none of these revolutionary movements did overseas Chinese take leadership roles. In Malaya, by contrast, overseas Chinese inspired and led the insurgency, and membership of the Malayan Communist Party (MCP) remained overwhelmingly Chinese. During the war, the Chinese community had been most oppressed by, and most opposed to, the Japanese occupation, and recruitment into the communist-controlled Malayan People's Anti-Japanese Army was also predominantly Chinese. After the war, the MCP fomented opposition to the British Military Administration through strikes and propaganda aimed mainly at the Chinese community. By mid-1948 the decision had been taken for an armed uprising. In response to growing terrorism, the British authorities announced a state of emergency. Vocal support (if little else), from Beijing after 1949 for liberation of the 'Malayan races' only served to exacerbate Malay distrust, despite being denounced by prominent Chinese leaders in Malaya.

The Malayan Emergency was to last beyond the declaration of Malayan independence. Though by far the majority of Chinese in Malaya gave no support to the MCP, the fact that the insurgency was predominantly a Chinese affair did nothing to improve relations between Chinese and Malays in the lead up to independence. Two key issues were citizenship and political representation, about which the Chinese community as a whole was unhappy. While under Malay law citizenship was automatic for Malays (even if immigrants from Indonesia), Chinese and Indians had to apply for registration and naturalisation. This left political control in the hands of the Malays, represented principally by the United Malays Nationalist Organization (UMNO). All attempts to form a multiracial party failed. By the time the independence of the Federation of Malaya was proclaimed in August 1957, an alliance had been struck between UMNO and the Malayan Chinese Association (with the Malayan Indian Congress a minor partner) that effectively traded off Malay political dominance against Chinese economic supremacy. It was hardly surprising that the new Malayan government refused to establish diplomatic relations with China.

In Indochina the situation was different again, with much more direct Chinese intervention in political developments. During the war years, Japanese troops were stationed throughout Indochina, though the French administration remained in place. Relations with the French became fraught only after the liberation of France, when the Japanese feared an American amphibious attack on coastal Vietnam to link up with Chinese Nationalist forces in southern China. In March 1945, all French personnel were interned in a lightning Japanese *coup de force*, but for a few who staged a fighting retreat into China, and small pockets in Laos.

Under Japanese inducement, the kings of Cambodia and Laos and Emperor Bao Dai of Vietnam all declared the independence of their countries. When Japan surrendered six months later, these royal declarations of independence were rescinded, but the genie was already out of the bottle, even where nationalism had been slow to develop. In Laos and Cambodia, Free Lao and Free Khmer movements fought the reimposition of French rule over the next several years.

Indochina was the one part of Southeast Asia where Chinese forces directly intervened after the war. Under the terms of the Potsdam Agreement, the surrender of Japanese troops north of the sixteenth parallel of latitude was taken by Nationalist Chinese forces and south of it by the British Southeast Asia Command. This did not apply to Burma, which the British had already reoccupied (a Chinese force briefly crossed the border near Myitkyina, but was prevailed upon to withdraw); or to Thailand, which had no common border with China. It did apply to Vietnam and Laos. Cambodia lay south of the sixteenth parallel.

It took time, however, for Chinese Nationalist forces to arrive. In the meantime the Free Lao established a government in Viang Chan that survived until the French reconquest of the country in 1946. In Vietnam, in an even more significant development, the Vietminh took advantage of the temporary power vacuum to force the abdication of Bao Dai and proclaim the independence of the Democratic Republic of Vietnam under the leadership of Ho Chi Minh.

By the time Chinese Nationalist forces arrived, remaining Japanese troops had retreated south to surrender to the British and French. In Laos, the Chinese favoured the Free Lao, but in Vietnam they brought with them the Dong Minh Hoi, members of which Ho prudently included in his provisional coalition government. No sooner had the Chinese arrived than the French began negotiations for them to leave. In the meantime, occupying Chinese forces systematically looted northern Vietnam. They were convinced, with the help of substantial bribes, to withdraw by 31 March 1946. (Withdrawal was delayed in Laos so the Chinese could buy up the opium crop.)

The way was at last open for the French reoccupation of Vietnam that led directly, in December 1946, to the outbreak of the First Indochina War. Had the French been in a position to return in force to northern Vietnam immediately following the Japanese surrender, the subsequent course of events might have been very different. (The French force that had retreated into China in March 1945 was prevented from returning by Chinese authorities.) The Chinese occupation, if only for a few months, had been crucial for the support given to Vietnamese nationalists of all political persuasions, but it left a nasty taste in Vietnamese mouths. Even the Vietminh were prepared to tolerate the temporary return of French forces to northern Vietnam if this would get rid of the Chinese.[11] Chinese withdrawal brought back the French, but it also deprived nationalist parties like the Dong Minh Hoi of their political patronage, and so left the Vietminh free to dispose of their political enemies.

For three years, from the outbreak of fighting until the arrival of communist Chinese forces on the Sino–Vietnamese border towards the end of 1949, neither the French nor the Vietminh was able to gain a decisive advantage. The Vietminh, borrowing extensively from Maoist theory of revolutionary warfare, established their Viet Bac base area in the northern mountains close to the border with China, and built up their political organisation in the countryside. But they obtained minimal Chinese support, for the GMD was by then well aware of the communist complexion of the Vietminh and its ties with the CCP. The French held the major towns and cities, and benefited from a degree of Chinese cooperation (despite the GMD's proclaimed sympathy for Vietnamese independence).

As Nationalist Chinese influence on and interest in the Vietminh-led independence struggle in Vietnam dwindled, so communist Chinese interest and influence increased. The Nationalists retained consulates in Saigon and Hanoi, but communist Chinese agents increasingly contested Nationalist influence in the Chinese community. Meanwhile in southern China, small locally recruited communist units worked closely with the Vietminh, seeking sanctuary in Vietnam when necessary, and offering sanctuary in China in return when Vietminh units were hard pressed. But this was a local initiative. The CCP was far too preoccupied with the civil war to formulate a considered policy towards the Vietminh, or to provide them with substantial assistance.

By December 1949, Chinese communist forces were approaching the Vietnamese frontier, pushing before them the remnants of the defeated Nationalist First Army Corps. Under an agreement with the French, 30 000 Nationalist troops and dependents were permitted to enter Vietnam, where they were disarmed and interned. Most were eventually repatriated to Taiwan, though not until 1953.[12] To the west, in Yunnan, remnants of the GMD Eighth Army retreated into north-eastern Shan state, without Burmese permission and against the government's wishes. Their presence would be a source of instability and diplomatic friction for years to come.

Conclusion

Like the late Qing, Nationalist China was intent on rebuilding Chinese prestige and status, and from an equally weak position. Attempts to expand Chinese influence in Southeast Asia were blocked, however, by the presence of European colonial powers. The only avenue remained the overseas Chinese. Whereas the Qing saw the overseas Chinese primarily in Middle Kingdom terms (that is, as subjects expected to assist China), the Nationalists saw them as a means of expanding Chinese influence in the region. Close contacts were developed between authorities in China and Chinese communities in Southeast Asia, while migration of unprecedented numbers of Chinese continued with little concern for indigenous sensitivities.

The interwar years were a period of competing nationalisms that gave both European authorities and local elites cause for concern. Chinese were urged to return to their roots by adopting Chinese values and education for their children. They were also encouraged to take an interest in Chinese politics. The struggle between communists and Nationalists was in this way transferred to Southeast Asia, where it interacted with local nationalist debate. The politicisation of the overseas Chinese had the untoward effect, however, of making them a political issue in the lands where they resided.

As a victor in the Second World War, China gained in international status. Thanks largely to the United States, Nationalist China was given a permanent seat on the United Nations Security Council. Beset, however, by civil war, the Chinese government was unable to exploit the country's international prominence, even among newly independent countries in Southeast Asia. How Nationalist determination to restore China's international prestige would have impacted on relations with Southeast Asia had communism in China been defeated must remain a matter of speculation. As it was, it was left to the communists to develop these relations, with the disadvantage that their contacts were predominantly with revolutionary movements intent on overthrowing Southeast Asian ruling elites. Little wonder that the process was fraught with tension and misunderstanding, and took over thirty years to work out.

8 COMMUNISM AND THE COLD WAR

中國

On 1 October 1949, Mao Zedong proclaimed the People's Republic of China (PRC) and informed the world that: 'Ours will no longer be a nation subject to insult and humiliation. We have stood up.'[1] Victory over the Nationalist forces of the Guomindang was all but complete. Chiang Kaishek and his Nationalist government had fled to Taiwan. A new and mighty communist state had been born, just days after the Soviet Union exploded its first nuclear weapon, into a world already deeply divided by the Cold War.

In Southeast Asia, Thailand had already reverted to military rule and sought alliance with the new hegemonic power in the region, the United States. Taking its lead from Washington, Bangkok continued to recognise the Republic of China (ROC) on Taiwan. So too did the newly independent Philippines, also closely aligned with the US and fighting its own communist insurgency. Independent Burma recognised Beijing in December 1949, the first Asian state to do so despite then combating both communist and ethnic Karen insurgencies. A few months later, independent Indonesia also hesitantly recognised

Top:
Meditating Buddha, Borobodur, Central Java, 9th century CE. Buddhism formed a common religious bond and stimulated trade between Southeast Asia and China.
PHOTOLIBRARY.COM

Bottom:
Ancient Buddhist pagodas, Pagan, central Burma (13th–15th centuries CE). As well as being Buddhist memorials, pagodas symbolised the axis of the world, a concept central to the Buddhist worldview. PHOTOLIBRARY.COM

CARTE D'UNE PARTIE DE LA CHINE, LES ISLES PHILIPPINES, DE LA SONDE, MOLUQUES, DE PAPOESI &c.
dreſsée ſur les Relations les plus nouvelles. A AMSTERDAM par COVENS et MORTIER.
ECHELLE
Tropique du Cancer
HAYNAN
LUZON ou LUZ
ISLES PHILIPPINES
GOLFE DE SIAM
BORNEO
LIGNE EQUINOCTIALE
HALEMAHERA
ISLES DE PAPOESI
NOUVELLE GUINEE ou TERRE DES PAPOESI
MOLUQUES
ISLES DE LA SONDE

Top left:
Ancient painting of Chinese junks and Malay trading vessels, Phuket Island, southern Thailand. Phuket was an important centre for trade between China and Southeast Asia. PHOTOLIBRARY.COM

Bottom left:
Engraved map of southern China and Southeast Asia drawn by the Dutch cartographers Johannes Covens and Cornelis Mortier, c. 1700 CE. During the 18th century, the Dutch gained a monopoly over the spice trade from the East Indies (Indonesia). PHOTOLIBRARY.COM

Top:
Painting of a riverside scene in Vietnam by the English artist George Chinnery (1774–1852). Rivers provided important arteries for trade in Southeast Asia. PHOTOLIBRARY.COM

Bottom:
Coloured engraving from a photograph (c. 1890) of three powerful Vietnamese mandarins. Note the strong Chinese influence on Vietnamese formal dress styles, even into the late 19th century. PHOTOLIBRARY.COM

Top:
Decoration detail from a Chinese Daoist temple. The dragon is a symbol of power and good luck. Daoist temples were constructed by overseas Chinese throughout Southeast Asia.
PHOTOLIBRARY.COM

Bottom:
Shipping containers in the port of Hong Kong. Chinese exports to Southeast Asia and other parts of the world have expanded greatly since China introduced its 'Open Door' policy in the mid-1980s. PHOTOLIBRARY.COM

the PRC. In Indochina and Malaya, communist forces were pitted against colonial regimes in wars that would delay independence—and thus formal relations with China—for years.

In both China and the four independent nations of Southeast Asia, new ruling elites faced the delicate task of forging new relations with each other. The Chinese Communist Party had long maintained clandestine contacts with communist parties in Southeast Asia, but these had almost entirely been through their overseas Chinese members. CCP contacts with indigenous communists had been few and insignificant, apart from the special case of Vietnam. One problem that confronted the PRC, therefore, was how to relate to non-communist ruling elites. It did so at first from the ideological perspective of Marxism–Leninism.

The Chinese Marxist–Leninist worldview

Like their Nationalist opponents, Chinese communists had looked to Europe for new ideas to replace discredited Confucianism. But whereas the GMD was eclectic in its borrowing (including even Marxist–Leninist 'democratic centralism' for its political organisation), the CCP was single-minded in its commitment to communism. Both parties, however, grafted sometimes ill-assimilated Western notions onto a Chinese base. From the late 1930s Marxism–Leninism in China carried with it a strong component of what came to be called 'Mao Zedong thought', and Mao was deeply Chinese. Unlike Ho Chi Minh (or Zhou Enlai), who had travelled the world and spoke European languages, Mao knew only China and Chinese. His education took in the Chinese classics on war and statecraft, and he was well versed in Chinese history and literature. Moreover, Mao was not only Chairman of the CCP, but also its leading theoretician. Thus, although the adoption of Marxism–Leninism entailed acceptance of a radically new view of the world, by 1949 that view was deeply imbued with 'Chinese characteristics'.

What the Chinese took from Marxism–Leninism was what also appealed to many political activists and intellectuals in Southeast Asia. First and foremost was a theory of history that explained their humiliation at the hands of Western imperialism, assured them of their inevitable triumph over it, and provided them with the revolutionary model by which this would be achieved. It gave them, in other words, both an intellectually satisfying worldview and a blueprint for political action. Imperialism, Lenin had argued, was the last internationalist phase of monopoly capitalism, seeking control over resources for its industries and markets for its products. It would be defeated at its weakest point, where its contradictions were most glaring, and that was in its colonies. Revolution would be achieved through mass action by peasants and workers led by the dedicated cadres of communist parties. What was taken on faith was Marx's belief that communism, as a mode of economic production, would prove superior to capitalism, so that the sooner a society adopted communism, the more rapidly it would catch up and overtake imperialist capitalist states. Proof lay in the rapid industrialisation of the Soviet Union, which had enabled it to defeat Nazi Germany. Such a view led to disastrous attempts to speed up economic development by 'by-passing' the capitalist mode of production entirely—a notion Marx would have found bizarre. Examples include the Great Leap Forward in China and Khmer Rouge agrarian communism in Cambodia.

In terms of international relations, the Marxist–Leninist worldview was global in conception, and class- rather than nation-based. The revolutionary leap from capitalism to communism was believed to be universal and inevitable, even though it would take place separately in each society (nation-state). The historical significance of each revolution lay in its contribution to this global historical process. This internationalist cause united workers across the world. By their revolutionary efforts the proletariat would seize state power (exercised by the communist party through dictatorship on the workers' behalf) leading ultimately to the communist utopia, to which all would contribute according to their abilities and from which all would benefit according to their needs. This heady brothers-in-arms vision went by the name of 'proletarian internationalism', and presupposed the equality of both fraternal parties and those states in which they had succeeded in seizing power.

The reality was rather different. Under Stalin, the Soviet Union arrogated to itself the right to guide and direct world communism. Just as previously Moscow had proclaimed itself the 'third Rome' of Orthodox Christianity (after Rome itself and Constantinople), under communism the Soviet Union was the fount of orthodoxy. Its model of urban proletarian revolution when applied in China, however, led only to disaster when the Shanghai uprising of 1927 was ruthlessly suppressed. The significance of the ultimate success of Mao's rural, peasant-based revolution lay in two things: it drew upon Chinese, not Soviet, historical experience; and it was shaped within the context of Chinese circumstances, including cultural beliefs and values. It thereby provided a new and different model of revolution, one that the Chinese believed, with some justification, was much more applicable in Asia than was the Soviet model.[2] One of the first demands made by China in its alliance with the Soviet Union was to be given primary responsibility for promoting communist revolution in Asia.

The countries of Southeast Asia, so the Chinese leadership believed, were ripe for revolution. In their analysis, imperialism was attempting to consolidate its hold either by handing power to compliant client elites (as in the Philippines and Burma) or by reasserting direct rule (as in Malaya, Indonesia and Indochina). Progressive forces in these countries, led by Marxist parties, were fighting to prevent this and to bring about genuine revolution. It was China's internationalist duty to support such forces. This meant backing both liberation movements fighting to expel colonial powers (the nationalist bourgeois–democratic phase) and revolutionary movements seeking to overthrow conservative indigenous ruling elites (to bring about the subsequent transition to socialism). The global struggle would be both relentless and prolonged, as imperialism (led by the United States) was bent on destroying the socialist commonwealth. And the primary arena would be the Third World.

This was the Chinese Marxist–Leninist view of the balance of global forces, one that was largely shared by leaders of revolutionary movements in Southeast Asia. The translation of this view of the world into foreign policy was another matter, however. Realistic analysis of the balance of military and economic power, and the pragmatic assessment of national interest were never absent from Chinese foreign policy, even if this was at times ideologically driven. As in other states, domestic politics also had a significant impact on international relations, especially at times of internal conflict. So, too, had the way in which foreign policy decisions were arrived at. In the case of the PRC, the highly centralised and hierarchical power structure limited input into foreign policy decision making. In fact, Mao Zedong and Zhou Enlai were personally responsible for all major foreign policy initiatives during their lifetimes.

It has frequently been pointed out how structurally similar communist government, as an authoritarian dictatorship exercised by the CCP, was at its upper levels to government as exercised by the equally authoritarian Confucian mandarinate. A similar power structure, it should be noted, also characterised the Nationalist government under the GMD. The ideological justification might have changed, but not belief about how power should be concentrated and exercised, and by whom. 'Democratic centralism' preserved the hierarchy of political power and the patriarchal exclusion (of all but a token few women) that had been characteristic of Confucianism. The CCP, like the mandarinate, retained a monopoly on both orthodoxy and the path to political power. A new orthodoxy had to be learned and recited, but it functioned in a structurally similar way to Confucianism to exclude not only all alternative views, but also all those not inducted into it. Lucian Pye has called the resulting system 'Confucian

Leninism'.[3] We should note in passing that neither equality nor individual rights were principles that figured significantly in this curious hybrid.

In the field of international relations a similar fusion occurred, merging Marxist–Leninist and deep-seated historically Chinese beliefs and values. One such belief related to the relative status of polities. Despite nominal membership of the Western system of formally equal sovereign nations, and of the communist commonwealth of fraternal socialist states, China has always had difficulty in seeing itself as just another nation-state. This is because China, in reality, remains both the last great empire, and a civilisation whose historical pretensions to superiority are deeply embedded in the national psyche. In the current world order, moreover, it is as obvious to the Chinese as to anyone else that nation-states are not equal, though Beijing has always been punctilious in treating all equally in a formal sense—just as under the tribute system all vassal kingdoms were treated equally and impartially by a benevolent emperor. The world of nation-states that China entered in reality consisted of a hierarchy of powers, which for China was a hierarchy of international status. If China was truly to stand up and erase the humiliation of the 'century of shame', then it was imperative to regain international standing and respect. This was the unquestioned national goal for all Chinese leaders, and it was a goal that had important implications for the region. For if China was to become a global great power, it would have to be recognised as such within its own immediate 'sphere of influence'. In other words, a regional political order would have to evolve in which China was the dominant power, which of course meant that the presence of outside imperialist powers would have to be reduced to a minimum.

A second element of the traditional Chinese view of international relations that carried through to the People's Republic was belief in the influence and superiority of Chinese example. In the past, the virtue of the emperor provided the supreme model for others to follow. The revolutionary leadership of the PRC believed their revolutionary praxis also provided a superior model for others to emulate. What carried over from Confucian to communist China was the assumption that China was in an important sense an example for other polities, and thus had a didactic leadership role to play. The patronising superiority with which Chinese envoys lectured vassal kings and their courts as to the proper behaviour expected of them, found its parallel in the way senior communist officials lectured visiting delegations from regional communist movements.[4]

A third element of traditional belief that carried over into the Chinese communist worldview was its moralism. The traditional worldview that the Chinese sought to impose on surrounding kingdoms was a moral order, suffused by the virtue of the emperor. Chinese moral superiority derived from acting in accordance with the will of Heaven, and found expression in the universal beneficence and concern of the emperor for the well-being of 'all under Heaven'. Vassal kingdoms failing to live up to Chinese expectations were rebuked in moral terms. Similar convictions of moral superiority and tendencies to make moral judgments were soon evident in the PRC's approach to international relations.[5] Chinese policies tended to be proclaimed as moral principles, whether the Bandung policy of coexistence and non-interference in the affairs of other countries, or the later policy of anti-hegemonism (outlined below). In each case, China claimed its view provided the sole moral basis for the fairer and more just international order that it sought to create. The tributary system and the trade that accompanied it had rested on a strong sense of moral commitment: tributary missions were generously recompensed and measures were taken to ensure that trade was fair. Similarly the concept of 'equal benefit' in PRC trade policy emphasised its moral basis in a way that reflected Chinese values more than socialist practice (at least if judged by Soviet example).

Other important elements of the Marxist–Leninist worldview replaced traditional notions entirely, with significant implications for foreign relations. One was the idea of history. The Confucian view of history, as elaborated by the great historians of the Han dynasty (Sima Qian and Ban Gu), conceived of it as a cyclical process. Each new dynasty, in gaining the mandate of Heaven, reinstated the moral order that the last emperor of the previous dynasty had neglected. Marx, by contrast, was a European progressivist, a true son of the Enlightenment, for whom time moved inexorably into the future. So it did for Chinese Marxists, who accepted that history was not just linear, but progressive in that it favoured progressive forces, notably the CCP. The victory of communism in China, Chinese Marxists believed, was the first surge in a new tide of revolution that would sweep across Asia and the world and free all subject peoples from imperial domination and exploitation.

Another major change was to Chinese beliefs about the significance of economic forces. Whereas in Confucian China interest in economic development focused principally on collection of taxation necessary to meet the costs of administration and the imperial court, for Marxists, economic production was the driving force of history and the primary source of social power. It was the role of the state actively to stimulate production and facilitate distribution. International trade was thus no longer a matter of little concern to government, to be left in the hands of merchants of lowly status. Rather, it became a key consideration in relations between states.

Finally, certain characteristics of communist parties, including the CCP, spilled over from domestic politics into state behaviour to influence international relations. Among these we shall note two: the role of ideology, and a tendency to paranoia. Because intra-party politics tended to be fought out in terms of ideological orthodoxy, foreign relations could never be immune to ideological criticism. The influence of ideology on foreign policy has been particularly marked in the case of China, at no time more so than during the Cultural Revolution. As for paranoia, since one-party states by definition allow no overt political opposition, any opposition that arises must remain clandestine. It must be conspiratorial. This is exactly what ruling communist parties were when they were still illegal, so historical experience adds to the paranoia. Enemies are all around, operating in secret, and this extends to the international arena. The Chinese regime has always believed that other governments were plotting its downfall. It was Mao himself who warned about the dangers of 'peaceful evolution' as an imperialist strategy to undermine and destroy the Chinese revolution. Such suspicion has been a hallmark of the PRC's international relations culture, as it has been of Southeast Asian communist states (Vietnam, Laos, and Cambodia under the Khmer Rouge).

Early PRC–Southeast Asia relations

The CCP came to power in the bipolar international environment of the Cold War, after years of civil conflict and in desperate need of foreign assistance. It saw no alternative, therefore, but to 'lean to one side' and enter into formal alliance with the Soviet Union, which it did in February 1950. It was always going to be a difficult relationship, for reasons outlined above, and one that in retrospect could not last, though this was not immediately apparent. For political elites in Southeast Asia, some already struggling against homegrown communist insurgencies, world communism not only had moved frighteningly closer, but also had new and powerful means at its disposal to support revolution.

Within a year, the PRC conclusively demonstrated its preparedness to use those means. In September 1950, a Vietminh offensive was launched with substantial Chinese assistance against French garrisons in northern Vietnam close to the border—with China. A month later, Chinese 'volunteers' poured into Korea, driving United Nations forces back below the 38th parallel. Together these two events caused considerable anxiety and hardened attitudes among non-communist Southeast Asian political elites already subject to blistering criticism over Radio Beijing as 'running dogs of imperialism'. It seemed that Beijing was ready to back its strong words of support for revolutionary movements by decisive deeds.

Nowhere did the spectre of Chinese intervention loom larger than in Burma with its long and porous land border with the PRC, and in Vietnam (see below). The government of Burmese Prime Minister U Nu feared direct Chinese support, including military 'volunteers', for the Burmese Communist Party's insurrection; or even invasion by Chinese communist forces on the pretext of pursuing GMD remnants that had crossed the Burmese border. In an effort to prevent such intervention, Burma adopted a policy of strict neutrality in foreign affairs, and dispatched units of its own hard-pressed army to harass the unwanted GMD troops. The Burmese severed all connections with Britain, gave no support to the UN in Korea (unlike Thailand), and refrained from commenting on China's brutal 'liberation' of Buddhist Tibet.

Burmese neutralism did not derive solely from a realistic assessment of immediate circumstances. That was obviously one factor, but the Burmese response also drew upon a bilateral relations regime with China that had deep historical and cultural roots. Geography made Burma and China neighbours, but frontiers were always ill defined—and still were in the 1950s. Between the Han Chinese and Burman heartlands lived a bewildering number of ethnic minorities, which each in the past had attempted to draw into its political orbit. Contacts had mostly been peaceful and commercial, but trade routes could always become routes of invasion. Even powerful Burmese dynasties had recognised the threat that China posed. Any Chinese incursion was vigorously resisted, though China was afterwards placated through the dispatch of a Burmese embassy. And while Burmese conquerors frequently marched their armies against the Tai world, they mostly refrained from provoking China.

Another important historical lesson for Burma has been that strength comes from unity enforced by strong centralised power. Power struggles at the centre, particularly succession disputes, weakened the Burmese *mandala* and left it open to intervention by its neighbours. Experience of the British colonial policy of divide and rule only reinforced this lesson. To a certain extent, the threat of intervention was reduced through isolation and reliance on geography to protect the core heartland of the Irrawaddy valley. But this needed to be backed by diplomacy. Neutrality was designed to minimise possible external interference while the government attempted to strengthen the power of the centre and unify the country.

Resistance and placation were the two poles of the traditional Burmese response to China. The Burmese accepted what they described as a *paukphaw* (sibling) relationship that accorded China seniority within the same family. Beijing was remote and unpredictable, so it was always wise to maintain formally friendly relations at comfortably extended intervals. In the meantime the Burmese were free to shape their own world, by the perennial means in a fluctuating *mandala* of conquest of Mon, Shan, and other minor principalities. A similar approach in 1950 seemed entirely logical to Rangoon. China would be placated, leaving the Burman ruling elite free to recreate an independent Burmese state through internal conquest (of the BCP, the Karen, and any other minority that might challenge Burman domination). Thus was the external security environment stabilised in order to focus on the internal environment.

The Burmese approach worked. During the Korean conflict, China wanted no second front in the south. Support for the Vietminh kept the French busy in Indochina; Thailand, allied with the US though it was, had no common border across which to threaten Yunnan. But an independent Burma allied with the West could have posed a danger, not least to the Chinese position in Tibet. Better to encourage Burmese neutrality (leaning to China), than to back the BCP. In its dealing with Burma, Beijing showed that vocal encouragement for revolutionary movements did not necessarily translate into material support. A gap opened up between words and deeds because

Chinese leaders were prepared to make a distinction between state-to-state and party-to-party relations in their pursuit of China's national interests. This provided a space which worried some Southeast Asian leaders, but in which others learned to move.

Indonesia, the other newly independent state in Southeast Asia to recognise the PRC, did so with some reluctance, and with very different motives. Like Burma, Indonesia was preoccupied with its own internal affairs. Like Burma, it sought to create a strong and unified state out of the wreckage of war and division. Both countries were multi-ethnic and both were vulnerable to regional and ethnic separatism. There similarities ended, however. Indonesia might be spread across more than 16 000 islands, but its frontiers were not in question (except with respect to West Irian), and did not abut China. Nor did Indonesia have to contend with a communist insurgency, though it did still have a small but active communist party. From an Indonesian point of view, therefore, China did not pose an immediate security threat.

From its inception, Indonesian security concerns were internal rather than external. The first priority was to build a nation. President Sukarno worked tirelessly to promote an 'archipelagic outlook', incorporating islands and waters in a single political whole that subsumed all ethnic and cultural differences. But differences remained. 'Unity in Diversity' was an appropriate national motto, but the unity had continuously to be constructed. Nationalist historiography harked back to the great Javanese kingdom of Majapahit to provide historical legitimisation for the modern Indonesian state. But though Javanese kingdoms had dominated parts of the archipelago, Majapahit had never extended its sway across all of Indonesia's islands, many of which resented Javanese domination. Territorial integrity was thus threatened more by the prospect of internal secession than by external aggression.

'Unity in Diversity' applied not only to ethnic and cultural divisions, but religious divisions as well. Though Indonesia was overwhelmingly Muslim, like India its nationalism was largely secular.

Only one of the 'five principles' (*PANCASILA*) to which all Indonesians were expected to give assent referred to belief in God. The other four covered humanitarianism, national unity, democracy and social justice. Even so, if Indonesians looked abroad, most looked to Mecca rather than Beijing. For centuries the islands had traded with China, but Indonesians had never considered themselves part of the Chinese world order. During this time Indonesia had become home to a large overseas Chinese community that had proved reluctant to support the Indonesian nationalist cause, and whose links with China were viewed with suspicion by the Muslim majority. In the early years of independence, it was the PRC's attitude towards overseas Chinese that was of most concern to the government in Jakarta.

The overseas Chinese were a problem, too, for the PRC. Beijing had inherited a legacy of suspicion throughout Southeast Asia, thanks mainly to the activities of the GMD and the policies of the Nationalist government, which had set back assimilation virtually everywhere. Chinese had been encouraged to see themselves as Chinese first and Southeast Asians second, and to direct their primary loyalties to China. The GMD had viewed overseas Chinese communities as a means of extending Chinese influence in the region, and as a resource for the government of China. Indeed, it had viewed them as citizens of China and thus under its own jurisdiction, a policy that had caused irritation, as we have seen, not only to colonial authorities, but also to the Thai government.

The PRC inherited this position, but tended to be more circumspect than the GMD. It accepted responsibility for protecting overseas Chinese, just as would any government, but was limited in doing so by lack of representation. In both Thailand and the Philippines, anti-Chinese discrimination continued. Schools were closed and newspapers censored. Several thousand Chinese were deported from Malaya for involvement with the Malayan Communist Party. Even in Indonesia, with which Beijing did have diplomatic relations, little could be done to prevent discrimination.

Part of the problem lay in the fact that the PRC had inherited the late Qing and Nationalist definition of nationality based on *jus sanguinis*; that is, that nationality was determined by paternal line, not country of birth. As a rough estimate, this put the overseas Chinese population at around twelve million, but made no allowance for choice of nationality, where this existed, let alone intermarriage.

In the period to 1954, the PRC was cautious about using the overseas Chinese as its own long arm into Southeast Asia to destabilise governments it denounced as 'tools of imperialism'. The reason was two-fold: the PRC was feeling its way with respect to the overseas Chinese; and it was not prepared in the meantime to jeopardise its own interests. In particular, Beijing was not prepared to allow the precipitate actions of overseas Chinese in Southeast Asia, over which it had limited control, to shape its policy towards the region. At the same time, the PRC did want its influence to prevail over that of Taiwan, and for overseas Chinese to support the PRC, both ideologically and financially. It therefore granted overseas Chinese the right to elect representatives to PRC political bodies, including the National People's Congress.

Nowhere was the need to tread a fine line with respect to overseas Chinese more evident than in Malaya, where not only was the insurgency inspired by Maoist revolutionary practice, but was actually led by overseas Chinese. China gave verbal support to the insurgents, and revolutionary literature was smuggled in; but only minimal material assistance was forthcoming. At the same time, Beijing protested the effect harsh control measures, taken during the emergency, had on ethnic Chinese. By 1951, however, the Chinese government was becoming concerned over both the terrorist tactics adopted by the MCP and the ethnic polarisation the insurgency was producing. In October Beijing obliquely criticised overseas Chinese dominance of the MCP by calling for formation of a broad united front of all the Malayan peoples. By the end of the year, the MCP had reduced its terrorist activities.

Over the next three years, the MCP gradually shifted emphasis from military to political struggle. By then it had been confined to jungle bases in northern Malaya along the Thai border, and it was clear that the insurgency could not succeed. The Korean War was at an end, the Geneva conference had brought temporary peace to Indochina, and Beijing had signalled a more amenable policy with respect to overseas Chinese. It was under these circumstances that the MCP called for a political resolution of the emergency that would legalise the party. Talks were held in December 1955, but as the MCP was reluctant to surrender its weapons, nothing came of them. A complicating factor from the point of view of the Malay political elite was what to do about Singapore. The fear was that an independent Singapore, with its overwhelmingly Chinese population and active left-wing unions, would succumb to communism. The favoured solution was to merge Malaya, Singapore and the British Borneo territories into a new political entity. But when the Federation of Malaya obtained independence in August 1957, Singapore remained under British rule. Not surprisingly, the new Malayan government made no move to enter into diplomatic relations with Beijing.

The First Indochina War

The first significant move made by the PRC in its relations with Southeast Asia came in January 1950, when China became the first nation to recognise the Democratic Republic of Vietnam (DRV). The Soviet Union followed suit, but the Chinese action was highly significant for it served notice that, under appropriate circumstances, the PRC would throw its support behind revolutionary independence movements in Asia. In the case of Vietnam, there were good strategic reasons for China to intervene. The Chinese leadership believed their fledgling regime faced threats to its very existence from Western imperialism poised to strike from Korea, Taiwan, and

Indochina. The French presence on China's southern border had, therefore, to be eliminated.

Chinese recognition of the DRV effectively internationalised the war in Indochina. France nominally transferred sovereignty to royal governments in Vietnam, Cambodia and Laos, which were promptly recognised by Washington and London. United States military assistance immediately began flowing to all three countries. From being a colonial war for independence, the war in Indochina became part of the global struggle against communism. By the time it ended in 1954, the United States was meeting three-quarters of the military cost, as well as providing economic assistance.

Apart from security, however, more complex motives lay behind the Chinese decision to back the Vietminh. Ideological support for revolution, and Beijing's 'international obligation' to assist the Vietnamese people were two factors, but so too was a desire to test the Chinese 'model' of revolution. The success of the CCP in coming to power in China had convinced its leadership that the Chinese model constituted a major theoretical advance for Marxism–Leninism. In November 1949, in his opening address to the Conference of Asian and Australasian Trade Unions, PRC President Liu Shaoqi had stated: 'The path of the Chinese people's victory . . . is the path which should be taken by the people of many colonial and semi-colonial nations who struggle for national independence and people's democracy.'[6] The means, Liu told delegates, should be through formation of a united front of classes, groups and individuals devoted to national liberation, led by a dedicated and disciplined communist party that would establish and lead a 'national army'. The first test of this model, the Chinese decided, was to be in Vietnam. Success there would powerfully strengthen China's revolutionary status.

There was yet another reason, however, why China was prepared to provide assistance to the Vietminh that harked back to historical precedent, one that both Chinese and Vietnamese were well aware of and viewed very differently: to re-establish the traditional status relationship that had previously existed between the two countries. Successive Vietnamese dynasties had over the centuries borrowed much of Chinese culture, from cosmography to Confucianism as a philosophy of government. So if the Vietminh took from the PRC an appropriate model of political organisation and revolutionary warfare, this would reinstate, in Chinese eyes, the former relationship between China as the source of orthodoxy and Vietnam as the grateful recipient; China as the teacher, Vietnam as the pupil; in a word, China as superior in status, Vietnam as inferior. Through generous assistance, Beijing would once again draw Vietnam into its status-structured political orbit.

As Vietnamese revolutionary leaders were enthusiastic about the Maoist model and needed international support, Chinese assistance was welcomed. A senior official was appointed to head the Chinese liaison mission in Vietnam; a Chinese Military Advisory Group was established, not just to oversee the training and equipping of Vietnamese units, but also to assist in military planning; and a senior Chinese general was sent to Vietnam to plan the first major Vietminh offensive. Vietminh military forces were renamed the People's Army of Vietnam (PAVN) and readied for battle, thanks to Chinese aid, on a scale not previously possible.

Beginning in mid-September, the Vietminh launched its offensive against French garrisons close the Chinese border. Victory was crushing. A series of attacks, ambushes and precipitous withdrawals resulted in heavy French losses of men and equipment and left all the mountainous northern China–Vietnam frontier area in Vietminh hands. The PAVN was led by General Vo Nguyen Giap, but the plan, as we now know from recently released Chinese documents, was drawn up by his Chinese advisers.[7]

Vietnamese historians have consistently minimised China's role in the First Indochina War, but bare statistics reveal how extensive this was: tens of thousands of small arms, hundreds of artillery pieces and heavy mortars, thousands of tons of ammunition, not to mention food, medical supplies, military uniforms, vehicles and other equipment. What was even more significant was the involvement of Chinese advisers in military planning for every major offensive campaign, including the Vietminh invasions of Laos in 1953 and 1954 (agreed upon as part of a grand strategic plan during a secret visit to Beijing by Ho Chi Minh in September 1952), and the battle of Dien Bien Phu that effectively brought the war to an end.

The extent to which Chinese advice was accepted and acted upon is still hotly disputed. The Vietnamese maintain that Chinese advice was often inappropriate, especially 'human wave' offensives modelled on Chinese tactics used in Korea. Friction occurred at times between Chinese advisers and Vietnamese commanders. Most Vietnamese venom, however, has been reserved for China's role not in prosecuting the war, but in the peace agreement that concluded it. The Vietnamese argue that it was Chinese machinations at Geneva in 1954 that deprived them of total victory against the French, and so condemned the Vietnamese people to twenty more years of conflict and suffering.[8]

The scene was set for the Geneva Conference on Indochina by conclusion of an armistice in Korea and victory at Dien Bien Phu. The DRV delegation went to Geneva hoping not only to secure the independence of Vietnam under communist rule, but also for a share in government for the Vietminh-backed revolutionary movements in Laos and Cambodia, formed after the Indochina Communist Party was disbanded in 1951. China attended with very different priorities in mind. The PRC still feared direct American military intervention in Indochina. But China needed a breathing space in which to concentrate on internal political matters and economic development. Beijing was prepared, therefore, to back the Soviet Union's policy of 'peaceful coexistence' (foreshadowed as early as October 1952)—provided that ensured security along China's southern border.

At Geneva, China's own security needs took precedence over Vietnamese interests. In the global context of the Cold War, however, Chinese security depended primarily on the attitude of the United States. Beijing sought a settlement in Indochina that would reduce the threat to China from American imperialism. The armistice in Korea had established North Korea as a protective shield along China's northeastern frontier. Beijing wanted a similar protective zone in Indochina. Support for the division of Vietnam, and for neutral, non-communist governments in Laos and Cambodia, was designed to head off a major American commitment to Indochina.

Chinese leaders had two additional goals, however, that reveal much about Chinese grand strategy. One was China's desire to be taken seriously as a major power; the other was to exert greater political influence in Southeast Asia. For the first five years of the regime's existence, during the Korean War, Beijing had been internationally isolated. China had no representation in the United Nations, and Britain alone among the great powers had recognised the PRC. Geneva provided a world stage, on which China could demonstrate that it was a major diplomatic player. Zhou Enlai, consummate diplomat that he was, set out to convince the more amenable Western powers (Britain and France) that China was both reasonable and responsible, and so divide them from the hard-line Americans. His success at Geneva greatly enhanced China's international standing, much to Beijing's satisfaction.[9]

China's success, however, came at the expense of the Vietnamese. First, under Chinese urging, the DRV was convinced to abandon its pretense that it had no forces in Laos or Cambodia and to agree to their withdrawal. This led to recognition of non-communist governments in both countries that were beholden to China for removing, if only temporarily, the threat of Vietnamese domination. Then, under intense pressure from both the Soviets and Chinese, the DRV delegation was forced to accept the interim partition of Vietnam at the seventeenth parallel. This was supposedly to allow the French to withdraw, and to allow a nationwide plebiscite to be held within two years. Five years of struggle had given the Vietminh half the country, and left revolutionaries in the south in limbo. It was a first bitter warning to Vietnam that China not only would put its own interests first, but that it would not endorse Vietnam's ambition to reduce Laos and Cambodia to satellite status.

The 'Bandung spirit'

If Geneva provided a stage for China to negotiate on equal terms with the great powers, Bandung was the forum at which Beijing attempted to increase its political influence in Southeast Asia. China's more moderate stance at Geneva had been welcomed in Southeast Asian capitals, even though suspicion remained of longer term Chinese intentions. The stage was also set for China at Bandung by the relatively lukewarm response of Southeast Asian nations to the South-East Asia Treaty Organization (SEATO).

SEATO was established under American auspices in September 1954, on the conclusion of the First Indochina War, to counter communist insurrection. The Philippines and Thailand, however, both close American allies, were the only two Southeast Asian nations to join. While the Philippines still feared communist insurgency, Thailand had been alarmed by the formation in 1953 of a 'Thai Autonomous Area' in southern Yunnan which, along with communist activity in Laos, Bangkok took to be part of a concerted Chinese strategy of subversion. A series of anti-government broadcasts by former Thai prime minister, Pridi Phanomyong, who had been granted political asylum in China, only added to Thai fears.

Laos and Cambodia were precluded from joining SEATO under the terms of the Geneva agreements, but were designated 'protocol states', invasion of which would trigger a SEATO response. Burma refused to join, preferring her policy of strict neutrality. For Rangoon,

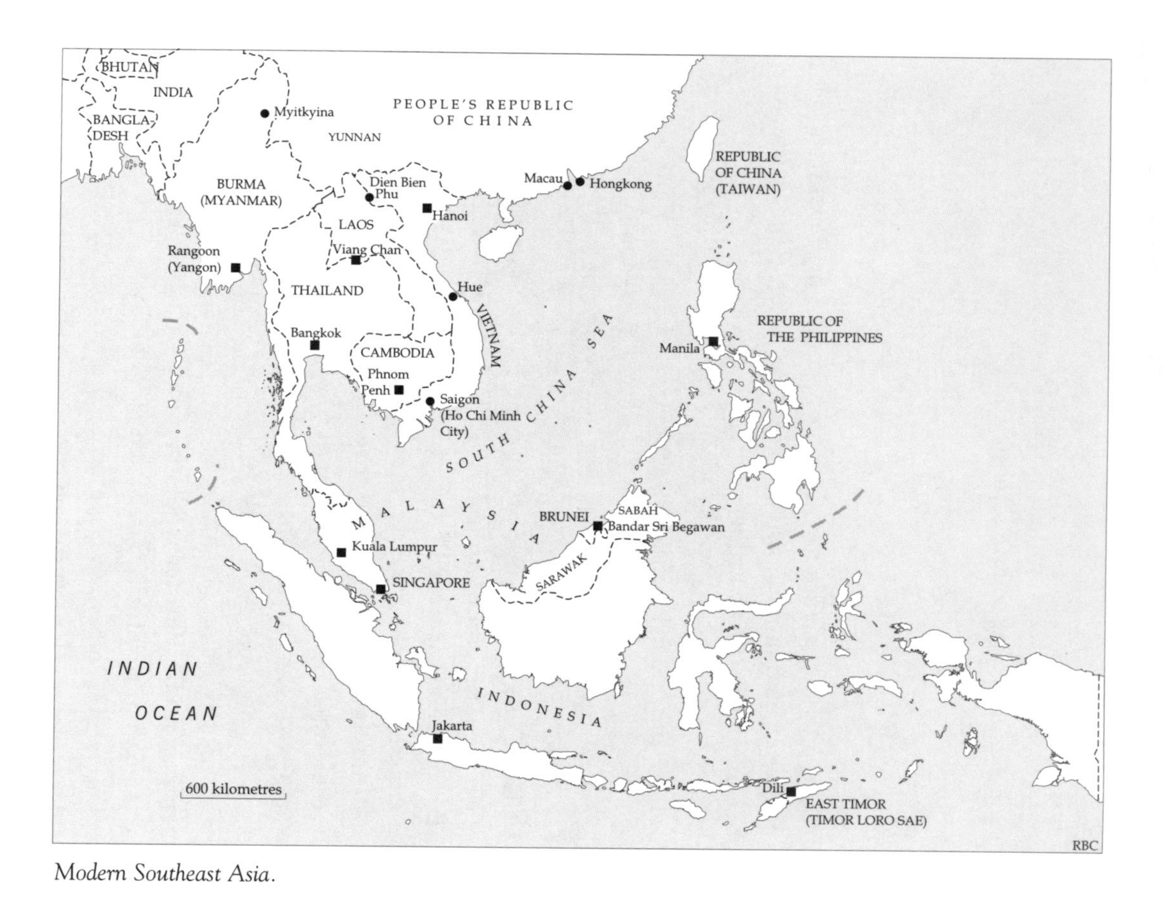

Modern Southeast Asia.

diplomacy had proved more effective than military alliance. The problem of the presence of Chinese Nationalist troops in Shan state had at last been resolved by taking the matter to the United Nations. The United States and Taiwan agreed to evacuate these forces, though in the end only about half (some 6000) actually left for Taiwan. The rest settled in the Burma–Thailand border area, where they turned to drug running.

Indonesia, too, refused to join SEATO. After three years of low-key relations, Jakarta dispatched its first ambassador to Beijing in October 1953, and began to promote trade. Indonesia was important for China as a principal member of the non-aligned group of nations, especially when, in April 1955, President Sukarno hosted the Bandung Asian–African Conference. The venue provided an opportunity for China to make friends and influence regional neighbours. Despite continuing support for revolutionary movements on a party-to-party basis, Beijing was eager to establish friendly state-to-state relations with neutral countries. The foundation for such relations were the 'Five Principles of Peaceful Coexistence' agreed upon the year before between Zhou Enlai and Prime Minister Jawaharlal Nehru of India. These were: mutual respect for sovereignty and territorial integrity, non-aggression, non-interference in internal affairs of other countries, equality of status, and mutual benefit.

For Indonesia, the Bandung conference marked a partial breakthrough on the vexed problem of the overseas Chinese. China agreed to a treaty that went some way towards eliminating dual nationality for Indonesian Chinese. Those who could claim dual nationality would be given the choice of either Indonesian or Chinese citizenship. Anyone not making an active choice would revert to Chinese nationality, and lose their Indonesian citizenship. Even so, tension continued over Indonesian anti-Chinese discrimination, particularly a 1959 ban by Jakarta on retail trade by aliens in rural areas that was directed mainly against Chinese. Attempts by Beijing to intervene on behalf of Chinese nationals were counterproductive, and China was forced to accept the return of almost 100 000 displaced Chinese.[10]

The Sino–Indonesian treaty on dual nationality was the only one signed. Discussions on a similar treaty with Burma lapsed. From the Chinese point of view, however, the Sino–Indonesian agreement had served its purpose. It had taken Beijing some time to become aware of how sensitive the overseas Chinese issue was in Southeast Asia. At first the PRC saw the Chinese overseas as citizens to be won over to the communist cause in its struggle with the Nationalists on Taiwan, and as representatives of China abroad. It was just this, however, that worried Southeast Asian governments and complicated relations with Beijing. Only later did Beijing come to see overseas Chinese as something of a liability, rather than an asset. Even their hard currency remittances (running at around $30 million a year during the PRC's first decade in power)[11] were insufficient to offset the cost of frayed relations with Southeast Asian nations.

The final elimination of dual nationality had to await enactment of the PRC Nationality Law of 1980. The treaty with Indonesia was significant, however, because it showed that China was prepared to abrogate the principle of citizenship by paternal descent that had been in force since 1909. Effectively therefore, Beijing was signalling that China's national interest took precedence over ties of descent and culture. Chinese in Southeast Asia could no longer look for redress to Beijing, even when, as in Indonesia, they were actively discriminated against. In other words, the PRC reverted to what essentially had been the traditional Chinese position on all those who chose to depart the Middle Kingdom: they were on their own.

The Bandung Conference had other positive benefits for China. Relations with Indonesia warmed, the more so after Sukarno introduced his 'guided democracy'. Trade, in particular, expanded rapidly. Personal relations between U Nu of Burma and Zhou Enlai blossomed, leading to negotiations on a principal issue of concern to the Burmese: demarcation of the frontier. Eventually, in January 1960, a boundary agreement was signed, along with a ten-year Treaty of Friendship and Mutual Non-Aggression. The agreement was generous in that Burma received most of the area under dispute. It was also the first such treaty China signed, and served as an example of Beijing's magnanimity. It was also proof that China's insistence that new treaties be signed to replace those forced upon it by imperialist powers was not an excuse to pursue irredentist claims.

Another positive outcome of the Bandung Conference, from China's point of view, came from Zhou Enlai's meeting with Prince Sihanouk of Cambodia. This led, in 1956, to trade and aid agreements and a visit from Zhou. It was friction with South Vietnam, however, that finally led Phnom Penh to establish diplomatic relations with Beijing in July 1958. Cambodia thus became the fourth country in Southeast Asia to recognise the PRC. It did so despite security concerns over communist influence among its Chinese community.

Nothing marked Cambodia's international relations culture so deeply as its own history. Modern Cambodia drew upon the heritage of the Khmer empire, which had spread from southern Vietnam to the Malay peninsula. After the thirteenth century, the empire contracted under pressure, first from the Thai to the west, and then from the Vietnamese to the east. In the 1830s Vietnam attempted to annex and assimilate Cambodia. Thai intervention forced Vietnam to accept joint suzerainty exercised by Bangkok and Hue. Only protection by France preserved Cambodia's territorial integrity, a point the French never tired of making. After independence, Cambodians still saw their country, even their race, as still under threat of extinction at the hands of their traditional enemies. Like the Thai, therefore, they sought a powerful protector. And since Thailand and Vietnam were both allies of the United States, where else was there to turn but to China?

Beijing responded sympathetically. Zhou Enlai assured Sihanouk on his second visit in May 1960 that China would come to Cambodia's assistance if it were externally threatened. A Treaty of Friendship and Mutual Non-Aggression was signed with Cambodia similar to the one concluded earlier with Burma. When Sihanouk terminated the American aid program three years later, China increased its assistance. Throughout the 1960s, Sihanouk maintained close relations with the PRC. When he was deposed in 1970, he took up residence in Beijing, from where he presided over a government-in-exile. What is interesting about Sihanouk's relations with the PRC is that he saw China, communist though it was, as the long-term guarantor of Cambodian independence, not just from threats from American-backed Thailand or South Vietnam, but also from a future, reunited communist Vietnam. Sihanouk was convinced that Hanoi would ultimately win the Second Indochina War. It was a powerful, aggressive, united Vietnam that he feared, and he understood long before most other leaders in the region that only China, with its determination to reassert its influence in Southeast Asia, would be prepared to rein in Vietnamese ambitions to dominate Cambodia (and Laos). In other words, Sihanouk foresaw a return to a traditional pattern in relations between China and Southeast Asia, and was prepared to accept this as the basis for a China–Cambodia bilateral relations regime. What he did not foresee was the Khmer Rouge, though in the end even they served merely as a catalyst in precipitating the very outcome Sihanouk took out his Chinese insurance against.

One other Southeast Asian leader shared something of Sihanouk's historical understanding of the importance of China for regional relations, and that was Prince Suvanna Phuma of Laos. The 1954 Geneva agreements had left Laos, like Vietnam, divided. Two northeastern provinces had been set aside for regroupment of pro-communist Pathet Lao forces. For three years Suvanna strove, in the face of American opposition, to reunify his country. In August 1956, Suvanna visited both Hanoi and Beijing to obtain North Vietnamese and Chinese agreement to the establishment of a neutral coalition government in Laos. Diplomatic relations were not on the agenda. All Suvanna promised was strict neutrality and adherence to the provisions of the Geneva agreements, which precluded foreign bases on Lao territory. This was enough for Beijing, since it would eliminate any American military threat from Laos. Hanoi, too, made no objection. The First Lao Coalition government (including two Pathet Lao ministers) took office in November 1957, with the blessing of the Chinese and to the fury of the United States.

Suvanna was of the royal clan of Luang Phrabang, a kingdom that had preserved a degree of autonomy by paying tribute simultaneously to Siam, Vietnam and China. He understood far better than most that Lao independence could only be preserved by taking account of China's security concerns, and by relying on China to bring pressure to bear on Vietnam. Suvanna's government lasted just eight months before the United States engineered his overthrow. His successor not only excluded Pathet Lao ministers from his government, but with American blessing established diplomatic relations with both South Vietnam and Taiwan. Within a year Laos had returned to civil war. It took a neutralist *coup d'état* in Viang Chan and substantial gains by communist forces to convince the incoming American administration of President John F. Kennedy to back the neutralist option for Laos. A new conference was convened in Geneva in 1962, attended by Beijing, which threw its support behind a Second Coalition government. That government established diplomatic relations with both the PRC and North Vietnam. But for Laos it was too late for neutrality, for the country's strategic location ensured it would be drawn inexorably into the Second Indochina War.

This series of Chinese foreign policy initiatives towards Southeast Asia in the 'Bandung spirit' should be seen, not apart from, but in conjunction with China's disastrous 'Great Leap Forward'. This is not to suggest, given the turmoil and famine in China between 1958 and 1962, that the PRC was acting from a position of weakness. The link, rather, is that through both its economic development policy and its foreign policy, China was seeking rapidly to augment both its economic power and its standing in the world. The two went together. In the end, neither achieved what had been hoped for: the former because the Great Leap Forward was ideologically driven and an economic disaster; the latter because leaders in Southeast Asia were still fearful of Chinese intentions, given Beijing's continuing support for revolutionary movements.

Complications and setbacks

The Great Leap Forward can only be understood in the context of Marxism–Leninist ideology, flavoured with a powerful dash of Mao Zedong thought. Ideologically driven, it sought to telescope the transition to a socialist mode of production in order to move directly to communism with the least possible delay. This, it was believed, would catapult the Chinese economy ahead of capitalist economies by releasing communism's greater productive potential. Not only was this theoretically naïve, but it relied to an impossible extent upon Maoist voluntarism. Agricultural communes were formed at a time when decentralised industry was absorbing an inordinate amount of labour. The result was plummeting production and an appalling famine in which tens of millions died. The Great Leap Forward set the Chinese economy back a decade and, with it, Chinese dreams of building influence in Asia, though it would take time for this lesson to sink in.

Nowhere did the Great Leap Forward encounter more doubt and hostility than in Moscow. An ideological gulf had been growing between China and the Soviet Union ever since Nikita Khrushchev's denunciation of Stalin in 1956. Thereafter, while the Soviet Union sought *détente* with the West, Chinese rhetoric became more radical. By 1960, the Russians were becoming increasingly annoyed at continuing Chinese criticism, and the decision was taken to terminate Soviet economic aid, including vital assistance for China's nuclear program. This was a devastating blow for Beijing, and one the Chinese never forgave. Not only did the Soviet action set back Chinese recovery after the Great Leap Forward, but China was denied the status it so desired of belonging to the nuclear club. Beijing immediately mounted a war of words against Khrushchev, culminating in a definitive break in July 1963 after Moscow signed the first nuclear test ban treaty with the United States. In foreign affairs Beijing thereupon adopted a policy of self-reliance that verged on isolationism.

The Sino–Soviet split had repercussions for China's relations with Southeast Asia. In an era of *détente* between the Soviet Union and the United States, China saw itself as leader of revolutionary forces throughout the Third World, including anti-colonial movements in Africa and Marxist revolutionary movements in Latin America. China pledged its support for all such rebel groups, in the form of finance, weapons and training. In practice, however, assistance went mainly to movements ideologically close to the CCP seeking to overthrow governments allied to the United States. In Southeast Asia, competition with Moscow for allegiance from communist parties was never in doubt. Most sided with Beijing, though some pro-Soviet splinter groups were formed. Only the Lao Dong (Workers' Party) in Vietnam and the Partai Komunis Indonesia (PKI) attempted to balance relations with both Moscow and Beijing, though the PKI soon came down on China's side.

Being ideologically close to the CCP did not guarantee substantial assistance, however. In Southeast Asia, China's increasingly radical foreign policy of 'exporting revolution' was selectively applied. As state-to-state relations with neutral Burma under the military regime of General Ne Win continued to be friendly, little assistance found its way to the Burmese Communist Party. Communist insurgencies in Malaya and the Philippines had been reduced to a security nuisance, so most assistance was directed to communist parties in Indochina and Thailand. The most interesting case, however, was China's relations with Indonesia, where Beijing established close ties both with the government of President Sukarno on the one hand, and with the PKI on the other.

The political discontent of the late 1950s in Indonesia culminated in Sukarno's decision, in July 1959, to replace parliamentary democracy with what he called 'guided democracy'. This allowed Sukarno to seize the political initiative by playing the PKI off against the army, but it meant that his ascendancy rested on a 'fragile balance' between antagonistic political forces. Only foreign policy offered an opportunity to unite these forces behind him. Sukarno enlisted both the PKI and the army in support of his revolutionary aims, first to 'liberate' West Irian from Dutch rule, and then to 'confront' the new state of Malaysia, formed in September 1963, comprising Malaya, Singapore and the British Borneo territories of Sabah and Sarawak. (Brunei was not included, and Singapore was expelled in August 1965.)

Indonesia's shift to an overtly anti-imperialist foreign policy was welcomed by Beijing, not least because it directed attention away from the internal problem of the Indonesian overseas Chinese. As the area of agreement expanded, a so-called 'Jakarta–Beijing axis' developed. Indonesia withdrew from the United Nations to become self-styled leader of the 'new emerging forces' challenging the 'old established forces' (principally the West), whose influence Sukarno believed was on the wane. When Sukarno challenged the creation of Malaysia, Beijing lent its support. Chinese aid was increased, though not enough to compensate for reductions not just in American aid, but in Soviet assistance as well. Confrontation, therefore, left Indonesia increasingly dependent on, and allied with, Beijing.

At the same time, party-to-party relations warmed between the CCP and the PKI. The PKI had attempted to tread a middle path in the Sino–Soviet dispute, while developing its own non-revolutionary strategy of seeking power through its political alliance with Sukarno. Though the Chinese had reservations about this non-Maoist strategy, they allowed that it might suit Indonesian conditions. Close relations between the PKI and the CCP were a poison chalice, however. Not only did they place the PKI in a difficult position with respect to the overseas Chinese, they also stirred army and orthodox Muslim fears of Chinese subversion and communist revolution.

Both external and internal factors contributed to the dramatic events following the murky and badly botched attempted coup of September 1965. Growing military doubts over confrontation had undermined the earlier foreign policy consensus. The Indonesian army was uncomfortable over the country's international isolation and dependency on Beijing. Meanwhile, as Sukarno came to rely increasingly on China externally, so he tended to rely more on the PKI internally. This undermined his ability to maintain the internal balance of power, which had in any case ignored political Islam. The coup provided the catalyst for the army to join forces with orthodox Muslims to destroy the PKI. China was accused of involvement in the coup attempt, a charge vehemently denied by Beijing. Relations between the PRC and the new government of General Suharto soured rapidly, however, until in October 1967 they were suspended unilaterally by Jakarta, along with all direct trade.

With the collapse of the Jakarta–Beijing axis, China's Southeast Asia policy suffered a severe setback. The PRC had targeted Indonesia as the largest, most populous, and most strategically situated country in the region. But in doing so it had made serious mistakes. It had depended far too much on the political skills of Sukarno, while failing to appreciate how fragile were the foundations of his power. It had underestimated the grim anti-communism of the army, ignored political Islam, and overestimated the organisational strength of the PKI.

China had been playing for high stakes. The Jakarta–Beijing Axis had been forged when the Second Indochina War was already underway, and Chinese–Vietnamese relations still close. A united communist Vietnam and the PKI in power in Indonesia, both beholden to China, might have brought all Southeast Asia (with the possible exception of the Philippines where there were still American bases) into Beijing's political orbit. In September 1963 Zhou Enlai had presided over a secret meeting in southern China, bringing together the leaders of the DRV, the Pathet Lao, and the PKI (represented by its secretary-general, D. N. Aidit), to develop a coordinated revolutionary strategy for Southeast Asia, based on communist movements in Indochina and Indonesia. Had this strategy been successful, China's influence in the region and the world would have taken a quantum leap forward. With the collapse of its Indonesia policy, China drew back, just as it had after the Ming voyages, to busy itself with the threat from the north (the Soviet Union) and with its own internal politics (during the Cultural Revolution). The impact of both reverberated, not in Indonesia, but in Indochina.

The Second Indochina War

Despite the disappointment of the Geneva agreements of 1954, relations between China and the Democratic Republic of Vietnam remained close and friendly. The nagging question of boundaries and possession of the Paracel and Spratly islands were put to one side. The Vietnamese were learning, however, that Chinese revolutionary precedent could not simply be applied in Vietnam. Nor did Chinese advice, despite the authoritative way in which it was given, always provide the best solution. A case in point was the land reform program in North Vietnam, whose excesses led to the first mass demonstrations against the regime. Vietnam declined to introduce communes, and was not tempted to emulate China's Great Leap Forward. As for southern Vietnam, Chinese advice, in the name of peaceful coexistence, was to pursue political struggle and avoid armed uprising. When the decision was taken in 1959 by a much more mature and experienced Vietnamese communist leadership to resume insurgency in the south, it was without seeking Chinese approval.[12]

Once the decision was taken, Beijing offered full support, even while coping with the aftermath of the Great Leap Forward. The

Chinese had been supplying the People's Army of Vietnam (PAVN) since 1956 when the government of South Vietnam, with American backing, refused to hold the plebiscite on reunification. More Chinese military assistance was promised in support of a protracted but limited insurgency in the south designed to minimise the likelihood of increased US intervention. The American decision to accept the neutrality of Laos, formally agreed upon in Geneva in 1962, indicated that if Washington intended to hold the line in Indochina, South Vietnam would be the principal theatre of anticommunist operations. By then the worry for Hanoi, and for Beijing too, was that the US might extend the war into North Vietnam.

As Chinese scholars have pointed out, China's more aggressive support for the escalating conflict in Vietnam after 1962 reflected Mao's determination to regain the revolutionary initiative, both internally after the Great Leap Forward, and internationally in his increasingly bitter opposition to the Soviet Union.[13] Internally Mao, in early 1963, launched his 'socialist education' campaign, forerunner of the Cultural Revolution. Externally, Moscow's decision to lean towards India in its border war with China exacerbated the Sino–Soviet conflict. China proclaimed that the centre of world revolution had moved from Moscow to Beijing, for the Soviet Union could no longer be relied upon to support armed insurgency. The proof that China, by contrast, could be relied upon lay in the backing Beijing gave to the war in Vietnam.

The Sino–Soviet split placed Hanoi in an awkward situation, for Vietnam needed all the help it could get in its escalating war in the south. Offers of greatly increased military assistance, if the DRV would join the Chinese camp, were politely turned down. Hanoi did begin, however, to lean towards Beijing; for example, by criticising 'revisionism'. As a result, relations between the DRV and the Soviet Union cooled appreciably in the mid-1960s.

The events spanning the period from the assassination of South Vietnamese President Ngo Dinh Diem in Saigon (just three weeks before US President John F. Kennedy, too, was assassinated), to the aftermath of the fall of Nikita Khrushchev in October 1964, changed both the face of the war in South Vietnam and its international context. In the political turmoil that followed the overthrow of Diem, the Viet Cong insurgency gained swift momentum, aided for the first time by PAVN units infiltrated down the Ho Chi Minh trail. The US response was to increase American aid and the American military presence in South Vietnam. In August 1964, in response to an incident in the Gulf of Tonkin in which American warships were reportedly attacked by DRV patrol boats, American aircraft bombed DRV military installations. Incremental escalation followed until, in 1965, the United States began systematically bombing North Vietnam and sent combat forces to South Vietnam.

The Second Indochina War soon spilled over the borders of Vietnam. In Laos the Second Coalition government had effectively collapsed following the assassination in April 1963 of the neutralist foreign minister. The neutralists themselves were divided, and neutrality was no longer a political option. PAVN forces assisted the Pathet Lao to seize control of the eastern third of the country, including most of the Plain of Jars and the Ho Chi Minh trail. In response, the US recruited its own 'secret army' in northern Laos and began bombing communist targets. In Thailand, the Communist Party of Thailand laid the organisational groundwork for its own Chinese backed and directed insurgency. Only Cambodia managed at this stage to insulate itself from the gathering storm.

Beijing closely monitored the growing American presence in Indochina. The Chinese response was to provide strong support for Hanoi, while reassuring the US that Chinese forces would only become involved if China itself were directly threatened. What would trigger Chinese intervention would be an American land invasion of North Vietnam. Short of that, Beijing would avoid confrontation with the US. This was not quite what Vietnamese leaders had in mind. Hanoi wanted China to deploy anti-aircraft batteries and send 'volunteer' pilots to engage US warplanes. No pilots arrived, and China stipulated that its anti-aircraft units were to defend only the northern part of the country. Tens of thousands of Chinese engineering troops built roads, railways and defence installations, and the level of military assistance was increased, but for Hanoi China's commitment was less than total, as it did little to prevent continued American bombing.[14]

The overthrow of Khrushchev did nothing to heal the Sino–Soviet rift, but it did lead to a rethinking of the Soviet Union's cautious policy towards revolutionary movements. Moscow called for a united effort by socialist countries to oppose American imperialism in Vietnam, and stepped up its aid to the DRV. This was welcomed by Hanoi, much to the annoyance of Beijing. The two countries differed in their approach to the war. For the Vietnamese it was a life-and-death struggle for national reunification, which they were determined to achieve as quickly as possible, even if that meant risking a widening war. Beijing favoured a protracted war that would wear away American staying power without risking an invasion of North Vietnam that might draw China into the conflict. Rejection of Chinese advice deepened these differences.

The Cultural Revolution launched in mid-1966 radicalised the CCP in order to destroy Mao's political enemies. Its success ensured not only that Mao regained his political eminence, but also that his personal view of global power relations and security threats would decide the direction of Chinese foreign policy. Despite the build-up of American forces in South Vietnam, Mao was convinced that an increasingly hegemonistic Soviet Union posed the principal threat to China's security. This acted as a self-fulfilling prophecy, for the irrationality of the Cultural Revolution convinced Moscow that Maoist China presented a security threat to the Soviet Union, and so led to a build-up of Soviet forces along the Chinese border.

By 1968, China's domestic turmoil had all but isolated it internationally and its standing in the world had plummeted. In Vietnam the Tet offensive, about which the Chinese were ambivalent, failed in its military objectives but succeeded in undermining whatever consensus existed on the war in the United States. US President Lyndon Johnson announced he would not seek re-election, limited bombing of North Vietnam, and called for substantive peace negotiations with Hanoi. Such negotiations made good sense to the DRV, which responded positively. The Vietnamese knew the United States could not be defeated militarily, so the only option was a political settlement that allowed for a face-saving American withdrawal. A strategy of 'talk and fight' was adopted, to be pursued until the Americans had had enough. This drew support from the Soviet Union, which continued to supply the DRV with heavy weapons, but angered Beijing, which had not been consulted and had consistently opposed peace negotiations.[15] The balance of influence in Vietnam was already shifting perceptibly from China to the Soviet Union.

The 1968 Soviet invasion of Czechoslovakia—justified by the Brezhnev doctrine of 'limited sovereignty' allowing Soviet intervention in socialist states in defence of socialism—and the outbreak of fighting along the Sino–Soviet border the following year, served to confirm China's perception of the Soviet Union as aggressively seeking global hegemony, at a time when the US was signalling its desire to withdraw from Vietnam. For its part, Washington saw China as aggressive and intransigent, and turned increasingly to Moscow to bring pressure to bear on Vietnam. It seemed increasingly likely to Beijing, therefore, that what happened in Indochina would be decided by the US and the Soviet Union with minimal consideration for Chinese interests.

Not only was the PRC being ignored by the great powers, but its standing in its own region was in decline. The repercussions of the Cultural Revolution had been felt throughout Southeast Asia. The radical turn in Chinese policy, leading to renewed support for pro-Beijing, anti-imperialist, and anti-hegemonist revolutionary movements alienated governments in the region. Thailand, in particular, was concerned as insurgency broke out in the north and northeast of the country, backed by the strident Voice of the People of Thailand broadcasting out of southern China. On the Thai–Malaya border, the Malayan Communist Party was again active, while in Burma, Beijing gave new encouragement to the Burmese Communist Party. The sight of radical overseas Chinese students chanting Maoist slogans in Southeast Asian capitals fanned fears of Chinese communist subversion. Even relations between Beijing and Rangoon became severely strained and ambassadors were withdrawn, while Cambodia, too, threatened to break diplomatic relations.

Chinese relations with Southeast Asia had reached their nadir. Dwindling Chinese influence in Indochina followed the fiasco in Indonesia. Suspicion of China and fear of communist subversion were factors in bringing together five anti-communist Southeast Asian countries—Indonesia, the Philippines, Malaysia, Singapore and Thailand—to form the Association of Southeast Asian Nations (ASEAN). Burma chose not to join in order to preserve its neutral status. ASEAN was immediately denounced by Beijing as an instrument of US policy, and subjected to vituperative abuse. Though the organisation was relatively ineffective in presenting a unified regional response to what was perceived as the growing communist threat, it did create some sense of regional solidarity.

As so often before in Chinese history, it was fear over the security threat along China's vulnerable northern frontier that led to a rethinking of the direction of Chinese foreign policy, rather than the failure of its Southeast Asian strategy. After the border clashes of 1969, Beijing decided it had no alternative but to 'play the American card' as protection against a hostile Soviet Union. A secret visit to Beijing by Henry Kissinger, then President Richard Nixon's national security adviser, laid the groundwork for Nixon's own visit to China in February 1972. The two sides agreed to work towards normalisation of relations, and to oppose hegemony in the Asia–Pacific region, a clause that made clear the anti-Soviet thrust of Sino–US reconciliation. As at Geneva in 1954, the immediate effect was that China gained international standing. Over the next decade, more than forty countries recognised the PRC, and China regained its seat as a permanent member of the United Nations Security Council from Taiwan.

China went out of its way to try to reassure Hanoi that the new strategic balance would not reduce Chinese support for Vietnam's war effort, yet it was clear that Beijing was less determined to expel the US from the region. For the DRV, the Chinese move proved once again that the PRC would place its own national interests before international communist solidarity, even if this meant betraying Vietnam. Subsequent Chinese advice over how to handle the peace negotiations in order to allow the US an honourable exit from the war only confirmed Vietnamese distrust; as did the suggestion that Hanoi should permit neutral regimes to be established not only in Cambodia and Laos, but also in South Vietnam, which would have delayed reunification for years.[16]

Another event that had long-term repercussions for Sino–Vietnamese relations was the 1970 overthrow of Sihanouk in Cambodia. The right-wing government of General Lon Nol severed diplomatic relations with the DRV and China, and abandoned Sihanouk's left-leaning neutrality. More importantly, the coup unleashed the Khmer Rouge. Over the next five years, while Beijing managed to retain some influence over Cambodian affairs through hosting Sihanouk's government-in-exile, Hanoi saw its forces expelled from the country and the cadres it had trained purged by the rabidly anti-Vietnamese Khmer Rouge.

Developing bilateral relations regimes

In just over two decades from its inception, the foreign policy of the People's Republic of China swung from formal alliance with the Soviet Union against the United States to de facto alliance with the United

States against the Soviet Union. In between, in the 1960s, Beijing attempted to go its own self-reliant way. The lesson from this period was that in a bipolar world, China made a difference when allied to one superpower or the other, but carried much less weight on its own, even (after 1964) as a nuclear power. To enhance its international standing, Beijing had to play the triangular game. It did so with two immediate concerns: regime survival and protection of national security; and one longer term goal: enhancement of international status.

After the 'century of shame', the PRC was determined to take its place as a major world power, not as the centre of its own world order, but definitely as a leader of other nations. In succession, Beijing proclaimed itself leader of revolutionary movements throughout Asia, by virtue of the superior model provided by its own revolution; of newly independent neutral Third World states; of armed insurgency throughout the world (in the radical 1960s); and of all opponents of Soviet hegemonism. Such leadership claims were difficult to sustain, however, in the face of reluctance by most nations to be led. Nowhere was this more evident than in the one region above all others that China wanted to exercise significant influence, and that was Southeast Asia.

Throughout this period Chinese foreign policy was weighed down by Marxist ideology. The small foreign policy decision-making elite was both communist and Chinese. Their worldview was an amalgam of ideology and their own historical experience, infused by traditional Chinese sinocentrism.[17] On the one hand, they wanted to enhance China's national standing; on the other, they believed they had a duty to promote world revolution. Given their Marxist belief in the progressivism of history and the superiority of the socialist economic mode of production, the Chinese leadership believed both goals could be achieved in tandem. As the leading force behind the global revolution that would inevitably sweep the world, China stood to regain her leadership among nations. It was a heady vision, but one that soon ran into the realities of global power relations.

Not only were the two superpowers reluctant to make way for China, in Southeast Asia nationalist elites were unimpressed by Chinese-backed attempts to overthrow them. With Western assistance, revolutionary movements were crushed in the Philippines and Malaya and, in different circumstances, brought under control in Burma and Indonesia. Largely as a result of its own policies, by 1970 China had been able to establish diplomatic relations with only five countries in Southeast Asia. These were, in order of recognition of the PRC, Burma, Indonesia (until 1967), the Democratic Republic of Vietnam, Cambodia and Laos. Let us look briefly at the development of bilateral relations regimes with the PRC by each of these states.

One point to note, first, is that of the five, four are continental states. Only Indonesia represented maritime Southeast Asia (including Malaysia). Only Thailand—among continental Southeast Asian states—did not recognise Beijing. This was in accordance with Thailand's historical international relations culture that has consistently sought to maintain Thai independence and security through alliance with the current hegemonic power in the region. From the end of the Second World War until the mid-1970s, this was the United States. With US backing, Thailand challenged Vietnamese influence in Laos, and to a lesser extent in Cambodia, but was itself vulnerable to peripheral insurgencies directed from outside the country.

Burma was most consistent in developing a bilateral relations regime with China, based on a clear set of mutual understandings. These had to do, above all, with mutual security. While China represented the principal threat to the Burmese government and state, Beijing feared imperialist encirclement. To this, both democratic and military regimes in Burma were sensitive. In return for strict Burmese neutrality, China limited its support for the Burmese Communist Party to a level that prevented the BCP from seriously challenging the government in Rangoon. Burma's Buddhist-impregnated international relations culture, which accepts impermanence as a universal

Mao Zedong welcoming Burmese president, General Ne Win, 13 November 1975. (Hsinhua News Agency)

characteristic, predisposed Rangoon to accommodate all but the most abrupt changes in the direction of Chinese foreign policy. Relations were at all times lubricated by understanding and deference on the part of the Burmese in regular, high-level exchanges. Even the provocations of the Cultural Revolution did not fatally disrupt the developing bilateral relations regime between the two countries.

Cambodia, too, developed a durable bilateral relations regime with China. Unlike Burma's, this was not based on mutual recognition of security concerns, but rather on Cambodia's need for a guarantor to ensure its continuing independence and survival in the face of threats and pressures from both Vietnam and Thailand, and China's readiness to perform this role. Cambodia turned to China when both its powerful neighbours were allies of the US. In providing some guarantee of Cambodian security, China was able to encourage Cambodian neutrality, project its influence into Southeast Asia and, at the same time, limit Vietnamese ambitions.

Had the Geneva agreements of 1962 been adhered to by all parties, Laos would probably have developed a bilateral relations regime with China similar to that of Cambodia. There was, after all, the historical precedent of Luang Phrabang's tributary relations simultaneously with Vietnam, Siam and China, in which China provided the ultimate court of appeal. Lao neutralism was unable, however, to withstand the political pressures of the Second Indochina War. Laos was divided into de facto areas of control with Vietnam and the Pathet Lao to the east, and the US and Thailand holding the Mekong valley. China, finding Vietnamese influence over the Pathet Lao impregnable, proceeded to carve out its own area of control in northern Laos as security for its southern frontier. Under these circumstances, no comprehensive Sino–Lao bilateral relations regime could evolve.

For a brief while, the Jakarta–Beijing axis defined a revolutionary bilateral relations regime between Indonesia and China that excited Beijing's hopes and ambitions. But this regime was highly ideosyncratic, and lacked any historical depth. It rested, in fact, not on shared security concerns or common interests, but on the political needs and ambitions of one man. Sukarno needed China and the PKI to balance the power of the army. His ambition was to lead the world's 'new emerging forces'. But in this he was effectively competing with China. What shattered the illusion was not the army alone, but the army in league with political Islam, whose horizons took little account of China. The New Order of President Suharto, once its political power was secure, sought leadership within Southeast Asia through ASEAN, and thus stood in the way of an extension of Chinese influence in the region. Just as historically strong Javanese regimes had resisted inclusion in the Chinese world order, so no bilateral relations regime developed between New Order Indonesia and the PRC.

Finally we come to Vietnam. Here elements of the traditional bilateral relationship resurfaced repeatedly—in the teacher-to-pupil relationship between revolutionary parties (Ho translated a number of Mao's works into Vietnamese); in Chinese generosity in support of the Vietnamese revolution in expectation that China's superior revolutionary status would be acknowledged; in Vietnamese deference and resentment. Between these two states, Marxism never succeeded in eliminating the burden of history. Even to proclaim that Chinese and Vietnamese were 'comrades and brothers' carried ancient allusions, for while comrades may be equal, brothers never are in either China or Vietnam. Brothers are older and younger, and respect is due from junior to senior.

Relations between China and Vietnam were deeply imbued with moral expectations. Chinese assistance was given in order to create an obligation on the part of Vietnam to recognise China's moral superiority in providing it.[18] It was this moral dimension, and the deep emotional hurt when principles were believed to have been violated, that made (and continues to make) the Sino–Vietnamese bilateral relations regime so fraught. The very language of criticism, once relations broke down entirely in 1979, carried a moral burden—of generosity unacknowledged, of trust betrayed. Revolutionary Vietnam looked for a new relationship with revolutionary China, but was unable to free itself of expectations of how China should behave that had deep historical roots. China tried to free itself of old attitudes of superiority, but the very effort revealed how firmly they remained in place.

The Vietnamese understood China better than anyone else in Southeast Asia, but because they shared so many of the assumptions underlying China's international relations culture, they tended to be uncritical of their own position. What the Vietnamese resented in their relationship with the Chinese they in turn assumed in their relations with the Cambodians and Lao. In the end, when China's turn to the US rekindled Vietnamese fears of Beijing's real intentions, there seemed no option but alliance with the Soviet Union, just as for Cambodia there was no option but to look to China. In the *mandala* world of Southeast Asia, the enemy of one's neighbour was one's friend, and the enmity of Cambodia's neighbour was unquestioned. By 1972, enmity and suspicion had replaced the revolutionary friendship between China and Vietnam, and the Marxist-coloured bilateral relations regime between the two states had all but broken down.

9
FRESH BEGINNINGS

The visit of President Nixon to Beijing in 1972 opened the way for several of America's Asian allies to follow suit. By the time full diplomatic relations were established between Washington and Beijing, Japan had signed a Treaty of Peace and Friendship with China, and three more Southeast Asian states (Malaysia, Thailand and the Philippines) had recognised the PRC. This left Indonesia and Singapore (and Brunei, which only gained full independence in 1984) as the only states in Southeast Asia that did not have diplomatic relations with Beijing.

The 1970s were thus a crucial decade for China–Southeast Asia relations. When the decade opened, the PRC—with an aging Mao still at the helm—was recovering from the excesses of the Cultural Revolution, still actively supporting revolutionary movements in the region, and was regarded with deep suspicion by Southeast Asian governments. China's only ally was North Vietnam, though even there appearances were misleading. Ten years later, Mao was dead, the radical 'Gang of Four' had been overthrown, and Deng Xiaoping had returned to power. China was pointed in a new direction in which economic development took precedence over revolution. And in Southeast Asia, the PRC was effectively allied with ASEAN against the reunited Socialist Republic of Vietnam (SRV).

Following America's defeat in the Second Indochina War, the late 1970s not only saw Cambodia and Laos become communist, but also witnessed a marked shift in superpower influence in Southeast Asia. As the United States withdrew from continental Southeast Asia to its sole remaining bases in the Philippines, its place was temporarily taken by the Soviet Union, which established a strong military presence in Vietnam. This change in the strategic balance was exacerbated by Vietnam's invasion of Cambodia in December 1979, a move viewed with considerable alarm, especially by Thailand.

Throughout the 1980s Southeast Asia was deeply divided, with the 'Indochina Bloc' of Vietnam, Laos and Cambodia on one side, backed by the Soviet Union, and the ASEAN countries on the other, supported by China and the United States. The issue was resolved through Moscow's change of direction towards reconciliation with China, reduction in its global commitments, and internal reform (leading in 1991–92 to the collapse of communism and dismemberment of the Soviet Union). Vietnam's withdrawal of its forces from Cambodia and Laos in 1989 was followed by normalisation of relations with China. In these events, insofar as they pertained to Southeast Asia, Beijing played a key role, which saw its political influence in the region increase dramatically.

In the 1990s, as globalisation gained momentum, economics replaced politics as the principal focus of attention. China's 'four modernisations' (in agriculture, industry, science and technology, and the military), inaugurated in the early 1980s, bore fruit in the form of double-digit economic growth. Projections even suggested that China would pass the United States as the world's largest economy early in the twenty-first century. This rapid economic development was fuelled by massive foreign investment, much of it coming from Taiwan and the Chinese diaspora in Southeast Asia. At the same time as China's economic power increased, so too did its military potential, provoking regional unease and stimulating increased military spending by the wealthier Southeast Asian states. Of the various matters of contention between Southeast Asia and China, none was more crucial than the conflicting claims to sovereignty over the islands of the South China Sea. At the end of the century, despite China's oft-repeated desire for peaceful regional relations, and the determination of Southeast Asian states to engage rather than confront Beijing, the future of China–Southeast Asia relations remained a primary concern in all ten capitals of the expanded Association of Southeast Asia Nations.

Shifting relations in continental Southeast Asia

After Nixon's visit to China, the countdown to American withdrawal not just from Vietnam, but from continental Southeast Asia, was just a matter of time. In Vietnam, the Spring Offensive and Christmas bombing of 1972 were, in retrospect, not much more than sparring for advantage prior to the ceasefire of January 1973 that cleared the way for release of American prisoners of war, and withdrawal of US ground forces. At that point no-one could foresee the collapse of the South Vietnamese regime and ignominious US exit two years later, but what was clear was that the balance of power in the region was about to change irrevocably. Superpower rivalry would continue, but China potentially stood to gain from any partial power vacuum.

In the early 1970s Beijing was already working to improve its image in Southeast Asia that had been so tarnished by the Cultural Revolution. Informal contacts were established with Southeast Asian governments, and criticism of them toned down in the Chinese media; trade was encouraged; and less was said about discrimination against overseas Chinese (a matter for criticism again during the Cultural Revolution). Support for revolutionary movements continued, but more and more these were encouraged to regard China as a source of inspiration rather than actual assistance.

An early target for improved relations was Malaysia, a state uninvolved in the Indochina conflict. China first dropped opposition to Malaysia itself, which Beijing had previously denounced as a 'neo-colonialist, imperialist plot', then embraced Malaysia's proposal for a Zone of Peace, Freedom and Neutrality (ZOPFAN) in Southeast Asia. Both moves made sense. Malaysia was a fait accompli and, if implemented, ZOPFAN would reduce the presence of both superpowers and so increase Chinese influence. Beijing also attempted to woo Indonesia, but with little response from Jakarta.

In the early 1970s China had no diplomatic relations with any of the five members of ASEAN. The breakthrough came in mid-1974, when Malaysia and China formally recognised each other. A joint *communiqué* reiterated the principles of peaceful coexistence, including non-interference in each other's internal affairs, a clause Malaysia took to apply specifically to the Communist Party of Malaya, even though no reference was made in the negotiations to party-to-party relations. As it was, the CCP continued to publish its communications with the CPM, much to Malaysian annoyance, until the latter finally gave up its armed struggle in 1989. Another clause (this one discussed at length) eliminated dual nationality, an undertaking given legal substance in China's 1980 Nationality Law. Even then China continued to reserve a welcome for Southeast Asians of Chinese ancestry that treated them more as kin than foreigners.

In 1975 the Philippines became the second ASEAN state to recognise Beijing when President Ferdinand Marcos signed a similar joint *communiqué*. As for Malaysia, recognition of the PRC meant accepting that there was only 'one China'. For Manila with its close ties to Taibei, this was a painful but necessary move, even though trade relations continued to flourish with Taiwan. Trade was also a factor in relations with the PRC. China sold oil to the Philippines at 'friendship prices' during the world oil crisis, and continued to do so. Even so, the value of Philippines trade with China remained substantially less than with Taiwan.

Thailand was the third ASEAN state to establish diplomatic relations with the PRC. This was a significant move because Thailand, even more than the Philippines, had been deeply involved in the Second Indochina War. Thai troops served in South Vietnam, while Thai bases were used by American aircraft to bomb communist positions. What facilitated establishment of diplomatic relations was the overthrow of the Thai military regime in 1973, which ushered in a brief spell of democracy. When Thai Prime Minister, Kukrit Pramoj, visited Beijing in July 1975, he met with a surprisingly friendly reception. Asked why he thought things had gone so well, Kukrit told reporters it was because he had 'used the Thai manner of approaching [Mao]—the idea that you are older and better'.[1] In other words, Kukrit accorded China the status Beijing desired. What Kukrit described as Thai politeness, the Chinese accepted as due deference. In return, they were gracious and accommodating.

The form of words Kukrit used is revealing, for it re-established a status hierarchy that the Thai often refer to as older brother–younger brother. This is a family relationship, but in Thai, as in Chinese, there is no word for 'brother' and the relationship not only is hierarchical, but also carries with it well understood obligations on both sides. What was just as significant about the Thai move was its timing, following so soon after the precipitous US withdrawal from Vietnam barely three months before. Thailand had turned from enjoying close relations with one regional hegemon to seeking a similar relationship with the state the Thai clearly believed would be the next. This was entirely in keeping with Thai international relations culture. When the Thai military retook power in a bloody coup a little over a year later, nothing was done to jeopardise blossoming relations with Beijing.

China's readiness to enter into diplomatic relations with countries in Southeast Asia in which it had previously supported revolution was justified by Mao's theory of the 'Three Worlds'. The First World comprised the two hegemonistic superpowers; their industrialised allies made up the Second; while all undeveloped countries were relegated to the Third World. The only way to prevent domination by the superpowers, Mao argued, was for the Second and Third worlds to combine to oppose and eventually replace the existing dual global political and economic system. This provided a new opportunity for China to play a leadership role, as champion of the Third World, in creating a more just international order—yet another example of China's use of a self-serving morality to pursue its quest for status recognition.

The theory of the Three Worlds was designed to focus attention on the threat posed by the Soviet Union. Nowhere did Beijing resent and fear growing Soviet influence more than in Southeast Asia, especially in Vietnam, because of the perceived 'two front' security threat this posed. Chinese advice to follow a strategy of 'people's war' in South Vietnam was disregarded in Hanoi. Instead, the DRV relied on heavy weapons supplied by Moscow to bring the Second Indochina War to an abrupt end. This rejection of the Chinese model, the rapidity with which Hanoi forced through the reunification of Vietnam, and discrimination against ethnic Chinese all soured relations further. So, too, did China's opportunistic seizure in 1974 of the Paracel (Xisha) Islands from South Vietnam. The following year Hanoi moved quickly to seize control of islands in the Spratly (Nansha) group, formerly garrisoned by South Vietnam.

The four years between the end of the Second Indochina War in 1975, and the outbreak of the Third in 1979, initiated by Vietnam's invasion of Cambodia, was a period of intense political manoeuvring in China. With the deaths in 1976 of Zhou Enlai and Mao Zedong, an era in Chinese history came to an end. Under Mao's compromise successor, Hua Guofeng, the radical 'Gang of Four' was overthrown before Hua himself was eased aside to make way for the return to power of former CCP Secretary-General, Deng Xiaoping. Deng was a pragmatist, famous for his quip that it did not matter what colour a cat was, just so long as it caught mice. He had been rehabilitated in 1973, in the aftermath of the Cultural Revolution, and had witnessed the shift in direction of Chinese foreign policy. Not until five years later, however, was Deng in a position to place his own stamp on China's relations with the world. By that time relations with Vietnam overshadowed all else in China's relations with Southeast Asia.

At first the depth of antagonism between China and Vietnam was hidden from public view. Relations had begun deteriorating, however, immediately upon the fall of Phnom Penh and Saigon in April 1975. The root of the problem lay in differing perceptions of the changing strategic balance in the region resulting from American withdrawal and closer Soviet–Vietnamese ties. What the Chinese saw as threatened encirclement by the Soviet Union, the Vietnamese saw as an opportunity both to reduce their dependency on China and to extend their influence in Southeast Asia. The key for both countries was Cambodia, and there China enjoyed an advantage, for the Khmer Rouge, led by Pol Pot, was already virulently anti-Vietnamese and closely allied to China.

The strategic security situations facing both China and Vietnam were, in fact, remarkably similar, as were their perceptions of them, resting as these did on similar international relations cultures. Just as China perceived a security threat from the Soviet Union on two fronts, so too did Vietnam perceive a security threat on two fronts from China. And just as the Soviet presence in Vietnam stood in the way of China's strategic goal of increasing its influence in Southeast Asia, so too did China's de facto alliance with the Khmer Rouge stand in the way of Vietnam's ambitions to extend its own influence in the region.

These parallel situations did not develop overnight, for the Soviet Union did not move immediately to take advantage of the US withdrawal. Chinese warnings to Vietnam about Moscow's hegemonic intentions seemed at first to have some effect. Pressured by Beijing to choose between the USSR and China, however, the Vietnamese chose Moscow, for two reasons: they resented Chinese attempts to reinstate the traditional superior–inferior relationship between the two countries; and more practically they knew that only the Soviet Union could provide the quantities of aid necessary to reconstruct their war-damaged country. Soviet aid was already propping up Laos, whose economy had virtually collapsed. In mid-1977 Vietnam cemented its position in Laos by signing a twenty-five-year Treaty of Friendship and Cooperation. For Hanoi, its 'special relationship' with Laos served as a model for relations with Cambodia, but it was not one the Khmer Rouge were prepared to accept.[2] Faced with increasing Cambodian truculence, Hanoi held Beijing responsible and strengthened ties with Moscow.

From mid-1977, relations between Cambodia and Vietnam rapidly unravelled. Fighting escalated along their common border until, in December, Vietnam retaliated in force. Phnom Penh promptly broke diplomatic relations with Hanoi. Beijing made some attempt to moderate the provocations of the Khmer Rouge, but to little effect. Meanwhile relations between China and Vietnam also deteriorated over Vietnamese treatment of ethnic Chinese. In southern Vietnam, Chinese were targeted as class enemies and sent to farm the New Economic Zones. In the north, Hanoi began expelling Chinese from provinces bordering the PRC. In the end as many as 200 000 were forced to leave, many evacuated on Chinese vessels.[3] By mid-1978 China had concluded that Vietnam was no longer open to reason and was determined to use the Soviet Union in order to pursue its 'regional hegemonist' ambitions, to the detriment of the PRC. In fact, Vietnam had decided that it was in an impossible situation. With border provocations escalating both north and south, Hanoi believed its only recourse was to overthrow the Khmer Rouge regime in Cambodia. In November 1978, Vietnam signed a Treaty of Friendship and Cooperation with the Soviet Union, a clause of which called for immediate consultations in the event that either was 'attacked or threatened with attack . . . with a view to eliminating that threat'.[4] The following month, the PRC and the United States agreed to normalise relations. Ten days later Vietnam invaded Cambodia.

The Vietnamese occupation of Cambodia and establishment of a pro-Vietnamese regime in Phnom Penh upset the strategic balance in Southeast Asia, to the anger of China and alarm of Thailand and other ASEAN states. The PRC did not respond immediately, however, as its military forces were not yet in place. Not until mid-February was China ready 'to teach the Vietnamese a lesson', by which time Chinese leaders had notified Washington that the invasion was imminent, and Moscow that it would be of short duration for limited objectives. This greatly reduced the risk of Soviet retaliation. The invasion itself was described as a 'self-defensive counter attack' in response to violations of the Sino–Vietnamese border by Vietnamese forces, though this was obviously not its real aim. The invasion had a strategic purpose to warn Moscow not to go too far in its support of Vietnam; a political purpose to reassure the Thai in particular that China was a reliable ally; and a military purpose to force Vietnam to commit troops on a second front and so relieve the pressure on the Cambodian resistance. There may also have been an internal political dimension. But the principal reason, as the Chinese themselves repeatedly stated, was to 'punish' Vietnam, and this needs further explanation.

The form of language is itself revealing. 'Punishment', to 'teach a lesson', is what parents do to obstreperous children, and carries with it strong moral overtones. A child who has erred needs correction; it needs to be taught the proper way to behave. Historically, China arrogated to itself the right to dictate how vassal kingdoms should behave. It did so from a position of assumed moral superiority that was never subjected to criticism, and still is not even in modern Chinese historiography.[5] Punishment was regretfully necessary, but there was never any doubt that China was morally justified in meting it out, as superior to inferior. These attitudes were palpably present in the Chinese decision to 'punish' Vietnam, and the Vietnamese were well aware of it. The irony was, that although they did not use the same language, similar attitudes were present in Vietnam's relations with Cambodia, where they were equally resented.

The Vietnamese invasion of Cambodia changed China's relations with the rest of Southeast Asia. As Sino–Vietnamese relations had deteriorated, both sides had attempted to explain their respective positions in Southeast Asian capitals. Only Jakarta had much sympathy for Hanoi. Other states were more receptive to Chinese warnings about Soviet support for Vietnamese ambitions to create an 'Indochina federation'. When the Vietnamese showed they were prepared to achieve this through military means, Beijing seemed to have been proved right, and the PRC was suddenly in a position to act as champion, not of radical social change, but of the status quo.

The Chinese invasion of Vietnam proved that China was prepared to use military force not just in defence of its own frontiers, but also in support of its broader interests, at least in continental Southeast Asia. This may have been reassuring to the Thai in the short term, but it carried with it worrying implications for future China–Southeast Asia relations. As for Vietnam, the Chinese invasion confirmed its historical experience that the price of independence has always to be paid in blood, and thereby reinforced core elements of its strategic and international relations culture.[6]

The Third Indochina War came at a time when Deng Xiaoping was already opening China's door to the West. This was designed to encourage foreign investment, technology transfer and tourism in order to bring in the foreign exchange that China needed to carry through its 'four modernisations'. The first modernisation was in agriculture. Collective farming was phased out in favour of families producing for a free market in agricultural produce. Private industry (the second modernisation) was allowed to compete with state-owned enterprises, with the watchword being improved technology (the third modernisation along with science).

Military modernisation, the fourth priority, proceeded more slowly. The invasion of Vietnam, effectively stopped in its tracks by the Vietnamese, showed up the deficiencies in the large but poorly equipped and led Chinese armed forces. Reforms followed, but twelve years later the Gulf War shocked Beijing by demonstrating just how high-tech modern warfare had become. In the face of American weapons superiority, the PRC had very little capacity for force projection beyond its shores. It did not even have the capability of taking Taiwan, unless through nuclear blackmail if the United States withdrew. Even if China remained militarily weak, however, the steady upgrading of its military capacity worried its Southeast Asian neighbours. Throughout the 1980s and early 1990s, the wealthier countries in Southeast Asia considerably increased their own defence spending, most of it on the latest weapons systems.

The Cambodian problem

What to do about the Vietnamese fait accompli in Cambodia dominated relations between China and Southeast Asia throughout the 1980s. In Beijing there was no doubt about what needed to be done: the Vietnamese had to be forced to withdraw and their 'puppet' Cambodian government replaced. Only thus could Chinese influence in Cambodia be restored and Vietnamese regional ambitions contained. The means chosen to bring this about were military, through support for the Khmer Rouge resistance; economic, to starve Vietnam of multilateral development aid; and diplomatic, to maintain a 'global united front' linking ASEAN, China and the West in opposition to Hanoi's 'regional hegemonism'.

Throughout the 1980s China was single-minded in its determination to bend Vietnam to its will. Chinese feelings towards Vietnam, as expressed by Chinese leaders, were remarkably bitter. Chinese estimates of their aid to Vietnam—military and economic—since 1949, ran into several billion dollars, for the most part non-repayable. Vietnam's lack of gratitude or any sense of obligation angered China. To turn around and side with the Soviet Union, China's principal enemy, was to Beijing an unforgivable act of betrayal that was all the more hurtful in that it repudiated a thousand years of close relations, during which Vietnam had always learned from China, and taken Chinese interests to heart.

History also figured largely in Vietnam's equally emotional view of China. China's actions and its advice over the years were interpreted as hypocritical. For while China pretended to support the Vietnamese revolution, what Beijing had really always wanted, according to Hanoi, was to weaken Vietnam in order to reimpose its traditional hegemony, not just over Vietnam, but over all Southeast Asia. Vietnamese leaders concluded that China would always be prepared to sacrifice Vietnam's interests for its own, and for this reason Beijing could never be trusted. As in the past, the only guarantee of Vietnam's independence lay in Vietnamese determination to preserve it—with some help from the Soviet Union.

The Chinese border invasion of 1979 did not deliver a significant military defeat to Vietnam. China withdrew voluntarily, leaving some 300 000 Chinese troops poised along Vietnam's northern border. Soon thereafter, Beijing came to an agreement with Bangkok to supply Cambodian resistance forces fighting the Vietnamese, notably the Khmer Rouge. But the Thais extracted a price. In return for the transit of Chinese arms through Thailand, China agreed to end its support for the Thai insurgency and close down its clandestine radio station in Yunnan. Vietnam thus found itself forced to mobilise armies on two fronts, at great economic and military cost. And because the Cambodian insurgents could always retreat to Thai territory, even the presence of 150 000 Vietnamese troops in Cambodia failed to guarantee the security of the Vietnamese-backed People's Republic of Kampuchea (PRK).

For Bangkok, the presence of Vietnamese forces in Cambodia posed a direct threat to Thai national security. Thai fears were exacerbated in June 1980 when Vietnamese troops crossed into Thailand in an attempt to close off Khmer Rouge resupply routes. Beijing immediately offered strong diplomatic support, and warned that China would come to the aid of Thailand in the event of a Vietnamese attack. This was exactly the response the Thais wanted. In the mid-1980s, the military relationship between China and Thailand was strengthened by the Thai purchase of Chinese heavy weapons, including surface-to-air missiles and naval vessels, at minimal 'friendship' prices. This burgeoning military relationship with China caused mounting concern among Thailand's ASEAN partners, especially Indonesia. There was recognition, however, that Thailand as the frontline state facing battle-hardened Vietnamese forces on its border had genuine security concerns, so despite some qualms, ASEAN solidarity held firm. In fact the security front forged during the Cambodian crisis significantly strengthened the sense of common purpose among ASEAN member states enshrined in the 1976 Treaty of Amity and Cooperation.

China and the United States also brought economic and political pressure to bear on Vietnam, through trade embargoes and vetoes on multinational financial lending. The Chinese strategy was to 'bleed' Vietnam into submission. The Vietnamese, good Marxists as they were, held to their belief that history was on their side and that 'contradictions' between members of the de facto coalition arrayed against them would lead to its disintegration. In the event, it was the Soviet Union that proved the weak reed, and the contradictions that developed were between an overextended Soviet Union bogged down in Afghanistan, and an overextended Vietnam approaching economic collapse.

By 1988 the shape of a solution to the Cambodian problem had begun to emerge. As of 1982, China had begun to distance itself from the United States and adopt a more even-handed policy towards the two superpowers. This opened up the possibility of normalisation of relations with the Soviet Union. From Beijing's point of view, however, 'three obstacles' stood in the way. The first two were the presence of Soviet forces in Afghanistan and along China's northern frontier. The third was Soviet support for the Vietnamese occupation of Cambodia. In the end the Soviets gave way: it was more important for Moscow to improve relations with Beijing than to go on backing a situation in Cambodia that drained Soviet resources and limited Soviet influence elsewhere in the region.

The Vietnamese, under severe pressure, promised to withdraw their forces from Cambodia and Laos by the end of 1989. This opened the way for Sino–Soviet rapprochment, all the more important for China as its relations with the West cooled after the Tiananmen massacre of pro-democracy student demonstrators. At the same time, Soviet economic and military assistance to Vietnam was reduced. This left Hanoi with no option but to mend its fences with ASEAN and China, even if that meant agreeing to a compromise political solution in Cambodia. Negotiations were complex and extended, with the crucial question being the role of the Khmer Rouge in whatever government in Cambodia replaced the PRK. A partial breakthrough came in 1990 when the UN Security Council took up the question of Cambodia and the United States withdrew recognition from the anti-Vietnamese Cambodian coalition. This created the conditions for negotiations in which several countries, including Indonesia, played a facilitating role. The shape of the final Comprehensive Political Settlement, however, was hammered out in discussions between the Cambodia parties, Vietnam, and China.

The details of the Cambodian Settlement need not detain us. What was significant was, first, the key role the PRC played in the political process; and second, that despite some compromise, the outcome was essentially what China wanted.[7] Vietnam was forced to make most of the concessions, its only reward being the normalisation of relations with China. As for Cambodia, the process provided a lesson for all political factions. The Khmer Rouge was forced under Chinese pressure to enter into coalition government with the hated Vietnamese-backed PRK regime, while the PRK learned that China, not Vietnam, was the real arbiter of Cambodia's destiny.

The restoration of relations between Vietnam and China provided a classic example of Chinese coercive diplomacy. Low level talks (between deputy foreign ministers) began early in 1989 and continued into 1990. Little progress was made, however, until at Chinese insistence Vietnam replaced its foreign minister. A secret summit followed between party secretary-generals and premiers of the two countries at Chengdu, at which Vietnam committed itself to resolve the Cambodian problem along the lines China wanted. This was a major concession on the part of Hanoi, for it marked the end of Vietnam's attempt to dominate Cambodia to the exclusion of Beijing. In the face of the collapse of communism in the Soviet Union, the Vietnamese Communist Party had no option but to rebuild relations with China: the few remaining socialist regimes clearly needed to stand together. Finally, in November 1991, relations between both states and parties were formally restored when Vietnamese leaders went to Beijing. More than a decade of conflict was finally resolved in the Chinese way, on Chinese terms, even if face-saving language was used. All Vietnam could do by way of a countermeasure was to improve its relations with ASEAN.

What was remarkable about this whole sequence of events was the way in which it echoed historical precedents, of which all sides were acutely aware, both in Vietnam's relations with Cambodia and in China's relations with Vietnam. For Cambodians, Vietnamese occupation recalled the 1830s when Vietnam not only occupied Cambodia, but forcibly tried to suppress Cambodian culture. Then it was Thailand that intervened to restore a degree of Cambodian autonomy. The lesson of the 1980s for Cambodians was that even after the interlude of French colonialism, Vietnam still sought to dominate their country. The Vietnamese drew similar conclusions with respect to China: no matter what the regime in Beijing, China was still determined to assert both its superiority and its own security priorities.

For Vietnam, the Chinese border incursion of 1979, though brief and limited in extent, conjured up all the previous occasions when Chinese forces had invaded Vietnam. In blunting the Chinese advance, Vietnam claimed once again to have defeated a Chinese army on

Chinese Prime Minister Li Peng greets Vietnamese foreign minister Nguyen Manh Cam, 11 September 1991. (Hsinhua News Agency)

Vietnamese soil. The lesson China sought to teach Vietnam was that Hanoi could never afford to disregard Chinese advice and warnings. These went unheeded for just so long as Vietnam could rely on the Soviet Union. But once that prop collapsed, there was nothing for it but to mend fences with Beijing. As so often in the past, protection of Vietnamese security required Vietnam to subscribe to China's view of how regional relations should be conducted. This in turn required Vietnamese leaders to make their submission symbolically and deferentially in Beijing. The formula of 'comrade plus brother', used by Beijing to characterise the restored relationship, made reference to shared ideology, linking what was by then a diminished Chinese-led 'Asian socialist community'[8] consisting of only four states: China,

Vietnam, Laos, and North Korea. In this community, Vietnam once again found itself looking to China, this time for its model of political control and economic liberalisation. The formula also made reference to a family relationship that, in the understanding of both China and Vietnam, restored the historical hierarchy between the two countries. China was the superior power, Vietnam the inferior, distasteful though this might be to Hanoi.

For China, resolution of the Cambodian problem and normalisation of relations with Vietnam restored a relationship that Vietnamese arrogance and ingratitude had temporarily disrupted. For Vietnam events going back to the founding of the PRC confirmed that even a radical change of ideology had not altered China's historic determination to dominate Southeast Asia. For a brief period of less than a century, Chinese weakness and Western imperialism had combined to alter the regional balance of power. Then the Soviet Union had taken advantage of America's withdrawal of Vietnam. By the 1990s, however, European imperialism and Soviet communism had both departed. The European age in Asia was at an end. Only America, as the sole remaining superpower, maintained a countervailing presence in Northeast and Southeast Asia to oppose an economically and militarily stronger, politically more influential, and ominously more nationalistic China.

The economic imperative

For China the 1990s were a decade of economic development. The Chinese economy grew for much of that time at rates averaging around 10 per cent per annum. This compared with substantially lower growth rates in most of Southeast Asia, especially towards the end of the decade due to the impact of the Asian economic crisis. China weathered the crisis remarkably well, earning gratitude in the process by not devaluing its currency.

The growth of the Chinese economy in the 1990s built upon the Open Door policy. This encouraged private foreign investment in the form of joint ventures centred initially on four Special Economic Zones in southern China. At the same time, the PRC began accepting multilateral and bilateral foreign aid. Trade not only expanded rapidly, but was diversified as well. By 1989 the Soviet Union was China's fourth largest trading partner (not counting Hong Kong), behind Japan, the US and West Germany. In the second half of the 1980s, trade rose to average over a quarter of Gross National Product for the first time in the history of the PRC.[9]

One thing of note about this rapid increase in trade was that a substantial proportion of it was in the hands of overseas Chinese in Taiwan and Southeast Asia. Trade was indirect in the case of Taiwan, so figures were impossible to pin down, but the total value of trade between the PRC and Hong Kong was, by 1989, running at close to double that for Japan, China's next most important trading partner. Of the countries in Southeast Asia, only Singapore ranked (at number six) among China's top dozen trading partners, though trade was rapidly increasing with other Southeast Asian states.

By the end of the 1980s, a rising proportion of foreign direct investment (FDI) was also coming from overseas Chinese, including Taiwan. In the 1990s, both overseas Chinese investment and investment from Southeast Asia rose absolutely and proportionally with the fall-off of Western and Japanese investment following the Tiananmen massacre. The principal jump occurred between 1991 and 1994, but the increase continued steadily through 1998.[10] Again, actual figures for overseas Chinese investment were difficult to determine because most capital came via Hong Kong. It was equally difficult to decide who was investing how much from where in Southeast Asia, as more than three-quarters of all investment from the region came from, or via, Singapore.

What is notable about the 1990s is, first, that both overall wealth and the ownership of liquid assets by overseas Chinese expanded greatly as Chinese business groups took advantage of globalisation. In fact, Chinese capital within ASEAN countries became more important than combined foreign investment in driving the economic development of Southeast Asia. While the share of foreign ownership in Southeast Asian economies fell, overseas Chinese ownership increased in absolute terms, even in countries like Malaysia where economic policy favoured Malays over Chinese and Indians.

A second point is that the PRC deliberately set out to attract overseas Chinese capital for the benefit of China, just as the Qing and the Nationalists had done. Paradoxically, it was able to do this because nationality was no longer an issue. Ethnic Chinese in Southeast Asia were citizens of the countries in which they resided, with no longer any call on China. Yet ethnic Chinese were encouraged to invest in China because they were Chinese, so possessing such advantages as language and business networks. They were prepared to invest in China in part because, as relations warmed between China and the countries of Southeast Asia, overseas Chinese felt less insecure about their ethnicity (except in Indonesia).

Together these developments caused some concern to governments in Southeast Asia. At the same time as ethnic Chinese were accumulating a disproportionate amount of the national wealth in their countries of citizenship, primary loyalties came once again to be questioned.[11] Even though Southeast Asian Chinese capital accounted for less than 8 per cent of total, foreign direct investment in China in 1997, over the decade the proportion of total investment in China, as compared with Southeast Asia, swung heavily in China's favour. From 1985 to 1990, FDI in Southeast Asia ran at approximately double that in China. By 1997, FDI in China was attracting almost double the figure for Southeast Asia.[12] The implications for increasing Chinese economic dominance of the region were obvious.

From ASEAN six to ASEAN ten

The burgeoning economic relationship between China and the wealthier Southeast Asian nations, with its dual components of increased trade and investment, may come to be seen as the most significant development of the 1990s, but the decade also saw a substantial increase in Chinese political influence in the region. Diplomatic relations were restored between China and Indonesia in 1990, followed immediately by Singapore's recognition of the PRC. Brunei was the last ASEAN state to establish relations with Beijing in the following year. It was in Burma, however, that Chinese political influence was most evident, with all that that implied for China's strategic relationship with the region.

As noted above, the strictly neutral, isolationist military regime in Burma successfully weathered the disruptions to relations with China resulting from the Cultural Revolution. Over the period from 1970 to 1985, China was particularly pleased by the way Burma kept both superpowers at bay, to the point in 1979 of withdrawing from the non-aligned movement when it began to tilt towards the Soviet Union, and by Burma's deferential consideration for China's national interests. From the Burmese point of view, this was sensible insurance against the ever-present threat of increased Chinese support for the Burmese Communist Party (BCP). With the return to power of Deng Xiaoping, even rhetorical Chinese support for the BCP decreased. In April 1989 an uprising by ethnic Wa cadres effectively destroyed the BCP, which accompanied the Thai and Malayan communist parties into oblivion.

In the late 1980s, two events conspired to bring China and Burma even closer together. These were the bloody seizure of power by the Burmese military in September 1988, followed by suppression of student demonstrators in Beijing the following year. Both were brutal attacks on popular movements calling for greater democracy; both caused considerable loss of life; and both were strongly condemned by the international community. Neither joined the chorus of condemnation of the other, however. On the contrary, each lent the other support in its hour of ostracism. In the early 1990s, Beijing began supplying large quantities of heavy weapons and other military equipment to the Burmese regime. In the wake of the collapse of the BCP insurgency a border trade agreement was signed that led within five years to annual two-way trade estimated at as much as $1.0 billion.[13] Chinese-manufactured goods flooded the Burmese market in exchange for illicit drugs, timber, pearls, and precious stones. Chinese engineers built new roads and bridges to facilitate this trade, while thousands of Chinese entrepreneurs, small traders and labourers migrated into northern Burma in search of economic opportunities.

As in the earlier relationship developed by Ne Win and Zhou Enlai, interstate relations were reinforced through the frequent exchange of high-level delegations. It was the developing military and strategic dimension of the relationship, however, that most worried Burma's neighbours. Not only did the Western arms embargo make Burma entirely dependent on China for its weapons purchases, but China also provided assistance in the construction of sensitive military and naval bases on the Bay of Bengal. At the same time, China constructed a transportation network linking the Chinese province of Yunnan with the Burmese river port of Bhamo, from where Chinese goods passed down the Irrawaddy River to Rangoon. This 'Irrawaddy corridor' gave China not just trade access to the Indian Ocean, but the means to support a naval presence as well. China's de facto alliance with Burma thus threatened greatly to extend Beijing's strategic reach.

India, in particular, worried over a potential Chinese naval presence in the Bay of Bengal, and became much more amenable towards Rangoon. ASEAN, too, was concerned. While Singaporean, Thai and Malaysian businessmen took advantage of new opportunities for investment in Burma, political leaders took note of the growing Chinese presence and influence. This was a principal reason for sounding out

Rangoon about membership of ASEAN, despite the military regime's unsavoury human rights record.

The inclusion of Brunei in 1984 had brought ASEAN membership to six. The next state to join, however, was not Burma but Vietnam. Vietnam (and Laos) signed the Treaty of Amity and Cooperation, the core document of ASEAN, in July 1992 and, three years later to the month, Vietnam joined the Association. This was a highly significant and symbolic addition, coming as it did so soon after Vietnam's loss of Soviet support. Vietnamese membership effectively healed the division that had existed between ASEAN and the 'Indochina bloc' during the Cold War. At the same time it signalled to China that Vietnam would henceforth consider itself a part of Southeast Asia, and so placed a little more distance between Hanoi and Beijing. The ASEAN seven went out of their way to reassure Beijing that they did not intend to act as a bloc to 'balance' China, but it was clear, nevertheless, that the addition of Vietnam did strengthen both ASEAN and Vietnam in their dealings with Beijing, especially with respect to overlapping claims in the South China Sea (see below).

In December 1995, the ASEAN summit in Bangkok was also attended by heads of government from Burma, Laos and Cambodia, the first time all Southeast Asian states had met at this level. Leaders marked the occasion by signing a treaty establishing a nuclear weapons-free zone in Southeast Asia. Laos indicated its intention to join the Association when it was better prepared to participate in the full range of ASEAN affairs. Member states, particularly Indonesia, were also eager to include Burma, specifically to reduce Rangoon's dependence on Beijing. The new coalition government in Cambodia also elected to join, but was delayed from doing so by internal political conflict. Laos and Burma both joined in 1997, with Cambodia finally becoming ASEAN's tenth member in April 1999.

Though ASEAN—as it entered the twenty-first century—was a much looser association than the European Union, the fact that it grouped all Southeast Asian states, and that it had already evolved a number of instruments to deal with international relations, trade and security, meant that it became a significant player in China's relations with the region. China's attitude towards ASEAN had been changing since the early 1980s, from ideological condemnation to pragmatic acceptance to 'friendship and cooperation'. At its own request, the PRC became one of ASEAN's 'dialogue partners' and a member of the ASEAN Regional Forum (ARF) for the discussion of security issues. In doing so, China went some way towards committing itself to dealing with Southeast Asia in the 'ASEAN way'.

The 'ASEAN way' refers to the form and principles of interaction between states developed by members of ASEAN since the founding of the organisation. As the preferred way of conducting relations between states, it is characterised by informality, the non-confrontational search for consensus through consultation, sensitivity to the views of others, and flexibility. This has produced what one commentator has called a 'regional security culture'[14] that both rests on widely held traditional Southeast Asian cultural values (including a sense of belonging together and respect for seniority), and reflects the 'process of interaction' that has grown up in ASEAN. That the 'ASEAN way' became generally accepted owed much to Indonesian leadership and to President Suharto's Javanese values and style. The 'five principles of peaceful coexistence' were enshrined as the basis for consensus (which does not necessarily mean unanimity), between participants in a region confronted far more than Europe by the need to manage diversity.

ASEAN has been reluctant to move towards formulating a common position on either international relations or regional security, however. There are various reasons for this. One is that this would seem to be too limiting and inflexible. Several states within ASEAN still face bilateral tensions, which must be bilaterally resolved. A more important reason is ASEAN's reluctance to antagonise Beijing by presenting a common front that could be construed as an alliance to contain or 'constrain' China.[15] ASEAN policy is to 'engage' China by involving it in as many international and regional 'dialogues' as possible. In a number of these (the Asia–Pacific Economic Cooperation [APEC] forum and ARF are examples), ASEAN speaks with a single voice. Even in bilateral discussions involving ASEAN member states, there is now a multilateral element present. How China conducts its bilateral relations with each Southeast Asian state, therefore, influences, to a much greater degree than previously, its relations with others. There is no better example of the implications of this than the way in which conflicting claims to the islands of the South China Sea impact on China–Southeast Asia relations.

The South China Sea

China claims two principal groups of islands in the South China Sea, the Paracel (Xisha) islands and the Spratly (Nansha) islands. While the former are entirely in Chinese hands, though also claimed by Vietnam, the latter are only partially occupied by the PRC. Vietnam, Malaysia, the Philippines and even Taiwan occupy one or more of the Spratlys. In fact, claims by ASEAN member states overlap each other as well as the comprehensive PRC claim.

The Paracel islands lie south of Hainan, an equal distance off the Vietnamese coast. Some were seized by the PRC from the Republic of (South) Vietnam in 1956, and the rest in 1974 when China apparently feared a unified Vietnam might allow a Soviet presence there. On neither occasion did Hanoi protest, though China's actions amounted to the forcible annexation of territory occupied by Vietnam. In fact, until 1974, Vietnam apparently recognised China's claim to both archipelagos. Only when relations broke down over Cambodia did Hanoi formally claim both island groups. For China, however, possession of the Paracels is a fait accompli and there is nothing to discuss. The boundary agreement signed between China and Vietnam in 2000 covered only the land frontier and territorial waters in the Gulf of

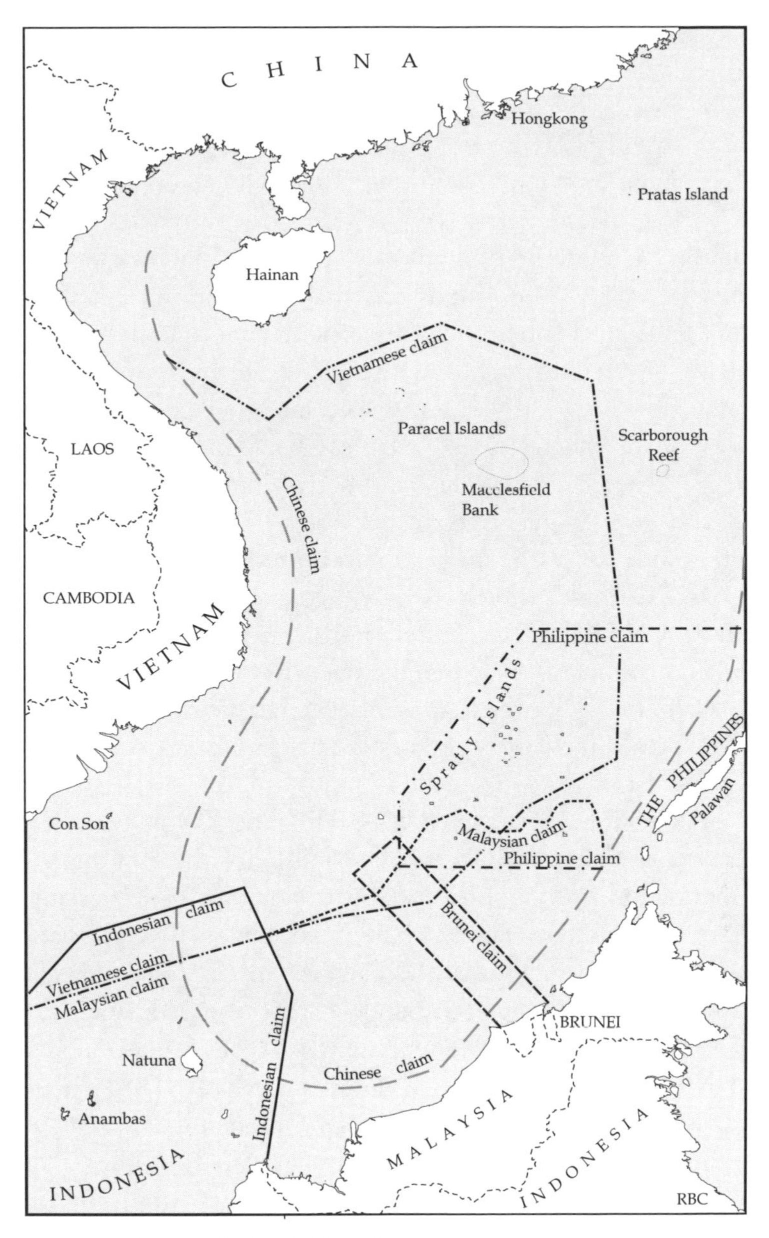

Territorial claims in the South China Sea.

Hainan. Sovereignty over the Paracels remains an issue, but between China and Vietnam only: it does not impinge on China–ASEAN relations in the way the Spratlys do.

The Spratly Islands present an altogether different and far more complex situation. The group lies 1000 kilometers from Hainan (though closer to the Paracels), but reach to within a 100 kilometres of Palawan Island in the Philippines. Geographically they form part of Southeast Asia. All the islands are small and barren, and the many reefs are submerged at high tide. Their significance lies in their natural resources (oil and fishing), and their strategic location. As China's economy grew in the 1990s, and it became a net importer of energy, exploitation of the oil reserves believed to exist under the South China Sea became increasingly attractive. Control of the Spratlys would also give China strategic control over major shipping lanes, though Beijing has stated it would never interfere with these. It would also project Chinese power very much closer to Southeast Asia.

Both China and Vietnam claim the entire group on grounds of 'historic use', primarily by fishermen over the centuries. The PRC laid formal claim to the Spratly islands in 1951, but did not move to occupy any. Then only the largest island in the group was occupied, by a Nationalist Chinese garrison. Philippines interest in the islands also dates back to the 1950s. In 1970–71 Filipino troops occupied five islands and even tried unsuccessfully to dislodge the Taiwanese garrison. Manila did not lay formal claim to any part of the group until 1978, however, after Hanoi, in 1975, occupied several islands in response to Chinese seizure of the Paracels. In 1979 Malaysia claimed a number of southern Spratly islands as part of its continental shelf, and later occupied three of these. Finally, in 1988, Brunei claimed one island lying within its Exclusive Economic Zone. Throughout this period, Vietnam was allied to the Soviet Union and so was an enemy of Beijing, while the ASEAN states were treated as allies. This led China vigorously to denounce Vietnamese occupation, but to offer only mild protests in response to the ASEAN claims.

China moved cautiously in backing its own claim to the Spratlys, first consolidating the Paracels as a strong naval and air base. In the early 1980s, China began a program of aerial surveys and naval patrols of the Spratlys. Not until 1987 did China establish its first permanent presence, on an artificial island constructed on a reef normally submerged at high tide. Vietnam protested and sent more troops to occupy other reefs and shoals. So too did the Philippines. In March 1988, an armed clash occurred when a Vietnamese naval force attempted to prevent Chinese troops from establishing a presence on Johnson Reef. By the early 1990s China was in possession of nine islands, compared to twenty-one for Vietnam. In February 1992, the PRC National People's Congress passed a law officially incorporating the entire archipelago as Chinese territory. At the same time China accepted the ASEAN position that force should not be used to resolve the sovereignty issue. There the matter rested until, in 1995, Filipino fishermen discovered that China had erected structures on Mischief Reef in the area claimed by Manila. The following year two shooting incidents occurred between Chinese and Philippines vessels. Beijing also alarmed Jakarta in 1995 by publishing a map showing Indonesia's Natuna gas field lying partly within China's claimed South China Sea territory. Indonesia was later reassured on this point, and in 1996 China ratified the UN Convention on the Law of the Sea (whose provisions it agreed to accept as a basis for further negotiations).

China has been reluctant to pursue a multilateral solution to the Spratlys problem, but the ASEAN countries have also failed to resolve their own overlapping claims. Though China has taken part in a series of multilateral workshops on the Spratlys, hosted by Indonesia, these have made little progress. Beijing is clearly more comfortable dealing with claimants bilaterally, and has proposed resource-sharing projects on this basis. Joint scientific research has also been suggested. ASEAN, by contrast, has preferred the security of numbers, and has attempted to internationalise the issue by raising it at ASEAN Ministerial Meetings and with Dialogue Partners.

In China's view, occupations of Spratly islands by other countries constitute provocative attempts to encroach on Chinese territory. Given the humiliation of previous loss of territory to European powers and Japan, not to mention Taiwan, this is a highly sensitive issue with domestic political implications. Arguably, therefore, China's response has been measured and restrained. It has asserted its rights by establishing a presence only on unoccupied reefs, and has not attempted to seize any island or reef from another claimant by force. This restraint has been designed to preserve a peaceful regional environment for economic development, but only by shelving the sovereignty question. With respect to sovereignty, Beijing's restraint can be interpreted in two ways: either as establishing a basis of trust on which to negotiate a settlement of rival claims; or as a temporary strategem to buy time for China to pursue its military modernisation program, with a view to seizing the remaining islands from a position of strength once it is in a position to do so.

As China has shown no inclination to pursue the former path, ASEAN countries fear the latter. How likely is this? Here several factors must be considered. The first set is internal and political, including inter-service rivalry in the People's Liberation Armed Forces (the Navy would have a stronger voice if it were responsible for capturing and defending the Spratlys), and inter-factional differences within the CCP (which might lead one to play the nationalist card). China is increasingly turning to nationalism to fill the ideological vacuum left as communism becomes irrelevant, and that is a worry for the region. Increasing population and environmental degradation may also impact on China's Spratly policy. Beijing needs new energy resources if it is to raise living standards and expand the economy. Then there are external factors. These include unilateral moves by claimant states to exploit resources that the Chinese believe are rightfully theirs, or direct interference by a major power (the US, or possibly Japan). In the meantime, the major factor preserving the status quo remains the American military presence.

If nothing is done to resolve the sovereignty issue, time will favour China. The Spratlys obviously fit into China's long-term plans to exert if not regional hegemony (which Beijing vigorously denies), then at least preponderant political influence, which amounts to much the same thing. South China Sea resources can contribute significantly to China's economic development; their distance from the Chinese mainland will stimulate China's naval capability to defend its territory; and this naval power projection plus the islands' strategic position will translate into strategic advantage vis-à-vis Southeast Asia. In all three ways the Spratlys would contribute to China's national goal of great power status. In the longer term, the US or Japan might prefer to settle for freedom of the seas rather than risk confrontation over the Spratlys, especially if China had already peacefully reabsorbed Taiwan. Under these circumstances, the chances of ASEAN countries holding onto their Spratlys claims would seem slim.

Patterns of interaction

From an historical perspective, certain patterns recur in relations between China and the countries of Southeast Asia. To begin with, in this longer perspective, despite the abrupt swings in Chinese foreign policy since the founding of the PRC, China has never lost sight of key strategic goals. While means have been influenced by ideology, internal politics (particularly during the Cultural Revolution), and the global balance of power as viewed from Beijing, ends have remained remarkably steady, not just for the life of the PRC, but reaching back to the Qing dynasty.

These ends are simply stated: China is determined to regain its 'rightful' place as a global great power, and to be recognised, respected and deferred to as such in the affairs of the world. To gain great power status, China sees it as essential to reunify its national territory, modernise and develop its economy, and build a powerful military.

Moreover, world standing necessarily entails exerting regional influence. In addition, China seeks to shape a world order that would better promote its national interests and standing. Such an order, in Beijing's view, would be more fair and just than the capitalist world order dominated by the United States, since it would promote peace, harmony and mutual respect in place of the contradictions the Chinese detect in global capitalism. China would not stand alone at the apex of this new world order, but it would, at the very least, be one of a handful of great powers responsible for maintaining it.

The means of achieving these ends have been difficult to decide upon. Like all revolutionary regimes, the PRC was in a hurry. Buoyed by ideological belief in the superiority of a socialist mode of production, it attempted first to 'bypass' capitalism in the disastrous Great Leap Forward. When this did not work, Maoist voluntaristic politics took the place of economics as the basis for an expansion of Chinese power through revolutionary means. At each stage, China sought status as the leader of one group of nations (or revolutionary movements) or another, while at the same time seeking to play in the superpower league of the US and USSR. What Beijing lacked, however, was power commensurate with its ambitions.

The newly independent countries of Southeast Asia were faced with the unenviable task of dealing with an erratic China. While some (Thailand, Burma) drew upon historically grounded international relations cultures to respond to China, if in different ways, for others (Indonesia, Malaysia) relations with China contributed to shaping newly evolving strategic and international relations cultures. For all, China was a threatening and disruptive presence, to be placated or kept at arm's length.

In the 1980s consensus developed among China's political elite on the need to lay a firmer foundation for Chinese claims to great power status. This realisation was forced on China both by the failure of Maoist policies and by the spiralling pace of scientific and technological change. China needed to modernise, through the application of science and technology to its economy, both industry and agriculture, and to its military capability. Of the sources of social power, China came to prioritise economic over ideological power. Political power still remained important, however, in Beijing's dealings with neighbouring states, backed as it increasingly was by a modernising military.

For China to develop economically required foreign investment, transfer of technology, and open markets for trade. In other words, China needed a peaceful and stable international environment, particularly in its own region, as a prerequisite for modernisation. Chinese foreign policy in the 1990s sought to create such an environment, by reassuring Southeast Asian countries that Beijing would no longer support armed insurgencies and would not pursue its claims to the Spratlys by force. Prioritising economics, however, reinforced links between the PRC and overseas Chinese. It was overwhelmingly overseas Chinese capital that found its way from Southeast Asia to China, while much of burgeoning regional trade was also in overseas Chinese hands. For some Southeast Asians the readiness of overseas Chinese to invest in China renewed doubts about their loyalty to their countries of residence.

More worrying, however, were the implications of China's long-term intention to achieve great power status. Southeast Asian countries went out of their way not to criticise or antagonise China. Engagement in the ASEAN way replaced balance-of-power thinking as the public face, at least, of the Southeast Asian relationship with China. Countries such as Vietnam, for all its distrust of China, swallowed their pride and reverted to traditional methods of dealing with Beijing. Deference to status replaced confrontation. At the same time, a new counterweight was provided through ASEAN solidarity. This placed China in something of a dilemma, as Beijing's preference for bilateral diplomacy came up against its increasing participation in multilateral forums also deemed necessary for world leadership. Whether such participation would 'socialise' China into becoming a good international citizen remained, however, an open question.

10
FUTURE DIRECTIONS

The rise of China and how to accommodate this will be one of the major international relations challenges of the twenty-first century. Whether or not this can be achieved peacefully is of particular importance for China's neighbours, and none more so than for the countries of Southeast Asia. Any attempt to foresee events is fraught with uncertainty. All we can do is sketch possible alternative scenarios, and suggest how these might play out given strategic interests, culturally embedded values and historical precedent. Of course, foreign policy decisions are made in response to contingent situations, both external due to the actions of other powers and internal in relation to the play of political forces. They are, in this sense, tactical. But behind these tactical responses lie broad strategic goals conceived in the context of the international relations and strategic cultures of the states in question. Not all tactical decisions will advance long-term strategic goals. But the two are connected, nonetheless, especially in the case of China, given its determination to regain great power status.

The China–Southeast Asia relationship is crucially important for both sides. For the nations of Southeast Asia, relations with China outweigh those with any other power, with the present exception of the United States. Relations with Southeast Asia would appear to be less significant for China, given Beijing's global great power ambitions, but in view of China's present economic and military weakness, its international standing will rest, to a large extent, on its regional influence. For the geopolitical reality is that China's influence beyond its frontiers is limited by large powers in three directions: to the east by Japan, to the north by Russia, and to the west by India. All historically have resisted any form of Chinese political influence. Traditionally, Chinese influence was greatest along the Silk Road into Central Asia and in Southeast Asia. But any influence Beijing hopes to exert among the Central Asian republics, formed from the breakup of the Soviet Union, will face strong competition from both Russia and political Islam. Moreover, Xinjiang hardly provides an ideal base from which to project Chinese influence, any more than Tibet does for the South Asian sub-continent.

The historic shift in economic importance from the Silk Road to maritime trade took place from the Tang through the Song dynasties. Thereafter Central Asia was usually more significant in terms of security than trade. The arrival of the West both intensified this economic shift, which today is overwhelming, and redirected the focus of China's security concerns. For now and into the future, the coastal provinces of central and southern China are where the country's economic development is, and will be, focused, not Xinjiang. Even given competition from the US and Japan, Southeast Asia offers far more inviting opportunities for Chinese political and economic ambitions than does Central Asia. The point I am making is simply that if China seeks to project political power beyond its borders, Southeast Asia is the prime target. For centuries the region has been seen by China as its 'natural' sphere of influence, and it still is, however unpalatable this might be to regional powers.

China: strategic goals and international relations culture

China has learned much from its history, and the rest of the world should too. Despite the pressures placed on China in the nineteenth century, the PRC remains the last great empire, in that it rules over subject non-Chinese peoples with ancient cultures of their own. In some areas these subject peoples still constitute a majority (in Tibet and Xinjiang); in others they are now a minority (Inner Mongolia and Yunnan). As in the past, it is state policy to increase Han Chinese settlement in all these nominally autonomous areas to ensure they remain forever Chinese. China's policy in the present-day context should be seen for what it is: a continuation of the means traditionally used to extend Chinese imperial rule through migration and administrative controls. In this sense Chinese policy carries with it expansionist implications.

The corollary to China's historical expansionism is that China has been remarkably reluctant to surrender any territory gained. Successive Chinese dynasties tried to reconquer Vietnam, the only formerly directly administered territory in Southeast Asia 'lost' to the Chinese empire. Chinese of all political persuasions are quite unsympathetic to Tibetan aspirations for independence, while the more recent 'loss' of (Outer) Mongolia and the Russian Far East still rankles. These two areas are probably now irretrievable, but two others are not: Taiwan and the islands of the South China Sea.

This brings us to a second historical lesson that Chinese strategic thinkers have taken very much to heart: the Chinese empire has been strongest (and thus most strategically invulnerable) when it has been united. A divided China, whether into competing empires (usually north and south), or when riven by internal disunity (as during the great rebellions of the mid-nineteenth century), was a weak China that invited humiliation and dismemberment. The importance of maintaining the territorial and political unity of China is today unquestioned by either communist or nationalist Chinese, despite often strong pressures for regional autonomy. The balance between central power and regional aspirations is something that has constantly to be negotiated, but it is negotiated within the context of the survival of the empire-state.

This historical lesson has a deep and emotional influence on the formulation of China's strategic goals and international relations culture. For China, after the return of Hong Kong and Macau, still remains divided: it is weaker than it would be if Taiwan, too, were to return to the empire-state. The importance of Taiwan in China's international relations culture bulks so large not only for historical, but also for strategic and political reasons, because of the quantum increase reunification would provide to Chinese power. The return of Taiwan would greatly benefit China's 'four modernisations'. A peaceful return would also bring with it Taiwan's considerable weapons stockpile. Geostrategically the gains would be just as great, and of greater long-term significance, for inclusion of Taiwan would advance Chinese power hundreds of kilometers east into the Pacific between Japan and Southeast Asia.

The return of Taiwan, by whatever means, would almost certainly strengthen China's determination to gain control of the islands of the South China Sea, for it would reinforce their geostrategic significance. Here the implications for Southeast Asia would be even more significant. Should Beijing refuse to compromise on its claim to sovereignty over the whole area and use its navy to seize the Spratlys, its reach into Southeast Asia would be greatly extended (always provided the US did not intervene). Vietnam would be outflanked and the island states threatened. The strains placed on ASEAN would be immense, and China's relations with the region would be changed forever. Not surprisingly, therefore, China's Spratly claims are seen in the region both as the latest example of Chinese expansionism, and as the litmus test of China's long-term intentions towards Southeast Asia.

China's intentions, of course, reflect its strategic goals. Two goals closely linked to that of reunification are the preservation of national security across all frontiers, and international status enhancement. Traditionally, China adopted a dual policy to protect the Chinese heartland combining the carrot of economic opportunity with the stick of forward defence. Central Asian kingdoms were alternatively bribed by gifts and access to trade under cover of the tribute system, and subjected to punishing raids and military occupation. Southeast Asian rulers were coopted into acting as 'pacification commissioners' to keep the peace along ill-defined frontiers. Mao's defence policy combined the protection of friendly (North Korea, North Vietnam) or neutral (Burma, Laos) buffer states to keep imperialist powers at a distance, combined with forward defence when necessary (as in Korea). More recently, the PRC has adopted a defence strategy aimed at maintaining China's security through a combination of frontier defence and limited force projection by smaller, more professional armed forces. Though Beijing works hard to ensure a ring of friendly powers along its frontiers through diplomatic overtures and economic incentives, forward defence still remains an option. The Yongle emperor reminded certain vassals of the fate of the Vietnamese emperor, Ho Quy Ly, but Beijing hardly needs to remind the Lao or Burmese of the 'punishment' meted out to Vietnam in 1979. As yet China does not have the means to project military power into those countries in Southeast Asia with which it does not share a common border, but both air and naval forces are developing force projection capabilities. In the future, therefore, China will have these means, if it wants to use them.

A constant in China's foreign policy, from the Qing to the PRC, has been the determination to enhance the country's international standing in order to wipe out the shame of the 'century of humiliation', and so restore China to its 'rightful' place in the world. The drive for status enhancement, fuelled, in the words of one Chinese political analyst, by a 'strong sense of status discrepancy', has motivated much of

Chinese foreign policy. Sheng Lijun argues that Chinese perceptions of status discrepancy have comprised four elements: between China's glorious past and less distinguished present; between China's sense of its own importance and the recognition accorded it by the world community; between China's desire to exercise political influence and its limited means of doing so; and between China's current power and influence and how it believes these will be enhanced in the future.[1] The Chinese believe they should stand at the apex of the status hierarchy of peoples (and states) that they have always taken to be the natural order of things. Status enhancement has been pursued, as we have seen, in several ways: through military means to demonstrate that China cannot be trifled with; through developing nuclear weapons; through manipulating relations with powerful states; through claiming leadership of one or another movement or group of nations (revolutionary forces, Third World countries, and so on); and through steady enhancement of Chinese power (political and economic, as well as military). Reunification (the definitive inclusion of Taiwan and the Spratlys in the empire-state) would powerfully contribute to the same goal.

In summary, China's strategic goals are to reunify the empire-state, prevent its disintegration (as happened to the Soviet Union), secure its frontiers, and enhance its international standing to the status of an undisputed 'great power'. Of course, status cannot simply be claimed; it has to be recognised by others, and that recognition must be expressed for the Chinese in appropriately deferential ways. Just as superiors are treated deferentially by inferiors in personal relationships, so, through the subtle rituals of diplomacy, can status be recognised among states.

How China's strategic goals are likely to impact on her relations with Southeast Asia depends on the great power strategic balance, and how this may change. The PRC, from its inception, encountered a bipolar world in which it first leaned to the Soviet Union, then to isolationism, then to the United States, and eventually tried to play a more independent role. The collapse of the Soviet Union, followed by the decline of Russian power, has now left the United States as the sole superpower. This is a situation that Beijing dislikes intensely, both because it places China in a subordinate position, and because the United States stands in the way of China's achievement of her strategic goals. What China would prefer is a multipolar world in which power is shared by six roughly equal great powers (the US, China, Europe, Russia, India, and Japan). Beijing believes that this is the way the world is moving, and that American power must inevitably decline in relative terms as that of other major states, or groupings of states, grows. In this scenario, the US might still remain *primus inter pares*, but it would no longer act as global hegemon.

China seeks not to replace the US as the new world leader, for this is not a practical possibility. What it does want is to be accepted as one of a handful of great powers, none inferior to another, which together would be responsible for shaping the world order. This is not a vision the US shares, or wants to move towards. Not only is US military power overwhelming, but, as it proved in the Gulf War and again in Kosovo, Washington also has the political means to bring together and lead a coalition of nations in support of its global strategy, thereby sharing the cost and avoiding imperial overstretch.[2] Added to this is the fact that the American economy monopolises the new post-industrial technology, and that the US acts as the global champion of democracy, and the array of American power—military, political, economic and ideological—is complete. Moreover, it is an array China cannot begin to match. It will take time for the 'four modernisations' to have their desired effect of increasing Chinese economic and military power. In the meantime, China is left to rely on political influence. What China now lacks, paradoxically, is any ideological claim to global leadership, for the 'restoration nationalism'[3] that has largely replaced communism as the driving inspiration behind Chinese foreign policy evokes no appeal outside China.

Not only the United States stands in the way of attainment of China's strategic goals: the country also faces enormous internal problems. Its population is still increasing; so is environmental degradation; and the pressure on land is becoming acute. A massive internal migration is underway as rural peasants seek employment and better living conditions in the cities of the eastern seaboard. Already these population movements are being felt outside China as increasing numbers of Chinese filter into northern Burma and Laos. Social turmoil in China would threaten not only to destabilise the regime, but also to spill over into Southeast Asia. This is one reason why few in Southeast Asia are critical of authoritarian central government in China (which gives a strategic twist to the Asian values debate).

China thus faces great obstacles in pursuing her strategic goals. But these goals are unlikely to change, and the Chinese are as patient as they are determined. The question is not, therefore, will China actively pursue her strategic goals, but when and how.

Three scenarios

In a recent study of China's 'grand strategy', Michael Swaine and Ashley Tellis of the Rand Corporation argue that China is currently pursuing what they term a 'calculative strategy'.[4] The key elements of this strategy are to promote a market economy in an amicable international environment in order to ensure rapid economic growth; to avoid the use of force while modernising military capability; and to expand China's international political influence, including through multilateral interaction. This is a pragmatic policy designed to lay the foundations for a strong and modern China. As long as it lasts, China is likely to be amenable in its international relations, both in its dealings with major powers and with its Southeast Asian neighbours. Thus China is ready to resolve relatively minor differences over land borders (as it has with Vietnam), while postponing decisions on sea frontiers.

In following this strategy, China remains determined to defend what it perceives as its long-term national interests, in particular its 'one China' policy in relation to Taiwan, and its sovereignty claim to the Spratly islands, both of which it intends to resolve from a position of greater strength.

What developments might derail the 'calculative strategy'? One would be internal political conflict in the event that the Chinese Communist Party is unable to deal with the problems outlined above. Another would be provocative Taiwanese moves towards independence. A third would be a change in the international environment that seriously undermined the 'calculative strategy', such as imposition of severe trade restrictions or formation of a hostile coalition of powers to contain China. But as Swaine and Tellis point out, the very success of the 'calculative strategy' carries risks.[5] Economic success may generate trade disputes internationally, or challenges to the CCP internally from a growing middle class; increasing military power, along with lack of transparency, may push smaller nations to seek US protection; the US itself may see China's success as a threat to its own global hegemony; or China may develop new strategic interests (such as control of shipping lanes) that bring it into conflict with other states.

Crucial to future Chinese foreign policy will be the role of the United States. In the post-Cold War world no power can challenge the US. Europe is an ally; so is Japan. India is fixated on South Asia. Russia is in temporary decline. In American eyes, only China looms as a likely future rival. Even so, it is ironical that most of the 'China as threat' literature comes out of the world's most powerful state. Strident voices argue that the US should prevent China's rise to power before it is too late. More moderate opinion is accommodationist, seeking ways to engage Beijing. Whatever the outcome of the American policy debate on how to deal with China, however, Washington will need allies. The American position is much stronger in Northeast Asia than in Southeast Asia, despite treaties with the Philippines and Thailand. American troops are stationed in Japan and South Korea, but nowhere in Southeast Asia. Yet if the US were to try to contain China, it would need the support of at least some Southeast Asian states. During the Second Indochina War, fought allegedly to prevent the southern thrust of Chinese communism, Washington managed to obtain the support of only two Southeast Asian states (Thailand and the Philippines). Whether the US would be more successful in the face of a more powerful and assertive China is a moot question.

If circumstances change, what might replace the present 'calculative strategy'?[6] One possibility is that China might collapse into internal chaos, and so be incapable of pursuing any coherent strategy. For Southeast Asia, this unlikely scenario would be catastrophic. Not only would Chinese foreign policy be unpredictable, but almost certainly population movements would result that would dwarf earlier Chinese migration to Southeast Asia. The tensions thus created in Southeast Asia would be politically explosive and socially divisive.

A strong China that had overcome its internal problems might, by contrast, move towards a cooperative strategy in which it would act as a responsible global citizen playing a constructive role in international forums to resolve outstanding conflicts, no longer primarily to the benefit of China (the 'calculative strategy'), but for the collective benefit of the community of nations. This rather idealistic possibility might evolve out of increased economic and multilateral political interdependence. It would be most clearly demonstrated for the nations of Southeast Asia if Beijing were to give way on its comprehensive sovereignty claim and divide up the islands and waters of the South China Sea.

A third scenario would be that China abandons the 'calculative strategy' for a more assertive one, either because its 'four modernisations' have had their desired effect and the Chinese feel they can act from a position of strength, or because Beijing is responding to what it perceives as hostile actions that threaten its national interests (see above). Essentially, a more assertive policy would see China pursue its strategic goals urgently and single-mindedly with little consideration for the interests of other states. Unification and sovereignty over all territory claimed as Chinese would be priorities, so once again for Southeast Asia the South China Sea would be the key indicator. This would seem to be the most likely scenario, *if the 'calculative strategy' is abandoned*, so what would the implications be for Southeast Asia?

To begin with, a more assertive Chinese posture towards Southeast Asia would be designed to increase China's influence in the region. For fifty years Southeast Asia has been a primary target area for Chinese foreign policy initiatives. In that time, Beijing has attempted to forge an 'axis' with Indonesia, contained Vietnamese ambitions, 'saved' Cambodia from Vietnamese domination, and developed close relations first with Burma, then Thailand, and more recently with Malaysia. China has been less successful in winning the confidence of post-Sukarno Indonesia or the Philippines. Relations with Vietnam are correct, but hardly cordial, while suspicion of longer-term Chinese intentions runs deep throughout the region.

Any considerable increase in Chinese influence in Southeast Asia could only come, however, at the expense of the US and Japan. In particular, it would require the United States to scale down its military presence in the region. This is not impossible to imagine. The reunification of Korea would obviate the need for a continuing US military presence, either in Korea or Japan (though Japan, faced with a competitive China and with few friends, might well opt to maintain its security treaty with Washington). The US has already withdrawn from continental Southeast Asia, and will not commit troops there again. US bases in the Philippines have been dismantled, and Indonesia, with pretensions to leadership of its own in the region, has never been a subservient ally, even during the Suharto era. If preceded by peaceful reunification with Taiwan, even an aggressive Chinese seizure of the islands of the South China Sea might not be opposed by a more isolationist US if the safety of shipping lanes were to be guaranteed. This is not to suggest that the US would abandon its interests in Southeast Asia entirely, just that the US, as a global power, might be prepared to make way for China as regional hegemon in Southeast Asia, even while retaining a more substantial presence in Northeast Asia. Southeast Asia, in other words, cannot rely on American power indefinitely.

Given its geographical position and regional economic interests, Japan might prove a more tenacious competitor, though it suffers certain historical disadvantages. Japan has never been prepared meekly to accept the Chinese world order. The competition that might have developed from the seventeenth century for influence in Southeast Asia was curtailed by Japanese isolationism. After the Meiji restoration of 1867, pent up Japanese national energies were channelled into rapid modernisation, the fruits of which were turned against China. Japanese aggression from 1895 to 1945 sowed seeds of deep distrust and resentment, not just in China, but throughout Southeast Asia. Fear of the resurgence of Japanese militarism, and the ugly side of Japanese nationalism, not to mention a lack of cultural affinity and Japanese racial arrogance, present barriers to the extension of Japanese influence in Southeast Asia. In view of these difficulties, Japan may well be content to rest its power on its global economic interests rather than attempt to compete politically with China in Southeast Asia. Even so, Japanese investment in, and aid to the region would be likely to continue as a welcome economic counterweight to China.

How might Southeast Asian nations respond to a more assertive China? Any answer to this question must take account of the historical and cultural context of Chinese–Southeast Asian relations. One point to note is that as the history of the relationship has shown, Southeast Asian kingdoms faced with the preponderance of Chinese power never concluded alliances to 'balance' it. Balance-of-power thinking that comes so naturally to Western international relations analysts[7] was never the way Southeast Asian kingdoms traditionally dealt with China. Only in the last fifty years, as a result of Western dominance in the region, have balance-of-power coalitions been constructed—and then Southeast Asian nations proved remarkably reluctant to join. It is significant that the ASEAN states are today just as opposed to any balance-of-power coalition that could be construed as aimed at China.

As we have seen, the kingdoms of Southeast Asia dealt with China on a bilateral basis through the tributary system. In so doing, they forged bilateral relations regimes not on the basis of similar world-views (except for Vietnam), but through accommodation of the Chinese world order, given key compatibilities and the moral obligations to which both sides were committed. China demanded recognition of both its status and its security interests (keeping peace on its frontiers) in return for trading privileges and political legitimisation (investiture). When Chinese armies marched into Southeast Asia against powerful kingdoms like Vietnam and Burma, however, whether to 'punish' or extend imperial frontiers, they encountered concerted resistance. Once Chinese armies were defeated, the Vietnamese and Burmese well understood that the only way to ensure their future security was to re-establish the tributary bilateral relations regime in recognition, if only symbolically, of China's superiority. A similar pattern of events marked the normalisation of Vietnamese relations with China a decade after their border war of 1979, as both Vietnamese and Chinese with their long historical memories were well aware.

The states of mainland Southeast Asia are most unlikely to be lured into a balance-of-power coalition orchestrated by Washington to contain China, as they well know the US would be most reluctant to commit troops to defend them. They must deal with China, therefore, in their own way. That way varies from ready alliance with the new regional hegemon in the case of Thailand, to the dour suspicion and tough self-reliance of Vietnam, from the opportunist realism of Burma to the weak dependency of Cambodia and Laos. The common element in all mainland Southeast Asian bilateral relations regimes with China, however, is that status recognition is the price of security.

History indicates that China is unlikely to invade mainland Southeast Asian countries that accord China de facto great power status, and respect China's security interests, as independent Burma consistently has done. The obverse face of status recognition is Chinese obligation to apply certain principles of international relations (non-intervention, fair economic exchange, political support for ruling regimes). It was not always thus during the revolutionary phase of China's relations with Southeast Asia. But that was, historically, something of an anomaly and Beijing has become more conservative and predictable—which is to say, more traditional—in its relations with its neighbours.

Maritime Southeast Asia (including the Malay peninsula) poses a much greater barrier to the extension of Chinese influence, for the historical bilateral relations regimes with China were much less developed. Relations depended far more than for continental states on the commercial activities of Malay merchants and Chinese migrants who had no official standing in their country of origin. It is interesting that in the map published in Beijing in 1954 in a history of modern China, Sulu was the only island territory in maritime Southeast Asia shown as formerly Chinese. None of the rest of the Philippines, nor Indonesia, were so designated (though the Malay peninsular was). Apparently the tributary relations of port principalities on Java and other islands with the Qing dynasty counted as qualitatively less binding, perhaps in the sense that they did not represent substantial polities with historical continuity through to modern independent states. The Chinese subsequently repudiated this map, but it is significant nonetheless for the distinction it drew between continental and maritime Southeast Asia.

Of all the countries of Southeast Asia, the one least likely to accept Chinese hegemony is Indonesia. No bilateral relations regime has historically linked Indonesia and China. The great inland kingdoms of Java never really acknowledged Chinese suzerainty: tributary missions to China were never more than for the purpose of trade. China's relations, as we have seen, were with various trading ports throughout the archipelago over which inland kingdoms such as Mataram exercised, at best, limited control. Trade in the hands of both Muslim and Chinese merchants took precedence over diplomacy in shaping the relationship with successive Chinese dynasties. Thus independent Indonesia could look back on no long historical kingdom-to-empire bilateral relations regime of the kind developed between China and Vietnam, or Thailand, or Burma. Even less could the Philippines, whose significant trade relations with China (apart from Sulu) post-date the arrival of the Spanish and were conducted under their auspices.

The relationship between Indonesia and China has indeed been 'troubled',[8] for several reasons. One is that nowhere else in Southeast Asia has the problem of overseas Chinese proved so prickly. This is because, for reasons of past policy and religious differences, nowhere else (with the exception of Malaysia) has the Chinese community been so poorly assimilated. Another reason is that Indonesia, despite its continuing focus on internal security, has seen itself as the natural leader in the region, and has been reluctant to allow room for China. A third reason is that Indonesia sees itself as an Islamic state and, as such, looks west to the great centres of the Islamic world more readily than it looks north to China. No other Southeast Asian nation, apart from the Philippines, has had its international relations culture less shaped historically by the need to accommodate China. There has, therefore, been correspondingly less historical basis on which to build a mutually acceptable Indonesia–China bilateral relations regime.

Given these factors, it would be in China's interests if Indonesia split into smaller polities more easily dominated by the PRC. This was the more prevalent pattern historically. Of course, China is not going to encourage the break-up of Indonesia: it would just not be too concerned if this happened. This is not the case for ASEAN, for which a strong and unified Indonesia provides a much more substantial counterweight to China than would a plethora of small states. Nor would it be in the interests of the West.

The Philippines also lacks a deep historical relationship with China, though its Chinese community is better assimilated than in Indonesia. Filipinos have looked east to America and west to Europe more than north to China in constructing their international relations culture. The Philippines is less sure of its position in Southeast Asia than is Indonesia, more ready to take offence and respond in a confrontational way to threatening situations, as the Mischief Reef incident illustrated. The Philippines–China bilateral relations regime remains, as a result of these factors, somewhat shallow and undeveloped.

As for Malaysia and Singapore, both historically formed part of the Malay trading world. Port cities on the Malay peninsula and Borneo have a long tradition of economic and political relations with China (Melaka, Brunei), but like Indonesia, these impinge little on the modern Sino–Malaysian bilateral relations regime. The exceptionally high proportion of Chinese in the population of Malaysia, and the fact that Singapore is majority Chinese, has injected an understandable ambiguity into their relations with China. Both claim to enjoy close relations with the PRC, while being acutely aware of possible adverse implications, either internally (Malaysia) or externally (Singapore).

Both prior to falling under European colonial domination and as independent states, the island nations of Southeast Asia have developed very different bilateral relations regimes with China to those of mainland Southeast Asian nations.[9] This has been due to a combination of geography and worldview (Muslim or Christian). The question is, therefore, would the maritime states be more ready to oppose Chinese regional hegemony? Would they, in the face of a more assertive China, even join an American-led balance-of-power alliance lying off the East Asian continent, comprising the US, Japan, Taiwan, the Philippines, Indonesia and Australia? Here another factor enters the equation: the Association of Southeast Asian Nations.

China and ASEAN

The division that exists between continental and maritime states, in the place China occupies in their international relations, has not prevented consensus so far on one point: balance-of-power containment of China is not the way to go. Far better to engage China in as many ways as possible, to build a set of common interests that will bind the PRC to the region. In large part this consensus has been arrived at through 'the ASEAN way' of non-confrontational consultation and discussion.[10] ASEAN has encouraged not just exchanges of views between member states that have enhanced mutual understanding of differing international relations cultures, but has also developed a sense of solidarity and common identity vis-à-vis outside powers, China included. But would this solidarity hold up in the face of an assertive China and an exigent United States?

It is significant that what forged a degree of solidarity between the original ASEAN five was not, as in the case of the European Union, the need to overcome a legacy of war between member states, but rather the need to confront a sudden external threat, and to agree on a role for China in what was a regional crisis. The external threat was to Thailand in the form of aggressive Indochinese communism. Thailand, as the front-line state, was much more eager to turn to China for support than was Indonesia, which then had no diplomatic relations with Beijing. Agreement came out of deliberations that drew upon the Indonesian concepts of consultation and consensus. The concerted policy agreed upon was to force the withdrawal of Vietnamese forces and restore the neutrality of Cambodia by allowing China an essential role in funnelling support to the despised Khmer Rouge via Thailand.

There are two things to note about the precedent set in ASEAN's response to the Third Indochina War for future relations with China. The first is that if the primacy given to the strategic needs of a frontline state is transferred to an expanded ASEAN in conflict with China, this would presumably commit ASEAN to the defence of Vietnam, Laos and Burma. It is unlikely, however, that ASEAN would, or could, respond to a threat from China to any of these three countries, yet failure to act would place both ASEAN's credibility and solidarity in question. The second point is that the consensus approach of ASEAN presents both a weakness and a strength in dealing with any crisis involving China. Though consensus for a concerted policy would make it more compelling, this will always be more difficult to achieve with ten than with six members. Consensus would confront China with a unified response that could severely embarrass Beijing, but China could exploit differences within ASEAN to divide members and prevent consensus. In an extreme situation, ASEAN could even disintegrate.

A common criticism of ASEAN is that it has failed to develop the institutional basis for a unified regional grouping of states, in the way that the European Union has. Nor is there any organisation to promote ASEAN security, apart from the amorphous ASEAN Regional Forum. Some of this, usually Western, criticism carries with it an edge of irritation: why can't Southeast Asians be more like Europeans? But there are good reasons for the ASEAN approach. How to accommodate the growing power of China will be the most important challenge ASEAN will face into the new millennium. 'Accommodation' is the key word, for given the strategic vulnerability and very different international relations cultures of the mainland Southeast Asian states, any attempt to contain, or even 'constrain', China would almost certainly divide ASEAN.

The ASEAN ten will do all in their power not to provoke China. What they want is to both slow and ease the changing power balance. They want the United States to remain a powerful presence, serving as a balancing force in the regional power equation, and have made this known; but they do not want to be part of any balance-of-power coalition. At the same time, they also want to make room for China. No

ASEAN state wants to be drawn into a US confrontation with China (for example, over Taiwan), so all reject any formal alliance. There is widespread agreement over a continuing US presence, though about Japan, even as a US ally, there is more ambivalence. Most ASEAN states would not be comfortable with either a militarily powerful or politically aggressive Japan, but they do want Japan to remain a major economic partner to offset growing Chinese economic penetration and competition.

For China, dealing with ASEAN as a group also presents challenges. Beijing has always preferred bilateral to multilateral relations. From at first refusing to deal with ASEAN, however, China has become an active Dialogue Partner. Partly this was to advance Chinese interests, but China also wants to encourage ASEAN not to turn to outside powers. As a Chinese goal remains a reduction in the US presence and US influence, China does not want to see the US return to bases in the Philippines, or anywhere else in the region.

To reiterate, however, the most important test of Chinese–ASEAN relations is what happens in the South China Sea. Possession of all the disputed islands by China would secure Beijing a strategic bridgehead into Southeast Asia, but any move to take possession would strengthen the alliance between continental (Vietnam) and maritime (the Philippines, Malaysia) states, and so risk armed conflict with a unified ASEAN, not to mention the United States. China's strategy has been to make maximum sovereignty claims, and then to place the whole question of sovereignty on hold while calling for joint resource development. This is a clever ploy. A peaceful and reasonable China pursuing its 'four modernisations' presents no immediate threat. In the longer term, when Beijing has had time to build its economic and military power, the balance of advantage will surely change.

Logically for China, reunification with Taiwan should precede any move in the South China Sea. This may also be a reason why the Spratlys are on hold. But this does not mean that China has abandoned its expansionist ambitions, and the possibility of greatly augmenting Chinese influence in Southeast Asia that possession of the Spratlys would offer. Only a negotiated settlement that met some of the claims of Southeast Asian nations would indicate that Beijing had a more benign agenda. What might a negotiated settlement offer China, given that the PRC would have to surrender part of the archipelago? The primary benefit would come from the reassurance it would give to Southeast Asian nations that China really did want peaceful and friendly relations. ASEAN states would be grateful, and ready to accommodate China in other ways. They would treat China with due deference as the regional great power. But there would be more. China would still stand to gain control of a good part of the South China Sea and its resources. A settlement would still project Chinese power far to the south and place China in a stronger strategic position. So China would still end up exerting greater influence in the region.

Would these benefits, substantial as they are, be enough for Beijing? Or is China determined to become the undisputed regional hegemon in its pursuit of global great power status? If so, China will reject all ASEAN attempts to negotiate a settlement of the South China Sea and, instead, pursue its long-term strategic goals, with all that entails for the countries of Southeast Asia.

Conclusion

In summary, the situation appears as follows. Changes are underway in the strategic balance and security environment in Southeast Asia as China's power increases. To this both the US and Japan must respond, as well as regional states. The US and Japan may oppose the rise of China, or make way for it. But whatever the two major powers do, continental Southeast Asian states will never be part of a balance-of-power coalition to contain China; and maritime states will be reluctant to join for fear of dividing ASEAN. Southeast Asian states will together prefer accommodation with China, and in doing so, will seek appropriate ways to evolve both their bilateral and combined multilateral relations regimes. For this they will naturally draw on their own histories and international relations cultures. Thus, as China assumes its former preponderant position in Asia, history and culture are likely to become more important, not less, in the evolving relationship between China and Southeast Asia.

How would an aggressively hegemonistic China affect the independence and security of Southeast Asia? There is no denying that, historically, China has been expansionist, to the south as well as to the north and west. But although Southeast Asian kingdoms were at times invaded, the tributary relationship was not unduly burdensome. Tributary states remained independent, and their security was guaranteed by status recognition and the acceptance of mutual moral obligations. Obviously no new tributary relationship is about to evolve, and China will never be in a position to reimpose its own world order. But certain elements central to historical bilateral relations regimes are likely to carry over. These include Chinese respect for the independence and territorial integrity of Southeast Asian nations in return for tacit acceptance of de facto Chinese regional hegemony. No kowtow will be performed, but Southeast Asia leaders are adept at polite, some might say deferential, diplomacy, and they understand how to deal with the Chinese.

The alternative to this kind of culturally and historically grounded accommodation would be for ASEAN to form its own NATO-like security organisation. But this would be relatively powerless unless it included alliance with a great power—and that would be seen by Beijing as directed against China. Tensions would increase as China stepped up pressure on selected states, to the point where disintegration of ASEAN would be a likely outcome. So despite the frustrations of Western security analysts who argue for a more robust security framework for ASEAN, even in the face of an increasingly powerful and assertive China, this is unlikely to happen.

This leaves open the fate of the islands of the South China Sea. An assertive China would certainly want control of the Spratlys, but is there anything ASEAN could do to prevent that happening? Solidarity would not be enough once China has a blue water navy, even given ASEAN's combined military resources. Besides, ASEAN states would have to sort out their own overlapping claims in order to present a common front to Beijing. Only the United States could stand in the way of a determined Chinese invasion of islands garrisoned by ASEAN states. But the Spratlys are not Taiwan, and the US might be reluctant to risk war for a few atolls. The political fallout might deter Beijing, though it hardly did during the Maoist period. The only policy for Southeast Asian states, therefore, would appear to be to continue to engage China while at the same time quietly encouraging a continued US presence without committing themselves to any balance-of-power alliance. It is a fine line to hew in the face of China's determined drive for status recognition and American arrogance of power, and it may still not be enough to save the Spratlys.

In the longer term, the countries of Southeast Asia must face the challenge of developing bilateral relations regimes with China that both protect their own interests and security and accommodate those of China, as the de facto regional hegemon and great power. It would hardly be surprising if in doing so they draw upon the cultural presuppositions and historical precedents that, as I have shown, lie buried deep within their respective international relations cultures.

NOTES

Chapter 1 Introduction

1. There is considerable debate about how relations between states should be understood. For a discussion of opposing views, see Robert Powell, 'Anarchy in international relations theory: the neorealist–neoliberal debate', *International Organization*, vol. 48, 1994, pp. 313–44.
2. This is well demonstrated in Stephen J. Morris, *Why Vietnam Invaded Cambodia: Political Culture and the Causes of War*, Stanford University Press, Stanford, Calif., 1999.
3. That states have different attitudes to the use of military force is recognised in the notion of 'strategic culture', defined as '*a distinctive and lasting set of beliefs, values and habits regarding the threat and use of force, which have their roots in such fundamental influences as geopolitical setting, history and political culture*'. Ken Booth and Russel Trood, eds, *Strategic Culture in the Asia-Pacific Region*, Macmillan, London, 1999, p. 8 (italics in original). For a useful discussion of different views on 'strategic culture', see Alastair Iain Johnston, 'Thinking about strategic culture', *International Security* vol. 19, 1995, pp. 32–64; and Colin S. Gray, 'Strategic culture as context: the first generation of theory strikes back', *Review of International Studies*, vol. 25, 1999, pp. 49–69.
4. A regime in international relations comprises agreed upon principles, norms, rules and procedures that form the basis for expected and acceptable state behaviour. States cooperate in regimes not primarily because they will be punished in some way for not doing so, but because it is in their interests that other states should accept the same principles, norms and obligations. See, for

example, Stephen Krasner, ed., *International Regimes*, Cornell University Press, Ithaca, NY, 1983; Volker Ritter, ed., *Regime Theory and International Relations*, Clarendon Press, Oxford, 1993; Marc A. Levy, Oran R. Young and Michael Zum, 'The study of international regimes', *European Journal of International Relations*, vol. 1, 1995, pp. 267–330.

Chapter 2 The Chinese view of the world

1. The translation is from Simon Leys, *The Analects of Confucius*, W. W. Norton and Co., New York, 1997, p. 60.
2. On Confucian qualities, see David L. Hall and Roger T. Ames, *Thinking Through Confucius*, State University Press of New York, New York, 1987.
3. Ralph Sawyer, *The Seven Military Classics of Ancient China*, Westview, Boulder, Colo., 1993.
4. The best study is Alastair Johnston's penetrating analysis of Chinese strategic culture during the Ming dynasty. Alastair Iain Johnston, *Cultural Realism: Strategic Culture and Grand Strategy in Chinese History*, Princeton University Press, Princeton, NJ, 1995.
5. Wang Gungwu, 'Early Ming relations with Southeast Asia: a background essay' in *The Chinese World Order: Traditional China's Foreign Relations*, ed. John King Fairbank, Harvard University Press, Cambridge, Mass., 1968, p. 43.
6. Aihe Wang, *Cosmology and Political Culture in Early China*, Cambridge University Press, Cambridge, 2000, especially chapter 5.
7. YüYing-Shih, 'Han foreign relations' in *The Cambridge History of China*, eds Denis Twitchett and John K. Fairbank, vol. 1, pp. 383–405.
8. ibid, pp. 379–80. See also Richard J. Smith, *Chinese Maps: Images of 'All Under Heaven'*, Oxford University Press, Hong Kong, 1996, pp. 23–4.

Chapter 3 Early relations

1. Claude Jacques, '"Funan", "Zhenla": The reality concealed by these Chinese views of Indochina' in *Early South East Asia: Essays in Archaeology, History and Historical Geography*, eds R. B. Smith and W. Watson, Oxford University Press, New York, 1979, pp. 371–9.
2. O. W. Wolters, *History, Culture, and Region in Southeast Asian Perspectives*, revised edition, Cornell University Southeast Program Publications, Ithaca, NY, 1999, pp. 18–21.
3. Kautilya's *Arthaśāstra*, translated by R. Shamasastry, 7th edn, Mysore Printing and Publishing, Mysore, 1951, p. 290.
4. Wang Gungwu, *The Nanhai Trade: The Early History of Chinese Trade in the South China Sea*, Times Academic Press, Singapore, 1998, pp. 46–8.
5. Joanna Waley-Cohen, *The Sextants of Beijing: Global Currents in Chinese History*, W. W. Norton and Co., New York, 1999, pp. 21–37.
6. O. W. Wolters, 'Restudying some Chinese writings on Sriwijaya', *Indonesia*, no. 42, 1986, p. 34.
7. Keith W. Taylor, *The Birth of Vietnam*, University of California Press, Berkeley, 1983, p. 113.
8. ibid, p. 286.
9. Alexander B. Woodside, *Vietnam and the Chinese Model: A Comparative Study of Nguyen and Ch'ing Civil Government in the First Half of the Nineteenth Century*, Harvard University Press, Cambridge, Mass., 1971, pp. 234–40.
10. Wang Gungwu, 'The rhetoric of a lesser empire' in *China Among Equals: The Middle Kingdom and Its Neighbours, 10th to 14th Centuries*, ed. Morris Rossabi, University of California Press, Berkeley, 1983, pp. 47–65.

Chapter 4 Mongol expansionism

1. Wang Gungwu, 'Song–Yuan–Ming relations with Southeast Asia: some comparisons' in Wang Gungwu, *China and the Overseas Chinese*, Times Academic Press, Singapore, 1991, pp. 106–10.
2. C. P. FitzGerald, *The Southern Expansion of the Chinese People*, White Lotus, Bangkok, 1993, pp. 42–9.
3. ibid, pp. 53–5.
4. This and the following account of the Mongol invasions of Vietnam are taken from Le Thanh Khoi, *Histoire du Viet Nam des origines à 1858*, Sudestasie, Paris, 1981, pp. 182–92.
5. My account here draws on Michael A. Aung-Thwin, *Myth and History in the Historiography of Early Burma: Paradigms, Primary Sources, and Prejudices*, Ohio Center for International Studies, Athens, 1998, pp. 33–92.
6. Grace Wong, *A Comment on the Tributary Trade Between China and Southeast Asia, and the Place of Porcelain in the Trade, During the Period of the Song Dynasty in China*, National Museum, Singapore, June 1979.
7. Morris Rossabi, 'The reign of Khubilai Khan' in *The Cambridge History of China*, vol. 6, eds H. Franke and D. Twitchett, Cambridge University Press, Cambridge, 1994, p. 487.
8. Anthony Reid has pointed out the close links that developed over the centuries between Champa and Java, in *Charting the Shape of Early Modern Southeast Asia*, Institute of Southeast Asian Studies, Singapore, 2000, pp. 32, 39–55.
9. The term *mandala* was coined by Oliver Wolters in the first edition of his *History, Culture, and Region in Southeast Asian Perspectives*, Institute of Southeast Asian Studies, Singapore, 1982. Cf. The concept of 'galactic polity' in S. J. Tambiah, *World Conqueror, World Renouncer: A Study of Buddhism and Polity in Thailand Against a Historical Background*, University of Cambridge Press, Cambridge, 1976.

10. On Islamic worldview, see Malise Ruthven, *Islam in the World*, Penguin, Harmondsworth, 1984.

Chapter 5 Sea power, tribute and trade

1. Wu Chi-hua, 'Basic foreign-policy attitudes of the early Ming dynasty', *Ming Studies*, vol. 12, Spring 1981, p. 67.
2. ibid, p. 66.
3. Wang Gungwu, 'Early Ming Relations with Southeast Asia: A Background Essay' in *The Chinese World Order: Traditional China's Foreign Relations*, ed. John King Fairbank, Harvard University Press, Cambridge, Mass., 1968, pp. 48–9.
4. ibid, p. 49.
5. ibid, p. 70.
6. Anthony Reid, *Charting the Shape of Early Modern Southeast Asia*, Institute of Southeast Asian Studies, Singapore, 2000, p. 66; and Promboon Suebsang, 'Sino–Siamese Tributary Relations, 1282–1853', PhD thesis, University of Michigan, 1971.
7. Geoff Wade, 'Chinese imperial expansion during the early Ming: two examples', paper presented to the International Convention of Asian Scholars, Noordwijkerhout, 25–28 June 1998, p. 3.
8. Cf. Wang Gungwu, 'Early Ming relations', p. 49.
9. The full list of twenty reasons is given in Wang Gungwu. 'China and South-East Asia 1402–1424' in *Studies in the Social History of China and South-East Asia: Essays in Memory of Victor Purcell*, eds Jerome Ch'en and Nicholas Tarling, Cambridge University Press, Cambridge, 1970, pp. 381–2.
10. For a Vietnamese account, see Le Thanh Khoi, *Histoire du Vietnam: des origines à 1858*, Sudestasie, Paris, 1981, pp. 199–202.
11. Wade, 'Chinese Imperial expansion', p. 14.
12. The account that follows is drawn from J. V. G. Mills, 'Introduction' to Ma Huan, *Ying-Yai Sheng-Lan: 'The Overall Survey of*

the Ocean's Shores', Cambridge University Press, Cambridge, 1970.

13. Wade, 'Chinese imperial expansion', p. 17.
14. Wang Gungwu, 'Early Ming relations with Southeast Asia', p. 56.
15. I am grateful to Geoff Wade for making available his translations from the Ming Shi-lu, from which this paragraph is drawn.
16. Nicolas Gervaise, *The Natural and Political History of the Kingdom of Siam*, translated and with an introduction by John Villiers, 2nd edn, White Lotus, Bangkok, 1998, pp. 191–3.

Chapter 6 Enter the Europeans

1. Anthony Reid, *Southeast Asia in the Age of Commerce, 1450–1680*, vol. 1, Yale University Press, New Haven, 1988.
2. John E. Wills Jr., *Embassies and Illusions: Dutch and Portuguese Envoys to K'ang-hsi, 1666–1687*, Harvard University Press, Cambridge, Mass., 1984, p. 19.
3. I am drawing here on Roderich Ptak, 'Ming maritime trade to Southeast Asia, 1368–1567: Visions of a "system"' in *From the Mediterranean to the China Sea: Miscellaneous Notes*, eds. Claude Guillot, Denys Lombard and Roderich Ptak, Harrassowitz Verlag, Wiesbaden, 1998, pp. 157–91.
4. Ptak, 'Ming maritime trade', p. 173.
5. Cf. Anthony Reid on the rise and fall of Ayutthaya in his *Charting the Shape of Modern Southeast Asia*, Institute of Southeast Asian Studies, Singapore, 2000, pp. 85–99.
6. John K. Fairbank and Ssu-yu Teng, 'On the Ch'ing tributary system' in John K. Fairbank and Ssu-yu Teng, *Ch'ing Administration: Three Studies*, Harvard University Press, Cambridge, Mass., 1961, pp. 135–45.
7. Wills, *Embassies*, pp. 1–5, 31–3.
8. Amounting to 58 per cent of the population. L. Blussé, *Strange*

Company: Chinese Settlers, Mestizo Women and the Dutch in VOC Batavia, KILTV, Dordrecht, 1986, p. 84. See also M. C. Ricklefs, *A History of Modern Indonesia since c. 1300*, 2nd edn, Macmillan, London, 1993, p. 90.

9. John K. Fairbank and Ssu-yu Teng, 'On the Ch'ing tributary system', p. 184.
10. Truong Buu Lam, 'Intervention versus tribute in Sino–Vietnamese Relations, 1788–1790' in *The Chinese World Order*, ed. J. K. Fairbank, Harvard University Press, Cambridge, Mass., 1968, pp. 165–79.
11. Quoted in Pei-kai Cheng and Michael Lestz, *The Search for Modern China: A Documentary Collection*, W. W. Norton, New York, 1993, p. 105.
12. ibid, pp. 107–109. The best account of the embassy is James L. Hevia, *Cherishing Men from Afar: Qing Guest Ritual and the Macartney Embassy* (Duke University Press, Durham, 1995).
13. Yoshiharu Tsuboï, *L'empire vietnamien face à la France et à la Chine*, L'Harmattan, Paris, 1987, pp. 263–4.
14. Sarasin Viraphol, *Tribute and Profit: Sino–Siamese Trade, 1652–1853*, Harvard University Press, Cambridge, Mass., 1977, p. 236–7.
15. These and subsequent figures are taken from Victor Purcell, *The Chinese in Southeast Asia*, 2nd edn, Oxford University Press, London, 1965, pp. 386, 232–4, 44, 175; and G. William Skinner, *Chinese Society in Thailand: An Analytical History*, Cornell University Press, Ithaca, NY, 1957, table 5, p. 79.

Chapter 7 The changing world order

1. George L. Hicks, 'Introduction', *Overseas Chinese Remittances from Southeast Asia, 1910–1940*, Select Books, Singapore, 1993, pp. xxx–xxxi.

2. Victor Purcell, *The Chinese in Southeast Asia*, 2nd edn, Oxford University Press, London, 1965, pp. 293–300.
3. ibid, p. 465.
4. King C. Chen, *Vietnam and China, 1938–1954*, Princeton University Press, Princeton, NJ, 1969, pp. 40–60.
5. Xiaoyuan Liu, 'China and the issue of postwar Indochina in the Second World War', *Modern Asian Studies*, vol. 33, 1999, pp. 459, 453. Liu argues that both were undertaken to enhance 'China's international status' (p. 453).
6. G. William Skinner, *Chinese Society in Thailand: An Analytical History*, Cornell University Press, Ithaca, NY, 1957, table 8, p. 183.
7. Anuson Chinvanno, *Thailand's Policies towards China, 1949–54*, Macmillan, London, 1992, p. 32.
8. David K. Wyatt, *Thailand: A Short History*, Silkworm Books, Chiang Mai, 1984, p. 229.
9. See Christopher E. Goscha, *Thailand and the Southeast Asian Networks of the Vietnamese Revolution, 1885–1954*, Curzon, Richmond, 1999.
10. Rizal Sukma, *Indonesia and China: The Politics of a Troubled Relationship*, Routledge, London, 1999, pp. 20–4.
11. Ho famously commented that it was 'better to sniff French shit for a while than to eat Chinese dung for the rest of our lives'. Paul Mus, *Sociologie d'une guerre*, Editions du Seuil, Paris, 1952, p. 85.
12. Chen, *Vietnam and China, 1938–1954*, pp. 204–11.

Chapter 8 Communism and the Cold War

1. Mao Zedong, *Selected Works of Mao Tsetung*, vol. 5, Foreign Languages Press, Peking, 1977, p. 17.
2. The idea of a 'Chinese model' evolved in Yan'an between 1937 and 1941. Steven M. Goldstein, 'The Chinese revolution and the

colonial areas: the view from Yenan, 1937–41', *China Quarterly*, no. 75 (September 1978), pp. 594–622.

3. Lucian W. Pye, 'China: erratic state, frustrated society', *Foreign Affairs*, vol. 69, no. 4, 1990, p. 60.
4. Odd Arne Westad, et al., eds, *77 Conversations Between Chinese and Foreign Leaders on the Wars in Indochina, 1964–1977*, Working Paper No. 22, Cold War International History Project, Woodrow Wilson International Center for Scholars, Washington, D.C., May 1998, pp. 68–71, 94–5, 105, 125. See also analysis by the editors on pp.14–15, 17–19.
5. Chih-yu Shih, *China's Just World: The Morality of China's Foreign Policy*, Lynn Rienner Publishers, Boulder, Colo., 1993.
6. King C. Chen, *Vietnam and China, 1938–1954*, Princeton University Press, Princeton, NJ, 1969, p. 217.
7. For China's involvement, see Chen Jian, 'China and the First Indo-China War, 1950–54', *China Quarterly*, no. 133 (March 1993), pp. 85–110; and Qiang Zhai, *China and the Vietnam Wars, 1950–1975*, University of North Carolina Press, Chapel Hill, NC, 2000, pp. 26–33 and 43–9.
8. Nguyen Khac Vien, *Vietnam: A Long History*, rev. edn, The Gioi Publishers, Hanoi, 1999, pp. 285–6.
9. *Renmin Ribao* (People's Daily) editorial of 22 July 1954 quoted in Zhai Qiang, 'China and the Geneva Conference of 1954', *China Quarterly*, no. 129 (March 1992), p. 121.
10. Stephen Fitzgerald, *China and the Overseas Chinese: A Study of Peking's Changing Policy 1949–1970*, Cambridge University Press, Cambridge, 1972, p. 146.
11. Harold C. Hinton, *Communist China in World Politics*, Macmillan, London, 1966, p. 407.
12. Chen Jian, 'China's involvement in the Vietnam War, 1964–69', *China Quarterly*, no. 142, June 1995, p. 358.
13. Qiang Zhai, *China and the Vietnam Wars*, pp. 114–17; Chan Jian, 'China's involvement in the Vietnam War', pp. 361–3.

14. Qiang Zhai, *China and the Vietnam Wars*, pp. 132–5; and Xiao-ming Zhang, 'The Vietnam War, 1964–1969: A Chinese Perspective', *The Journal of Military History*, vol. 60, 1996, pp. 756–9, for figures on Chinese military assistance and casualties.
15. Qiang Zhai, 'Opposing Negotiations: China and the Vietnam Peace Talks, 1965–1968', *Pacific Historical Review*, vol. 68, 1999, pp. 21–49.
16. Qiang Zhai, *China and the Vietnam Wars*, p. 207.
17. Chen Jian, 'China's involvement in the Vietnam War', p. 386.
18. Chen Jian, 'Personal–Historical puzzles about China and the Vietnam War', in Westad, et al., eds, *77 Conversations*, p. 28.

Chapter 9 Fresh beginnings

1. Quoted in Michael Vatikiotis, 'Ties That Bind', *Far Eastern Economic Review*, 11 January 1996.
2. Martin Stuart-Fox, *Vietnam in Laos: Hanoi's Model for Kampuchea*, Keck Center for International Strategic Studies, Claremont, Calif., 1987.
3. Andrew J. Nathan and Robert S. Ross, *The Great Wall and the Empty Fortress: China's Search for Security*, W. W. Norton and Co., New York, 1997, p. 103.
4. Robert S. Ross, *The Indochina Tangle: China's Vietnam Policy 1975–1979*, Columbia University Press, New York, 1988, p. 209.
5. Geoff Wade, 'Some Topoi in Southern Border historiography during the Ming (and their modern relevance)', in *China and Her Neighbours: Borders, Visions of the Other, Foreign Policy 10th to 19th century*, eds Sabine Dabringhaus and Roderich Ptak, Harrassowitz Verlag, Wiesbaden, 1997, pp. 135–58.
6. Cf. David W. P. Elliot, 'Vietnam: tradition under challenge', in *Strategic Cultures in the Asia–Pacific Region*, eds Ken Booth and Russell Trood, Macmillan, London, 1999, pp. 111–45.

7. Cf. Robert S. Ross, 'China and the Cambodian Peace Process', *Asian Survey*, vol. 31, 1991, 1169–85.
8. Carl Thayer, 'Comrade plus brother: the new Sino–Vietnamese Relations', *The Pacific Review*, vol. 5, 1992, pp. 402–6.
9. Madelyn C. Ross, 'China's international economic behaviour' in *Chinese Foreign Policy: Theory and Practice*, Clarendon Press, Oxford, 1994, pp. 435–52.
10. Paul J. Bolt, *China and Southeast Asia's Ethnic Chinese: State and Diaspora in Contemporary Asia*, Praeger, Westport, Conn., 2000, table 4.1, p. 66.
11. Dewi Fortuna Anwar, 'Indonesia: domestic priorities define national security', in *Asian Security Practice: Material and Ideational Influences*, ed. Muthiah Alagappa, Stanford University Press, Stanford, Calif., 1998, p. 498.
12. Bolt, *China and Southeast Asia's Ethnic Chinese*, table 6.1, p. 111.
13. Mya Maung, 'On the road to Mandalay: a case study of the Sinonization of Upper Burma', *Asian Survey*, vol. 34, 1994, p. 449.
14. Amitav Acharya, *Constructing a Security Community in Southeast Asia: ASEAN and the problem of regional order*, Routledge, London, 2001.
15. Gerald Segal, 'East Asia and the "constrainment" of China', *International Security*, vol. 20, 1996, pp. 107–29.

Chapter 10 Future directions

1. Sheng Lijun, 'China's foreign policy under status discrepancy, status enhancement', *Contemporary Southeast Asia*, vol. 17, 1993, p. 242.
2. America's political leaders appear to have taken Paul M. Kennedy's warnings seriously in *The Rise and Fall of the Great Powers: Economic Change and Military Conflict from 1500 to 2000*, Unwin Hyman, London, 1988.

3. The term is Wang Gungwu's, which he defines as having several layers that tie in 'the faith in a glorious past more directly [than other forms of nationalism] with a vision of a great future'. Wang Gungwu, *The Revival of Chinese Nationalism*, International Institute for Asian Studies, Leiden, 1996, p. 7.
4. Michael D. Swaine and Ashley J. Tellis, *Interpreting China's Grand Strategy: Past, Present, and Future*, Rand Corporation, Santa Monica, Calif., 2000.
5. ibid, pp. 142–50.
6. These alternatives are also taken from ibid, pp. 183–204.
7. Paul Dibb, *Towards a New Balance of Power in Asia*, Adelphi Papers No. 295, 1995.
8. Rizal Sukma, *Indonesia and China: The Politics of a Troubled Relationship*, Routledge, London, 1999.
9. This difference is symbolised in the readiness of mainland states to use superior–inferior family metaphors in describing their relations with China, a form of words resisted by Indonesia and the Philippines.
10. Amitav Acharya has defined 'the ASEAN way' as characterised by 'compromise, consensus building, ambiguity, avoidance of strict reciprocity, and rejection of legally binding obligations'. In *Constructing a Security Community in Southeast Asia: ASEAN and the Problem of Regional Order*, Routledge, London, 2001, p. 55.

SUGGESTED READING

A number of references to the history of relations between China and Southeast Asia can be found in the notes. Only the more significant are included below.

The best histories of China and Southeast Asia are the respective multi-volume Cambridge University Press publications. John King Fairbank, *China: A New History* (Harvard University Press, Cambridge, Mass., 1992) provides a one-volume overview, while Jonathan Spence, *The Search for Modern China*, 2nd edn (W. W. Norton, New York, 1999) is a fine study from the Qing dynasty on. Joanna Waley-Cohen emphasises China's cosmopolitanism in *The Sextants of Beijing: Global Currents in Chinese History* (W. W. Norton, New York, 1999). For Southeast Asia, Milton Osborne, *Southeast Asia: A History*, 8th edn (Allen & Unwin, Sydney, NSW, 2000) covers the whole period, while David Joel Steinberg, ed., *In Search of Southeast Asia: A Modern History*, rev. edn (Allen & Unwin, Sydney, 1987) begins with the eighteeenth century. Single volume histories of the ten countries of Southeast Asia can also be consulted, though most say little about relations with China. The exception is Vietnam, on which see K. W. Taylor, *The Birth of Vietnam* (University of California Press, Berkeley, 1983), and Le Thanh Khoi, *Histoire du Vietnam des origines à 1858* (Sudestasie, Paris, 1981).

John King Fairbank, ed., *The Chinese World Order: Traditional China's Foreign Relations* (Harvard University Press, Cambridge, Mass., 1968) still provides the best study of the tributary system. Aihe Wang, *Cosmology and Political Culture in Early China* (Cambridge University Press, Cambridge, 2000) provides a revealing analysis of the origins of the Chinese worldview. On Confucius, see David L. Hall and Roger T.

Ames, *Thinking Through Confucius* (State University of New York Press, New York, 1987). No comprehensive study exists of the worldviews of early Southeast Asian kingdoms, but Lorraine Gesick, ed., *Centers, Symbols, and Hierarchies: Essays on the Classical States of Southeast Asia* (Yale University Press, New Haven, 1983), provides some indication. The idea of the *mandala* and the amalgam of indigenous and Indian notions that underlies it are discussed in O. W. Wolters, *History, Culture and Region in Southeast Asian Perspectives*, revised edn (Institute of Southeast Asian Studies, Singapore, 1999).

On strategic culture, for China see Alastair Iain Johnston, *Cultural Realism: Strategic Culture and Grand Strategy in Chinese History* (Princeton University Press, Princeton, 1995); and for Southeast Asia (and China), Ken Booth and Russell Trood, eds, *Strategic Cultures in the Asia–Pacific Region* (Macmillan, London, 1999). On Chinese military thinking, see Ralph Sawyer, *The Seven Military Classics of Ancient China* (Westview, Boulder, 1993); and Chen-Ya Tien, *Chinese Military Theory: Ancient and Modern* (Mosaic Press, Oakville, NY, 1992).

On early Chinese expansion south, see C. P. Fitzgerald, *The Southern Expansion of the Chinese People* (White Lotus, Bangkok, 1993); Ying-shih Yu, *Trade and Expansion in Han China: A Study in the Structure of Sino–Barbarian Economic Relations* (University of California Press, Berkeley, 1967); and Edward H. Schafer, *The Vermilion Bird: T'ang Images of the South* (University of California Press, Berkeley, 1967). Chinese attempts to preserve the tributary system are examined in Morris Rossabi, ed., *China Among Equals: The Middle Kingdom and Its Neighbours, 10th–14th Centuries* (University of California Press, Berkeley, 1983).

On early trading relations between China and Southeast Asia, the classic study is Wang Gungwu, *The Nanhai Trade* (Times Academic Books, Singapore, 1998), and for early Southeast Asian commerce O. W. Wolters, *Early Indonesian Commerce: A Study of the Origins of Srivijaya* (Cornell University Press, Ithaca, NY, 1967) and its sequel *The Fall of Srivijaya in Malay History* (Asia Major Library, London,

1970). Denys Lombard, *Le carrefour javanais: essai d'histoire globale*, 3 vols (Editions de l'Ecole des Hautes Etudes en Sciences Sociales, Paris, 1990) is magisterial in its coverage. William Lytle Schurz, *The Manila Galleon* (E. P. Dutton, New York, 1959) is still a good read. Other useful studies include Anthony Reid, *Southeast Asia in the Age of Commerce 1450–1680*, 2 vols (Yale University Press, New Haven, 1988 and 1993) and *Charting the Shape of Early Modern Southeast Asia* (Institute of Southeast Asian Studies, Singapore, 2000); Sarasin Viraphol, *Tribute and Profit: Sino–Siamese Trade, 1652–1853* (Harvard University Press, Cambridge, Mass., 1977); Kenneth R. Hall, *Maritime Trade and State Development in Early Southeast Asia* (University of Hawaii Press, Honolulu, 1985); Jennifer Cushman, *Fields from the Sea: Chinese Junk Trade with Siam during the Late Eighteenth and Early Nineteenth Centuries* (Cornell University Press, Ithaca, NY, 1993); Roderich Ptak, *China and the Asian Seas: Trade, Travel, and Visions of the Other (1400–1750)* (Ashgate, Aldershot, 1998); and Gang Deng, *Maritime Sector, Institutions, and Sea Power of Premodern China* (Greenwood Press, Westport, Conn., 1999).

Two fascinating records of Chinese who visited Southeast Asia are: Chou Ta-kuan, *The Customs of Cambodia*, 2nd edn (The Siam Society, Bangkok, 1992) and Ma Huan, *Ying-yai Sheng-lan: 'The Overall Survey of the Ocean's Shores'* (Cambridge University Press, Cambridge, 1970). Ma Huan is the best source for the Ming voyages. A more popular account is Louise Levathes, *When China Ruled the Seas: The Treasure Fleet of the Dragon Throne 1405–1433* (Simon and Schuster, New York, 1994).

On early European embassies to the Qing, excellent studies include John E. Wills, Jr., *Pepper, Guns and Parlays: The Dutch East India Company and China 1622–1681* (Harvard University Press, Cambridge, Mass., 1974) and *Embassies and Illusions: Dutch and Portuguese Envoys to K'ang-hsi, 1666–1687* (Harvard University Press, Cambridge, Mass., 1984); and James L. Heria, *Cherishing Men from Afar: Qing Guest Ritual and the Macartney Embassy* (Duke University Press,

Durham, 1995). Earl H. Pritchard, *The Crucial Years of Early Anglo-Chinese Relations 1750–1800* (Octagon Books, New York, 1970); and John K. Fairbank, *Trade and Diplomacy on the China Coast: The Opening of the Treaty Ports 1842–1854* (Harvard University Press, Cambridge, Mass., 1964) both contain much useful information.

The Republic of China's relations with Southeast Asia are touched upon in John Gittings, *The World and China 1922–1972* (Eyre Methuen, London, 1974). The most important aspect of these relations was with overseas Chinese, on which the classic study is Victor Purcell, *The Chinese in Southeast Asia*, 2nd edn (Oxford University Press, London, 1965). The best recent studies are by Wang Gungwu: *China and the Overseas Chinese* (Times Academic Press, Singapore, 1991); and *The Chinese Overseas: From Earthbound China to the Quest for Autonomy* (Harvard University Press, Cambridge, Mass., 2000). Other useful works include Stephen Fitzgerald, *China and the Overseas Chinese: A Study of Peking's Changing Policy, 1949–1970* (Cambridge University Press, Cambridge, 1972); Lynn Pan, *Sons of the Yellow Emperor: A History of the Chinese Diaspora* (Little, Brown, Boston, 1990); Leo Suryadinata, ed., *Southeast Asian Chinese and China: The Politico-Economic Dimension* (Times Academic Press, Singapore, 1995); Constance Lever-Tracy, David Ip, and Noel Tracy, *The Chinese Diaspora and Mainland China: An Emerging Economic Synergy* (St Martin's Press, New York, 1996); Anthony Reid, ed., *Sojourners and Settlers: Histories of Southeast Asia and the Chinese in Honour of Jennifer Cushman* (Allen & Unwin, Sydney, NSW, 1996); and Paul J. Bolt, *China and Southeast Asia's Ethnic Chinese: State and Diaspora in Contemporary Asia* (Praeger, Westport, Conn., 2000).

On the foreign and security relations of the PRC, the best studies include Harold C. Hinton, *China's Turbulent Quest: An Analysis of China's Foreign Relations Since 1949* (Indiana University Press, Bloomington, 1970); Joseph Camilleri, *Chinese Foreign Policy: The Maoist Era and Its Aftermath* (Martin Robertson, Oxford, 1980); Harry Harding, ed., *China's Foreign Relations in the 1980s* (Yale University Press, New

Haven, 1984); John Wong, *The Political Economy of China's Changing Relations with Southeast Asia* (Macmillan, London, 1984); Lim Joo-Jock, *Territorial Power Domains, Southeast Asia and China: The Geo-strategy of an Overarching Massif* (Institute of Southeast Asian Studies, Singapore, 1984); John W. Garver, *Foreign Relations of the People's Republic of China* (Prentice Hall, Englewood Cliffs, NJ, 1993); Chih-Yu Shih, *China's Just World: The Morality of Chinese Foreign Policy* (Lynn Rienner, Boulder, 1993); Thomas W. Robinson and David Shanbaugh, eds, *Chinese Foreign Policy: Theory and Practice* (Oxford University Press, New York, 1994); Samuel S. Kim, *China and the World: Chinese Foreign Relations in the Post-Cold War Era* (Westview, Boulder, 1994); Stuart Harris and Gary Klintworth, eds, *China as a Great Power: Myths, Realities and Challenges in the Asia–Pacific Region* (St Martin's Press, New York, 1995); Michael H. Hunt, *The Genesis of Chinese Communist Foreign Policy* (Columbia University Press, New York, 1996); Andrew J. Nathan and Robert S. Ross, *The Great Wall and the Empty Fortress: China's Search for Security* (W. W. Norton, New York, 1997); Denny Roy, *China's Foreign Relations* (Macmillan, London, 1998); Samuel S. Kim, ed., *China and the World: Chinese Foreign Policy Faces the New Millennium* (Westview, Boulder, 1998); and Michael D. Swaine and Ashley J. Tellis, *Interpreting China's Grand Strategy: Past, Present, and Future* (Rand Corporation, Santa Monica, Calif., 2000). A fascinating study of the Chinese point of view is Yong Deng and Fei-Ling Wang, eds, *In the Eyes of the Dragon: China Views the World* (Rowman and Littlefield, Lanham, Md., 1999).

On relations between the PRC and Southeast Asia, useful studies include Melvin Gurtov, *China and Southeast Asia: The Politics of Survival: A Study of Foreign Policy Interaction* (Heath Lexington Books, Lexington, Mass., 1971); Jay Taylor, *China and Southeast Asia: Peking's Relations with Revolutionary Movements*, 2nd edn (Westview, Boulder, 1976); Joyce K. Kallgren, Noordin Sopiee, and Soedjati Djiwandono, eds, *ASEAN and China: An Evolving Relationship* (University of California Press, Berkeley, 1988); Mutiah Aliagappa, ed., *Asian Security*

Practice: Material and Ideational Influences (Stanford University Press, Stanford, 1998); and William T. Tow, *Asia Pacific Security Relations: Seeking Convergent Security* (Cambridge University Press, Cambridge, 2001).

On China's relations with Vietnam, the pioneering study is King C. Chen, *Vietnam and China, 1938–1954* (Princeton University Press, Princeton, NJ, 1969). More recent are William J. Duiker, *China and Vietnam: The Roots of Conflict* (University of California Press, Berkeley, 1986); Robert S. Ross, *The Indochina Tangle: China's Vietnam Policy 1975–1979* (Columbia University Press, New York, 1988); Anne Gilks, *The Breakdown of the Sino–Vietnamese Alliance, 1970–1979* (University of California Press, Berkeley, 1992); Carlyle A. Thayer and Ramses Amer, eds, *Vietnamese Foreign Policy in Transition* (St Martin's Press, New York, 1999); Ang Cheng Guan, *Vietnamese Communists' Relations with China and the Second Indochina Conflict, 1956–1962* (McFarland, Jefferson, NC, 1997); Stephen J. Morris, *Why Vietnam Invaded Cambodia: Political Culture and the Causes of War* (Stanford University Press, Stanford, Calif., 1999); and Zhai Qiang, *China and the Vietnam Wars: 1950–1975* (University of North Carolina Press, Chapel Hill, 2000).

China's relations with Cambodia are covered in Chang Pao-Min, *Kampuchea between China and Vietnam* (Singapore University Press, Singapore, 1985); and with Laos in Lee Chae-Jin, *Communist China's Policy Towards Laos: A Case Study 1954–67* (University of Kansas Press, Lawrence, 1970).

For relations between Burma and China, see Ralph Pettman, *China in Burma's Foreign Policy* (Australian National University Press, Canberra, 1973); Daw Than Han, *Common Vision: Burma's Regional Outlook* (Georgetown University Press, Washington, DC, 1988); and between Thailand and China, Anuson Chinvanno, *Thailand's Policies towards China, 1949–54* (Macmillan, London, 1992); and Sukhumbhand Paribatra, *From Enmity to Alignment: Thailand's Evolving Relations with China* (Chulalongkorn University Press, Bangkok, 1987).

Studies of relations between China and Indonesia include Sheldon W. Simon, *The Broken Triangle: Peking, Djakarta and the PKI* (Johns Hopkins Press, Baltimore, 1969); David Mozingo, *Chinese Policy toward Indonesia, 1949–1967* (Cornell University Press, Ithaca, NY, 1976); and Rizal Sukma, *Indonesia and China: The Politics of a Troubled Relationship* (Routledge, London, 1999). There is no book-length study of Sino–Malaysian relations, except for R. K. Jain's collection of documents, *China and Malaysia 1949–1983* (Sangam, London, 1987). Sino–Philippine relations are examined in Theresa C. Cariño and Bernardita R. Churchill, eds, *Perspectives on Philippine Policy Towards China* (Philippine Association for Chinese Studies, Manila, 1993).

On the South China Sea, the best recent studies are Mark J. Valencia, *China and the South China Sea Disputes: Conflicting Claims and Potential Solutions in the South China Sea* Adelphi Paper No. 298 (Oxford University Press, London, 1995); Bob Catley and Makmur Keliat, *Spratlys: The Dispute in the South China Sea* (Ashgate, Aldershot, 1997); and Greg Austin, *China's Ocean Frontier: International Law, Military Force and National Development* (Allen & Unwin, Sydney, NSW, 1998).

INDEX